CLASSICS IN EDUCATION

Lawrence A. Cremin, General Editor

☆ ☆ ☆

THE REPUBLIC AND THE SCHOOL
Horace Mann on the Education of Free Men
Edited by Lawrence A. Cremin

AMERICAN IDEAS ABOUT ADULT EDUCATION
1710–1951
Edited by C. Hartley Grattan

DEWEY ON EDUCATION
Introduction and Notes by Martin S. Dworkin

THE SUPREME COURT AND EDUCATION
Edited by David Fellman

INTERNATIONAL EDUCATION
A Documentary History
Edited by David G. Scanlon

CRUSADE AGAINST IGNORANCE
Thomas Jefferson on Education
Edited by Gordon C. Lee

CHINESE EDUCATION UNDER COMMUNISM
Edited by Chang-tu Hu

CHARLES W. ELIOT AND POPULAR EDUCATION
Edited by Edward A. Krug

WILLIAM T. HARRIS ON EDUCATION
(in preparation)
Edited by Martin S. Dworkin

THE *EMILE* OF JEAN JACQUES ROUSSEAU
Selections
Translated and Edited by William Boyd

THE MINOR EDUCATIONAL WRITINGS OF
JEAN JACQUES ROUSSEAU
Selected and Translated by William Boyd

PSYCHOLOGY AND THE SCIENCE OF EDUCATION
Selected Writings of Edward L. Thorndike
Edited by Geraldine M. Joncich

THE NEW-ENGLAND PRIMER
Introduction by Paul Leicester Ford

BENJAMIN FRANKLIN ON EDUCATION
Edited by John Hardin Best

THE COLLEGES AND THE PUBLIC
1787–1862
Edited by Theodore Rawson Crane

TRADITIONS OF AFRICAN EDUCATION
Edited by David G. Scanlon

NOAH WEBSTER'S AMERICAN SPELLING BOOK
Introductory Essay by Henry Steele Commager

VITTORINO DA FELTRE
AND OTHER HUMANIST EDUCATORS
By William Harrison Woodward
Foreword by Eugene F. Rice, Jr.

DESIDERIUS ERASMUS
CONCERNING THE AIM AND METHOD
OF EDUCATION
By William Harrison Woodward
Foreword by Craig R. Thompson

JOHN LOCKE ON EDUCATION
Edited by Peter Gay

CATHOLIC EDUCATION IN AMERICA
A Documentary History
Edited by Neil G. McCluskey, S.J.

THE AGE OF THE ACADEMIES
Edited by Theodore R. Sizer

HEALTH, GROWTH, AND HEREDITY
G. Stanley Hall on Natural Education
Edited by Charles E. Strickland and Charles Burgess

TEACHER EDUCATION IN AMERICA
A Documentary History
Edited by Merle L. Borrowman

THE EDUCATED WOMAN IN AMERICA
Selected Writings of Catharine Beecher,
Margaret Fuller, and M. Carey Thomas
Edited by Barbara M. Cross

EMERSON ON EDUCATION
Selections
Edited by Howard Mumford Jones

ECONOMIC INFLUENCES UPON EDUCATIONAL
PROGRESS IN THE UNITED STATES, 1820–1850
By Frank Tracy Carlton
Foreword by Lawrence A. Cremin

QUINTILIAN ON EDUCATION
Selected and Translated by William M. Smail

ROMAN EDUCATION FROM CICERO
TO QUINTILIAN
By Aubrey Gwynn, S.J.

HERBERT SPENCER ON EDUCATION
Edited by Andreas M. Kazamias

JOHN LOCKE'S *OF THE CONDUCT*
OF THE UNDERSTANDING
Edited by Francis W. Garforth

STUDIES IN EDUCATION DURING THE
AGE OF THE RENAISSANCE, 1400–1600
By William Harrison Woodward
Foreword by Lawrence Stone

JOHN AMOS COMENIUS ON EDUCATION
Introduction by Jean Piaget

HUMANISM AND THE SOCIAL ORDER
IN TUDOR ENGLAND
By Fritz Caspari

VIVES' *INTRODUCTION TO WISDOM*
Edited by Marian Leona Tobriner, S.N.J.M.

THE THEORY OF EDUCATION IN
THE *REPUBLIC* OF PLATO
By Richard Lewis Nettleship
Foreword by Robert McClintock

UTOPIANISM AND EDUCATION
Robert Owen and the Owenites
Edited by John F. C. Harrison

SCHOOLS OF HELLAS
By Kenneth J. Freeman
Foreword by William M. Calder III

Schools of Hellas

By KENNETH J. FREEMAN

With a Foreword by
WILLIAM M. CALDER III

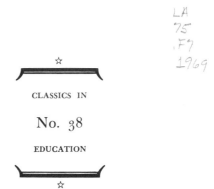

CLASSICS IN

No. 38

EDUCATION

TEACHERS COLLEGE PRESS
TEACHERS COLLEGE, COLUMBIA UNIVERSITY
NEW YORK

Library of Congress Catalog
Card Number 73-79994

Manufactured in the United States of America

Contents

PART III

Illustrations

Foreword

By WILLIAM M. CALDER III

Certain books inform. Others grind axes. The informative ones survive and deserve reprinting. Kenneth J. Freeman's *Schools of Hellas* is one of these. After sixty years it still has much to say pleasingly. Because it was written as a kind of dissertation, much of the book gathers and arranges useful information. Because he was an educated Englishman rather than German or American, the author wrote prose both learned and readable. Because he was still a youth (twenty-four years old), he wrote with a candor both naïve and charming. Learning, readability, and candor, therefore, were the recipe for this book's longevity.

Kenneth J. Freeman (1882–1906) enjoyed a classical education of a sort that no longer exists in any part of the world. He was prepared at Winchester (his Greek poetry proves the caliber of his training there) and graduated in 1904 from the college of Richard Bentley, Trinity, Cambridge. This was the Golden Age of classical studies at Cambridge. Freeman could hear among traditionalists, Sir Richard Jebb, the austere Sophoclean, his pupil Walter Headlam, Sir John Sandys, and the popular rather than scholarly Henry Jackson, famous for the number of books dedicated to him. But the talented classicist of the time must have been especially attracted by the brilliant circle of A. W. Verrall, Miss Jane Harrison, Francis MacDonald Cornford, and the young Aus-

tralian from Oxford who, we know, often visited his
Cambridge friends, Gilbert Murray.[1] Verrall (1851–
1912)—he wrote the preface to his pupil's posthumous
volume—and his friends worked a sort of revolution in
English classical studies. The glory of the discipline in
England had traditionally resided in the remote and
meticulous field of textual criticism, the discovery and
correction of minute linguistic and metrical errors in
classical texts. Bentley, Richard Porson, and A. E. Hous-
man, all Cambridge dons, were England's greatest textual
critics. B. L. Gildersleeve was right but malicious to call
their activity a kind of "proofreading." The discipline
required a combination of expertise and intuition granted
few, and such work was indispensable to the editing of
intelligible texts, antiquity's most precious legacy as well
as the sources of most of what we know of the period.

Verrall and his friends, influenced by the unprece-
dented rise of historical scholarship in Germany, began
to apply to the classics contemporary techniques from
other disciplines, whether literary criticism (in February
1911, Verrall became the first King Edward VII Professor of English Literature), social anthropology, or the
comparative history of religion (Sir James George Frazer
was also a Cambridge don). The scent of revolution appealed to the young. Verrall exalted a new Euripides
called the rationalist, a poet whose name Jebb could
not pronounce without a physical quiver of pain. Miss
Harrison and her favorite Cornford flirted with Karl
Marx. A new historicism that preferred Greeks, warts
and all, demanded critical, informative books that presented the Greeks as people rather than as rules of
grammar. Freeman's study, the first proper treatment

[1] See Jessie Stewart, *Jane Ellen Harrison: A Portrait from Letters*
(London, 1959).

of its subject in English, derives from this need, and its theme, education, presumably reflects a deep concern of Verrall.

The book is the product of a precocious, well-trained, slightly insular young man, writing in the Edwardian England of 1904–1906. A reader must know the author's assumptions in order to detect his anachronisms. I may, however, say at the start that in only a few places has subsequent research proved the author objectively wrong. This is the best evidence that he avoided unsubstantiated theory. Yet readers would do well to note the following: Xenophon (p. 61 with n. 1) was not the author of the so-called *Constitution of the Athenians;* the work is rather an anonymous political pamphlet of about 431 B.C. The spelling-drama of Kallias (p. 88) was not a comedy but a tragedy, whose structure influenced Euripides' *Medea.*[2] "Cheironeia" (*sic*) on the Berlin vase (p. 96) probably refers to a girl's name rather than the title of a lost Hesiodic poem.[3] Sokrates and Kritoboulos (p. 98) were not "two Athenian school friends" but adult and boy. Plato is not the author of the erotic epigrams ascribed to him (pp. 201–202).[4] I cannot imagine a modern Hellenist describing Periklean Athens (p. 290) as "a hereditary aristocracy of birth," although such a view is not indefensible and Freeman is right to stress that even under the extreme democracy only a minority of those living in Attica possessed the franchise. Women, slaves, resident aliens, and minors could never vote. Freeman also, like many of his contemporaries who thought of Athens in Roman terms, overestimates (p.

[2] See P. D. Arnott, in *Classical Philology,* LV (1960), 178–180.

[3] See Sir John Beazley, in *American Journal of Archaeology,* LII (1948), 337.

[4] See W. Ludwig, in *Greek, Roman, and Byzantine Studies,* IV (1963), 59–82.

43) the abundance of slaves; and the corollary that "a large proportion of the free population" lived "in idleness" is untrue. Nor did "upper-class Athenians" scorn trade. Sophocles' father owned an arms factory, and there were few people more "upper-class" than Sophocles. Literacy in Athens, if we may judge from the number of preserved inscriptions, was far higher than in any other Greek state, but it is optimistic to assert (p. 204) that "every Athenian could read." The presence of illiterate shepherds in Euripides shows that this was not the case.

Freeman too, as a German reviewer long ago remarked, lacks a sense for source criticism. A pseudo-Platonic tract of unknown date and provenience ought not to be used (p. 158) as evidence for historical truth concerning the life of Sokrates. We learn (p. 243) that Theophrastus held Phrygian flute music to be a cure for lumbago and that Kleinias calmed himself with harp music when angry. For both bits of information Freeman cites Athenaeus. This writer, a learned cook of Commodus' time, composed a valuable but uncritical compilation from earlier sources of widely varying worth. Inspection of Athenaeus reveals that his statements about Theophrastus are based on a fragment of the philosopher himself, and therefore we may believe that Theophrastus did in fact think music cured disease. But in what he says of Kleinias, Athenaeus is quoting a highly untrustworthy source, Chamaeleon of Heraclea Pontica; and we should probably be right to assume that what he says is merely Hellenistic sensational fiction. In both cases, Freeman ought to have cited, not simply Athenaeus, but the sources that Athenaeus used. A modern and more critical scholar would do so.

I lament, too, Freeman's decision to present ancient monetary sums in pre-World War I pounds sterling (e.g., pp. 168–169). Such localization will provide a hopeless puzzle to those who, as Dante says, will call that time (1904) ancient. The key to remember when dealing with Athenian figures is that one drachma provided a daily living wage for a laborer and his family. Any other kind of conversion leads only to misunderstanding. The monetary units were:

$$6 \text{ obols } = 1 \text{ drachma}$$
$$100 \text{ drachmas } = 1 \text{ mna}$$
$$60 \text{ mnai } = 1 \text{ talent.}$$

Certainly the most shocking feature of Freeman's book for a contemporary reader is that he exalts the Spartan system of education over the Athenian. "Brilliant but corrupt Socratic Athens" (p. 75) revolted the author's moral sense. The most amusing sentence in the whole is found on the same page: "The free discussion with children of ethical subjects probably ceased with the death of Sokrates; this can hardly be regretted, if Plato's evidence as to the nature of Socratic dialogues is to be believed." Most revealing of his Spartan bias is the following passage (p. 284):[5]

The somewhat hedonistic Attic visitor must have watched Spartan games and exercises with much the feelings of a French visitor at an English public school; he found it difficult to realize that the boys underwent such hardships of their own free will. Then we must remember what the Spartan boys were. They were a picked breed of peculiar toughness, strength, and health; for centuries every invalid had been exposed at birth or rejected as incapable of the school-system. Generation after generation had been trained to be thick-skinned and stout-hearted; pluck and endurance were hereditary, and asceticism was a national characteristic. The whole system, with its perpetual fighting, its rough games, its hardships, its fagging and "roughing-it" in the woods,

[5] Cf. pp. 32–33: "The Spartans deserve all credit for their experiments with the boarding-school system."

is just what boys of this sort might be expected to evolve
for themselves because they liked it. I have already pointed
out, in my account of the Spartan schools, how very similar
are many of the customs which grew up at the older English
public schools, mainly on the boys' own initiative. If English
boys, brought up on the whole much less roughly, evolved
such customs of their own free will, the young Spartans may
reasonably be supposed to have accepted them gladly.

This betrays a naïve and uncritical equation of Lace-
daemon with Eton, of the Eurotas with the Cam. Both
produced austere and obedient servants of the state,
and in both cases boys allegedly enjoyed the process.
The brutality and unnaturalness of the nineteenth-
century English public school, despite its practical success in breeding a succession of viceroys of India, revolt
modern educators and parents. I doubt whether Tom
Brown was a particularly happy child while smarting
under the rod of Dr. Arnold.[6] But even if we admit the
virtue of the school system of which Freeman was product and part (for the last year of his brief life, he was
classical master at Winchester), any analogy with Sparta
is superficial and misleading. The Lycurgan system
smothered all the finer instincts of men: art and literature ceased to exist; family life was obliterated; perver-
sion thrived to the degree that on their wedding nights
Spartan brides disguised themselves as men; citizens became merciless, unthinking creatures of the state, mere
engines of war and savage exploiters of a servile class,
the Helots, far exceeding in number themselves. Plato,
the discoverer of totalitarianism, modeled his blueprint,
the *Republic,* in great part on their repellant system.
Athenian writers on Spartan matters were no French
visitors to English public schools. *O Sancta Simplicitas!*

[6] On flogging, see T. W. Bamford, *Thomas Arnold* (London,
1960), pp. 49 ff.

They were disappointed autocrats, called politely oligarchs, who with friends had sought—ultimately without success—to overthrow Athenian democracy. Our "best source," Xenophon, could not risk remaining in his native Athens but fled to Sparta, the Argentina of his day. Indeed, the pernicious influence of "the Spartan mirage" has endured to our own time. The French historian H. I. Marrou says forcefully what must be said:[7]

From K. O. Müller (1824) to W. Jaeger (1932), German scholarship lauded it [Spartan education] to the skies as a product of the Nordic spirit possessed by the Dorians—the conscious embodiment of a racial, militarist, totalitarian policy—a model, miraculously before its time, of the ideal which from the time of Frederick II, Scharnhorst and Bismarck to the Nazi Third Reich, never ceased to inspire the German soul.

Marrou concludes, and he is right, that to glorify the Spartan system of education against all the teaching of sound history is "moral obliquity." A leading ancient historian in West Germany today, Helmut Berve, in 1937 wrote a book called *Sparta*, which begins with the sentence "Few phenomena of the ancient world meet today with such general and vital interest as the Spartan state."[8] He lists "the education of youth, the spirit of fellowship, the soldier's life, order and heroic endurance," all virtues which "have risen again for us," and continues to assure his readers that the Spartans were "indo-germanic and of nordic race." In short, I caution the reader to beware of Freeman's gross errors of judgment in respect to Sparta.

[7] *A History of Education in Antiquity,* translated by George Lamb (New York, 1956), p. 23.

[8] See Helmut Berve, *Sparta* (Leipzig, 1937) and further, but typically, Gottfried Benn, *Essays* (Wiesbaden, 1951), pp. 9-48 ("Dorische Welt" originally published 1933).

SUGGESTIONS FOR FURTHER READING

Certain readers of Freeman will wish to pursue the subject further, and the following remarks are intended
for them. The fundamental modern study, originally
written in French but now available in English, is H. I.
Marrou, *A History of Education in Antiquity,* translated
by George Lamb (New York and London, 1956). There
is an important review of the book by Glanville Downey
in the *Classical Journal,* LII (1957), 337–343. The book
covers the period from Homer to the rise of Christian
schools and the notes provide excellent leads to specialized
literature. Of especial importance as supplements to
Freeman are the chapters on pederasty in classical
education (pp. 26 ff.), a subject hopelessly misrepre-
sented by Freeman (pp. 279–280), and on Isocrates (pp.
79 ff.) whose crucial importance in the history of liberal
education Freeman ignored. Attention ought also to be
drawn to an excellent American book, John W. H.
Walden, *The Universities of Ancient Greece* (New York,
1909). Walden is generally concerned with the period
after the Roman conquest and so provides a continua-
tion of the earlier book, discussing such subjects as the
relation of education to the state, courses of study, the
appointment of professors and their position in society,
and student life. These years saw the emergence of the
academic "chair," the first "degree," and the wearing
of academic gowns; the evidence for these is gathered
and assessed by Walden.

Finally, I wish to direct attention to four books on
subjects Freeman treats in some detail. The remarks on
education at Plato's Academy (Freeman, pp. 195 ff.)
should be supplemented by Paul Friedländer, *Plato: An
Introduction,* translated from the German by Hans

Meyerhoff (New York and London, 1958), pp. 85 ff. We have learned a great deal about what Freeman calls "tertiary education" (pp. 210 ff.), that is, the ephebes. The authoritative modern treatment is C. Pélékidis, *Histoire de l'Éphébie attique des Origines à 31 avant Jésus-Christ* (Paris, 1962). For the highly complex subject of Greek music, discussed by Freeman at pp. 240 ff., I urge interested students to consult the masterful account by Isobel Henderson in *The New Oxford History of Music,* Vol. I: *Ancient and Oriental Music,* edited by Egon Wellesz (Oxford, 1957). A recording is available with the volume, on which one may hear attempts to reproduce ancient music. Finally, Freeman's discussion of Xenophon (pp. 259 ff.) should be supplemented by the intelligent study of É. Delebecque, entitled *Essai sur la Vie de Xénophon* (Paris, 1957).

Columbia University
September 1968

IN A RIDING-SCHOOL

From a Kulix by Euphronios, now in the Louvre.   Hartwig's *Meisterschalen*, Plate 53.

Schools of Hellas

AN ESSAY ON THE PRACTICE AND THEORY
OF ANCIENT GREEK EDUCATION

FROM

600 TO 300 B.C.

BY

KENNETH J. FREEMAN

SCHOLAR OF TRINITY COLLEGE, CAMBRIDGE ; BROWNE UNIVERSITY SCHOLAR ;
CRAVEN UNIVERSITY SCHOLAR ; SENIOR CHANCELLOR'S MEDALLIST, ETC.

EDITED BY

M. J. RENDALL

SECOND MASTER OF WINCHESTER COLLEGE

WITH A PREFACE BY A. W. VERRALL, LITT.DOC.

ILLUSTRATED

MACMILLAN AND CO., LIMITED
ST. MARTIN'S STREET, LONDON

1907

ΦΙΛΟΚΑΛΟΙΣ

ΚΑΙ

ΦΙΛΟΣΟΦΟΙΣ

PREFACE

THE Dissertation here published was written by the late Mr. K. J. Freeman, in the course of the year following his graduation at Cambridge as a Bachelor of Arts, with a view to his candidature for a Fellowship of Trinity College, for which purpose the rules of the College require the production of some original work. In the summer of 1906, three months before the autumn election of that year, his brilliant and promising career was arrested by death.

We have been encouraged to publish the work, as it was left, by several judgments of great weight; nor does it, in my opinion, require anything in the nature of an apology. It is of course, under the circumstances, incomplete, and it is in some respects immature. But, within the limits, the execution is adequate for practical purposes; and the actual achievement has a substantive value independent of any personal consideration. No English book, perhaps no extant book, covers the same ground, or brings together so conveniently the materials for studying the subject of ancient Greek education—education as treated in practice and theory during the most fertile and characteristic age of Hellas. It would be regrettable that this useful, though preliminary, labour should be lost and suppressed, only because it was decreed that the author should not build upon his own foundation.

Novelty of view he disclaimed; but he claimed,

with evident truth, that the work is not second-hand, but based upon wide and direct study of the sources, which are made accessible by copious references.

The subject is in one respect specially appropriate to a youthful hand. Perhaps at no time is a man more likely to have fresh and living impressions about education than when he has himself just ceased to be a pupil, when he has just completed the subordinate stages of a long and strenuous self-culture. It will be seen, in more than one place, that the author is not content with the purely historical aspect of his theme, but suggests criticisms and even practical applications. It may be thought that these remarks upon a matter of pressing and growing importance are by no means the less deserving of consideration because the writer, when he speaks of the schoolboy and the undergraduate, is unquestionably an authentic witness.

But, as I have already said, the work will commend itself sufficiently to those interested in the topic, if only as a conspectus of facts, presented with orderly arrangement and in a simple and perspicuous style.

It is not my part here to express personal feelings. But I cannot dismiss this, the first and only fruit of the classical studies of Kenneth Freeman, without a word of profound sorrow for the premature loss of a most honourable heart and vigorous mind. He was one whom a teacher may freely praise, without suspicion of partiality ; for, whatever he was, he was no mere product of lessons, as this, his first essay, will sufficiently show. It is not what he would have made it ; but it is his own, and it is worthy of him.

A. W. VERRALL.

TRINITY COLLEGE, CAMBRIDGE,
January 1907.

EDITOR'S STATEMENT

It has fallen to my lot to edit this essay, the first, and last, work of Kenneth John Freeman, a brilliant young Scholar of Winchester College and Trinity College, Cambridge, whose short life closed in the summer of 1906.

He was born in London on June 19, 1882, and died at Winchester on July 15, 1906,—a brief span of twenty-four years, the greater part of which was spent in the strenuous pursuit of truth and beauty, both in literature and in the book of Nature, but above all among the Classics.

Scholarly traditions and interests he inherited in no small measure : he was the son of Mr. G. Broke Freeman, a member of the Chancery Bar, and a Classical graduate of Trinity College, Cambridge, and the grandson of Philip Freeman, Archdeacon of Exeter, himself a Scholar of the same great Foundation, Craven University Scholar and Senior Classic in 1839. He was also a great-grandson of the Rev. Henry Hervey Baber, for many years Principal Librarian of the British Museum, and Editor of the *editio princeps* of the *Codex Alexandrinus*. From them he inherited a passion for Classical study, a keen sense of form, and a determined pursuit of knowledge, which nothing could daunt, not even the recurrent shadow of a long and distressing illness.

Through his mother, a daughter of Dr. Horace Dobell, of Harley Street, London, he was also a great-nephew of the poet Sydney Dobell ; and thus he may well have derived that poetic feeling which distinguished a number of verses found among his papers, since printed for private circulation.

His School and University career was uniformly successful. At Winchester he won prizes in many subjects and several tongues, and carried off the Goddard Scholarship, the intellectual blue ribbon, at the age of sixteen.

At Cambridge he was Browne University Scholar in 1903, and in the first "division" of the Classical Tripos in 1904, in which year he also won the Craven Scholarship. The senior Chancellor's medal fell to him in the following year.

There is no need to enumerate his other distinctions, but the epigram with which he won the Browne Medal in 1903 is so beautiful in itself and so true an epitome of the boy and the man, that I am tempted to quote it here :

> ξεῖνε, καλὸν τὸ ζῆν καταγώγιόν ἐστιν ἅπασιν,
> νηπυτίους γὰρ ὅμως νυκτιπλανεῖς τε φιλεῖ,
> δῶρα χαριζόμενον φιλίας καὶ τερπνὸν ἔρωτα
> καὶ πόνον εὐάνδρον φροντίδα τ' οὐρανίαν ·
> τρυχομένους δ' ἤδη κοιμᾷ τὸν ἀκήρατον ὕπνον
> πέμπει δ' ὥστε λαθεῖν οἰκάδ' ἐληλυθότας.

He was always an optimist, who regarded life as a "fair Inn," which provided much good cheer. Shyness and ill-health limited sadly the range of his friends, but not his capacity and desire for "friendship." "Manly toil," both physical and intellectual, was dear to his soul : thus, though no great athlete, he was an ardent Volunteer both at School and College, and declared that, had he not chosen the teacher's profession, he would have wished to be a soldier : he writes of Sparta and Xenophon with evident sympathy. Also he fought and won many an intellectual battle against great odds ; to quote one instance, he wrote the papers for his Craven Scholarship while convalescent in his old nursery. His poems, to complete the parallel, may justly be described as the " aspiring thoughts " of a singularly pure and reverent heart.

It is a simple, uneventful record : six happy years as a Winchester Scholar ; three as a Scholar of Trinity College, Cambridge ; one year of travel and study, mainly devoted to the subject of Education, which always had a special attraction for him ; and lastly, one year, the happiest of his life, when he returned to teach at his old school.

All appeared bright and promising ; he was doing the work he desired at the school of his choice, health and vigour seemed fully restored, and a strenuous life as a Winchester Master lay before him, when an acute attack of the old trouble, borne with perfect patience, cut him off in the prime of his promise.

Then, to quote his own translation of his epigram :

> When I was aweary, last and best
> They gave me dreamless rest ;
> And sent me on my way that I might come
> Unknown, unknowing, Home.

The work itself was never finished for the press ; indeed, some chapters, dealing with Sokrates, Plato, and Aristotle, did not appear sufficiently complete to justify publication : these, therefore, we have withheld. But this book is in substance what he left it, and he was fully aware that the omitted chapters were in need of further revision.

In any case, it would have been a labour of love to me to edit this dissertation ; but the labour has been lightened at every turn by the ungrudging help and friendship of many Scholars. Dr. Verrall, besides contributing a Preface, has contributed much advice in general and in detail ; Dr. Sandys has revised the proofs and given me the benefit of his comprehensive knowledge of the subject ; Dr. Henry Jackson went through some of the later chapters and discussed points of general interest. The original Essay or the proofs have in addition been revised, from different points of view, by Mr. Edmund D. A. Morshead, late Fellow of New College, Oxford, and Mr. F. M. Cornford, Fellow of Trinity College, Cambridge. Mr. G. S. Freeman (brother of the author) is responsible for the Index ; while Mr. W. R. H. Merriman has spent much pains upon verifying the numerous quotations. In a few cases Dr. F. G. Kenyon's erudition came to the rescue. To all these my best thanks are due. Mr. A. Hamilton Smith of the British Museum was most helpful in identifying the vases from which the illustrations are derived. The author, who was a considerable draughtsman, had drawn scenes from Greek vases with his own hand; but of course our illustrations are derived from published reproductions, with two exceptions. The two British Museum vase-scenes (Illustrations III. and IV.) were specially drawn for this book : they have never been carefully reproduced before. I must thank the Syndics of the Pitt Press at Cambridge for their kind permission to reproduce their print of Douris' Educational Vase from

Dr. Sandys' *History of Classical Scholarship.* The design which appears on the cover of this volume is also adapted from this vase.

It remains to add a few sentences from a Statement which the author himself drew up :

"I have," he says, "confined my attention very largely for several years to original texts and eschewed the aid of commentaries." This will be patent to the reader.

"As to accepted interpretations, I have, purposely and on principle, neither read nor heard much of them, since I wished, in pursuance of the bidding of Plato himself, not to receive unquestioningly the authority of those whom to hear is to believe, but to develop views and interpretations of my own. For I have always believed that education suffers immensely from the study of books about books, in preference to the study of the books themselves. M. Paul Girard's book in French (*L'Éducation Athénienne*) and Grasberger's in German (*Erziehung und Unterricht im klassischen Alterthum*), the latter of which I have only read in part, have set me on the track of authorities whom I should otherwise have missed, but I believe that my acknowledgments in the text and in the notes fully cover my direct obligations to them in other respects, although my indirect obligations to M. Girard's stimulating book, which are great, remain unexpressed.

"An apology is, perhaps, needed for the peculiar, and not wholly consistent, spelling of the Greek words. I had meant to employ the Latinised spelling. But when I came to write Lyceum, Academy, and pedagogue, my heart failed me. For I did not wish to suggest modern music-halls, modern art, and, worst of all, modern 'pedagogy. In adopting the ancient spelling I had

Browning on my side. But again, when I wrote Thou-kudides, my heart sank, for I could hardly recognise an old friend in such a guise. So I decided, perhaps weakly, to steer a middle course, and preserve the Latinised forms in the case of the more familiar words. Thus I put Plato, not Platon, but Menon and Phaidon." We have adhered to this principle in the main ; we need hardly say that Lakedaimon is the transliteration of a Greek word : Lacedaemonian is an English adjective. So a citizen of Troizen is a Troezenian, and of Boiotia a Boeotian. "I have," the author concludes, "preferred *Hellas* and *Hellene* to *Greece* and *Greek*. For a rose by any other name does not always smell as sweet."

M. J. RENDALL.

WINCHESTER COLLEGE,
March 1907.

INTRODUCTION

THE meeting-place of two streams has always a curious fascination for the traveller. There is a strange charm in watching the two currents blend and lose their individuality in a new whole. The discoloured, foam-flecked torrent, swirling on remorselessly its pebbles and minuter particles of granite from the mountains, and the calm, translucent stream, bearing in invisible solution the clays and sands of the plains through which its slow coils have wound, melt into a single river, mightier than either, which has received and will carry onward the burdens of both and lay them side by side in some far-off delta, where they will form "the dust of continents to be."

To the student of history or of psychology the meeting-place of two civilisations has a similar charm. To watch the immemorial culture of the East, slow-moving with the weight of years, dreamy with centuries of deep meditation, accept and assimilate, as in a moment of time, the science, the machinery, the restless energy and practical activity of the West is a fascinating employment ; for the process is big with hope of some glorious product from this union of the two. Those who live while such a union is in progress cannot esti-mate its value or its probable result ; they are but

conscious of the discomforts and confusion arising from
the ending of the old order that passes away, and can
hardly presage the glories of the new, to which it is
yielding place. It is in past history, not in the contemporary world, that such combinations must be
studied.

The chief historical instance of two distinct civilisations blending into one is the Renaissance, that mighty
union of the spirit of ancient Hellas and her pupil
Rome with the spirit of medieval Europe, which has
hardly been perfected even now. But it is often forgotten that there were at least two dress-rehearsals for
the great drama of the Renaissance, in the course of
which Hellenism learnt its own charm and adapted
itself to the task of educating the world. Alexander
carried the arts, the literature, and the spirit of Hellas
far into the heart of Asia ; and, though his great experiment of blending West with East was interrupted
by his early death and the consequent disruption of his
world-empire, yet, even so, something of his object was
effected in the Hellenistic culture of Alexandria, Syria,
and Asia Minor. Within a century of his death began
the second dress-rehearsal, this time in the West.
Conquered Hellas led her fierce conqueror captive, and
the strength of Rome bowed before the intellect and
imagination of the Hellene. Once more the great
man who designed to unite the two currents into one
stream without loss to either was cut off before his
plans could be carried out, and the murder of Julius
Cæsar caused incalculable damage to this earlier Renaissance, for the education of Rome, the second
scholar of Hellas, was not too wisely conducted. Yet
the schooling produced Virgil and Horace and that
Greco-Roman civilisation in which the Teutonic nations

of the North received their first lessons in culture. After several premature attempts, medieval Europe rediscovered ancient Hellas and her pupil Rome at the time of the Renaissance. Since that time the influence exerted by Hellenism upon modern civilisation has been continuous and incalculable. How much of that influence remains unassimilated, how far it is still needed, may perhaps be realised best by passing straight from the Elgin marbles or a play of Sophocles to a modern crowd or to modern literature.

Hellas has thus been the educator of the world to an extent of which not even Perikles ever dreamed. How then, it may naturally be asked, did the teacher of the nations teach her own sons and daughters ? If so many peoples have been at school to learn the lessons of Hellenism, what was the nature of the schools of ancient Hellas ? How did those wonderful city-states, which produced in the course of a few centuries a wealth of unsurpassed literature, philosophy and art, whose history is immortalised by the names of Thermopylae and Marathon, train their young citizens to be at once patriots and art-critics, statesmen and philosophers, money-makers and lovers of literature? They must have known not a little about education, those old Hellenes, it is natural to suppose. Have the schools, like the arts and literature and spirit, of Hellas any lesson for the modern world? These are the questions which the present work will attempt in some measure to answer.

In some measure only ; for the spirit of Hellas cannot be caught at second hand : it consists in just those subtler elements of refined taste and perfect choice of expression which cannot but be lost in a translation or a photograph. In like manner, the

secret of Hellenic education cannot be reproduced by
any mere accumulation of bald facts and wiseacres'
deductions. It is easy for the modern theorist to give
an exact account of his ideal school; he has only to
tabulate the subjects which are to be studied, the books
which are to be read, and the hours at which his
mechanical children are to be stuffed with the required
mass of facts. But the Hellenic schoolmaster held
that education dealt not with machines but with
children, not with facts but with character. His
object was to mould the taste of his pupils, to make
them "love what is beautiful and hate what is ugly."
And because he wished them to love what is beautiful
in art and literature, in nature and in human life, he
sought to make his lessons attractive, in order that the
subjects learnt at school might not be regarded with
loathing in after life. Education had to be charming
to the young; its field was largely music and art and
the literature which appeals most to children, adventure
and heroism and tales of romance expressed in verse.
The music is all but gone, and of the art only a
few fragments remain; the primary schools of Hellas
have left to modern research only portions of their
literature. Their attractiveness must be judged from
the poems of Homer. But the charm of education
lies mainly in the methods of the teacher; and of these
posterity can know little. Scholars may piece together
the books which were read and the exercises which
were practised, but of the method in which they were
taught, of their order and arrangement and respective
quantities, nothing can be known. There is the raw
material, the human boy, and of the tools wherewith the
masters fashioned him, some relics are left; but of the
way in which the artist used those tools, of the true

inwardness of his handicraft and skill, not all the diligence of Teutonic research can recover a trace. The
young art-student will learn little of Michel Angelo or
Raphael, if he focusses his attention simply on the
materials and the tools which they employed: to
grasp their spirit he must go to the Sistine Chapel or
to the Dresden Gallery, and contemplate their masterpieces. In like manner the student of Hellenic education ought to consider not its materials and tools, but
rather its results and ideals. He must look with his
own eyes and imagination upon the Aegina pediment or
the " Hermes " of Praxiteles, if he wishes to comprehend
the objects of the Doric and Ionic schools. This he must
do for himself, since no book can do it for him. All
that this work can hope to do is to furnish some few
ideas about the tools wherewith the Hellenic schoolmasters tried to fashion the boys at their disposal into
the masterpieces bodied forth in the " Hermes " and the
Aeginetan figures : the skilled fingers and the imaginative brains which used the tools are for ever beyond the
reach of the scholar and the archæologist.

The " Hermes," with his physical perfection and his
plenitude of intellect, with the features of an artist and
the brow of a thinker, may be taken as the ideal of the
fully developed Athenian education of the early fourth
century B.C. The Aeginetan figures stand in the same
relation to the Spartan and Cretan schools ; these heroic
figures have the bodily harmoniousness, the narrow if
deep thought, the hardness of the Dorian temper.
Perhaps it is not fanciful to see in the so-called
" Theseus " of the Parthenon an earlier ideal of
Athenian training, when it aimed at rather less of
dreamy contemplation, at a less sensuous and more
strenuous mode of life. If this be so, that glorious

figure bodies forth the very ideal of Periclean and Imperial Athens at her grandest moment, before the ruin caused by the long war with Sparta.

The stream of Hellenism ran in two currents. Underlying the local diversity, which made every little town ethically and artistically distinct from its neighbour, was the fundamental difference between Dorian and Ionian. Clearly marked in every aspect of life, this difference was most marked in the schools. Sparta and Crete on the one hand, and Athens, followed closely by her Ionian and Aeolic allies and at a greater distance by the rest of civilised Hellas, on the other, develop totally different types of education. The young Spartan is enrolled at a fixed age in a boarding-school : everything he learns or does is under State-supervision. Perfect grace and harmony of body is his sole object : he is hardly taught his letters or numbers. The young Athenian goes to school when and where his parents like ; learns, within certain wide limits, what they please ; ends his schooling when they choose. He learns his letters and arithmetic, studies literature and music, and, at a later date, painting, besides his athletic exercises, at a day-school. When he grows older, he may add rhetoric or philosophy or science or any subject he pleases to this earlier course. The State interferes only to protect his morals, and to enforce upon him two years of military training between the ages of eighteen and twenty.

The superficial differences between the Athenian and the Spartan type of school are so striking that at first sight they appear to have no one principle in common. It will therefore be necessary to keep the two types apart at first and discuss their details separately. But the Hellenic thinkers recognised certain deep-seated similarities beneath the superficial contradictions, and it became the object of educational philosophy to blend the two types into a perfect system. As soon as a deeper study has been made of the theory of education in Hellas, the distinctions of practice begin to vanish away and the similarities of ideal and aim become more and more apparent. When the survey of both practice and theory, which is the object of this work, has been completed, it should be possible to grasp and estimate the common principles, which, amid much variety of detail, governed the schools of Hellas.

PART I

THE PRACTICE OF EDUCATION

CHAPTER I

EDUCATION AT SPARTA AND IN CRETE

ACCORDING to a current legend, which Herodotos, owing to his Ionian patriotism, is eager to contradict, Anacharsis the Scythian, on his return from his travels, declared that the Spartans seemed to him to be the only Hellenic people with whom it was possible to converse sensibly, for they alone had time to be wise.[1] The full Spartan citizen certainly had abundant leisure. He was absolutely free from the cares of money-making, for he was supported by an hereditary allotment which was cultivated for him by State-serfs. He had no profession or trade to occupy him. His whole time was spent in educating himself and his younger countrymen in accordance with Spartan ideas, and in practising the Spartan mode of life. The Spartans divided their day between various gymnastic and military exercises, hunting, public affairs, and "leschai" or conversation-clubs, at which no talk of business was permitted ; the members discussed only what was honourable and noble, or blamed what was cowardly and base.[2] They were on the whole a grave and silent people, but they had a terse wit of their own, and there

[1] Herodotos, 4. 77.
[2] Plutarch, *Lukourgos*, 25. Kratinos (Athen. 138) ridicules these clubs and says that the attraction of them was that sausages hung there on pegs to be nibbled.

was a statue of Laughter in their city. They were
always in a state of perfect training, like the "wiry
dogs" of Plato's Republic. They were strong conservatives; innovation was strictly forbidden. The
unfortunate who made a change in the rules of the
Ball-game was scourged. In the Skias or Council-
chamber still hung in Pausanias' time the eleven-stringed
lyre which Timotheos had brought to Sparta, only to
have it broken; [1] and the nine-stringed lyre of Phrunis
met the same fate. Having once accepted the seven-
stringed lyre from Terpander, the Spartans never permitted it to be changed. They had also a talent for
minute organisation; both their army and their
children were greatly subdivided. Every one at Sparta
was a part of a beautifully organised machine, designed
almost exclusively for military purposes.

In this strangely artificial State, it was essential
that the future citizens should be saturated with
the spirit of the place at an early age. There were
practically no written laws. Judges and rulers acted
on their own discretion.[2] This was only possible if a
particular stamp of character, a particular outlook
and attitude, were impressed upon every citizen.
Consequently, education was the most important thing
at Sparta. It was both regulated and enforced by the
State. It was exactly the same for all. The boys were
taken away from home and brought up in great
boarding-schools, so that the individualising tendencies
of family life and hereditary instincts might be stamped
out, and a general type of character, the Spartan type,
alone be left in all the boys. For boarding-schools
have admittedly this result, that they impose a recognis-

---

[1] Pausanias, 3. 12. A similar event happened at Argos. Plutarch, *On Music*, 37.
[2] Aristot. *Pol.* ii. 9, 10.

able stamp, a certain similarity of manner and attitude, upon all the boys who pass through them.

Therefore, as soon as a child was born at Sparta, it was taken before the elders of the tribe to which its parents belonged.[1] If they decided that it was likely to prove sickly, it was exposed on Mount Taügetos, there to die or be brought up by Helots or Perioikoi. Sparta was no place for invalids. If the infant was approved, it was taken back to its home, to be brought up by its mother. Spartan women were famous for their skill in bringing up children. Spartan nurses were in great demand in Hellas. They were eagerly sought after for boys of rank and wealth like Alkibiades. The songs which they sang to their charges and the rules which they enforced made the children " not afraid of the dark " or terrified if they were left alone ; not addicted "to daintiness or naughty tempers or screaming " ; in fact, "little gentlemen " in every way.

No doubt the discipline of the children was strict, but then the parents lived just as strictly themselves. There were no luxuries for any one at Sparta : the houses and furniture were as plain as the food. But there is a charming picture of Agesilaos riding on a stick to amuse his children ; and the Spartan mothers, if stern towards cowardice, seem to have been keenly interested in their children's development ; they were by no means nonentities like Athenian ladies.

The children slept at home till they were seven ; but at an early age were taken by their fathers to the "Pheiditia " or clubs where the grown men spent those hours during which they stayed indoors and took their meals. About fifty men attended each of these clubs. The children sat on the floor near their fathers.

[1] Plutarch, *Lyk.* 16.

Each member contributed monthly a " medimnos " of barley-meal, eight " choes " of wine, five " mnai " of cheese, two and a half " mnai " of figs,[1] and some very cheap relish ; if he sacrificed to a god, he gave part of the victim to his " mess," and if he was successful in hunting (which was a frequent occupation), he brought his spoils to the common table. There was also the famous black broth, made by the hereditary guild of State cooks, which only a life of Spartan training and cold baths in the Eurotas could make appetising ; yet elderly Spartans preferred it to meat. Perhaps a fragment of Alkman represents a high-day at one of these clubs : " Seven couches and as many tables, brimming full of poppy-flavoured loaves, and linseed and sesamum, and in bowls honey and linseed for the children." [2]

A Spartan who became too poor to pay his contribution to his club lost his rights as a citizen, and so could not have his children educated in the State-system. But as long as the allotments were not alienated, such cases were not common. The contribution was κατὰ κεφαλήν,[3] that is, the fixed quantity of provisions had to be supplied for every member of the family who attended a club, *i.e.* for every male, since the women took their meals at home. There is no reason whatever for supposing that the boys, either before or after they went to the boarding-schools, were fed at the expense of the State. It is expressly stated that the number of foster-children, who accompanied their benefactors' sons to school, varied according to the extent of their patron's means.[4] Parents must there-

---

[1] Say, 1½ bushels of meal, 5 gallons of wine, 5 lbs. of cheese, and 2½ lbs. of figs.
[2] Smyth, *Melic Poets*, " Alkman," 26, if the emendation παίδεσσι be correct.
[3] Aristot. *Pol.* ii. 9.   [4] Phularchos (Athen. vi. 271).

fore have paid something for their boys while they were
at school. The teaching involved no expenses ; hence
it must have been the food for which they paid.
Thus, only those boys could attend the Spartan schools
whose parents could afford to pay the customary subscription in kind for their own and their children's food
at the common meals. Xenophon, the admirer of all
things Spartan, adopts the same system in his State,
since he makes the children of the poor drop out
automatically from the public schools. It must be
remembered that at Sparta families were always small,
and the population tended to decrease steadily ; the
number of males for whom subscriptions had to be paid
by the head of the family can rarely have been large.

Generally speaking, therefore, the Spartan schools
were only for the sons of " Peers " (ὅμοιοι),[1] that
is, those who paid the subscriptions. But a certain
number of other boys were admitted, provided that
their food was paid for. A rich Spartan might, if he
chose, select certain other boys to be educated with his
own son or sons, and pay their expenses meanwhile. [2]
The number of these school-companions depended on
the number of contributions in kind which he was
capable of supplying. The school-companions could
thus attend the Spartan schools ; but they did not
become citizens when they grew up, unless they revealed
so much merit that the Spartan State gave them the
franchise.

From what classes were these school-companions
drawn ? Sometimes they were foreigners, sons either
of distinguished guest-friends of leading Spartans, or
of refugee-settlers in Laconia. Thus Xenophon's

---

[1] Xen. *Anab.* iv. 6. 14 ; Aristot. *Pol.* ii. 9. 31.
[2] Phularchos (Athen. vi. 271 e).

two sons were educated at Sparta. These foreign boys were called τρόφιμοι or Foster - children. Xenophon mentions "foreigners from among the τρόφιμοι."[1] If these Foster-children, when grown up, remained in Sparta they possessed no civic rights. A passage in Plato refers to the difficulty which was experienced in getting these Foster-children to accept this humble position.[2] It is interesting to note that Sparta thus precedes Athens as an educational centre to which boys from foreign cities came to receive their schooling.

More often Spartan parents chose Helots to be school-companions of their sons. Thus Plutarch speaks of "two of the foster-brothers of Kleomenes, whom they call Mothakes."[3] The name Mothax was applied to these educated Helots. They seem to have been notorious for the way in which they presumed upon their position, if we may assume a connection between Mothax and Mothon, a term which is used for the patron deity of impudence in Aristophanes, and elsewhere is the name of a vulgar dance.[4] They were not enfranchised when their school-days were over, and had to settle down to slavish duties, unless they showed peculiar merit. But several of the most distinguished Spartans, including Lusandros, were enfranchised Mothakes.

Xenophon, in a passage which has already been quoted, mentions "gentlemen - volunteers of the Perioikoi and certain foreigners of the so-called Foster-children and bastards of the Spartiatai, very goodly men and not without share in the honourable things in the State."[5] If most of the authorities are

---

[1] Xen. *Hellen.* v. 3. 9.   [2] Plato, *Rep.* 520 D.   [3] Plut. *Kleom.* 8.
[4] Aristoph. *Knights*, 635, 695 (with Schol. on 697, φορτικὸν ὀρχήσεως εἶδος);
Eurip. *Bacch.* 1060.   [5] Xen. *Hellen.* v. 3. 9.

right in regarding "the honourable things"[1] as a
Spartan phrase for their educational system—and there
is good ground for this view—then this passage shows
that illegitimate sons, and perhaps eminent Perioikoi,
passed through the public schools at Sparta although,
however, neither were called Foster-children, a name
reserved for distinguished foreigners.   The Helots
who shared the education were known as Mothakes,
and sometimes as σύντροφοι, school-companions ; but
they do not seem to have been called τρόφιμοι,
" Foster-children."

During the best period of Spartan history, none of
these extra pupils, τρόφιμοι, Mothakes, illegitimate
children, and eminent Perioikoi, were enfranchised
unless they showed peculiar merit.   At a later date,
perhaps, any one who passed through the schools became
a Spartan citizen.   Plutarch makes this a part of
Lukourgos' system ; but that is improbable.   Such a
custom would only arise in the days of Spartan decay
and depopulation.   On the other hand, any Spartan
boys who flinched before the hardships of their national
education, lost their status, and were disfranchised, if
they did not persevere.[2]

Till they were seven, the boys were taken to
their fathers' clubs : the girls had all their meals with
their mothers at home, for the women did not have
dining-clubs.   By seeing the hardships which their
fathers endured, and hearing their discussions on
political subjects and their terse humour, the boys were
already being trained in the Spartan mode of life ; for
the clubs served as an elementary school.   There, too,
they learnt to play with their contemporaries, and to

[1] Xen. *Constit. of Lak.* iii. 3 ; *Hellen.* v. 4. 32.
[2] Xen. *Constit. of Lak.* iii. 3.

exchange rough jests without flinching.   To take a
jest without annoyance was part of the Spartan character ; but if the jester went too far for endurance, he
might be asked to stop.

At seven the boys were taken away from home, and
organised in a most systematic way into " packs " and
" divisions."   These were the " ilai," which probably
contained sixty-four boys, and the " agelai," whose
numbers are unknown.[1]   These packs fed together,
slept together on bundles of reeds for bedding, and
played together.   The boys had to go barefoot always,
and wore only a single garment summer and winter
alike.   They   were   all   under   the   control   of   a
" Paidonomos "   or   " Superintendent   of   the   boys,"
a citizen of rank, repute, and position, who might at
any moment call them together, and punish them
severely if they had been idle : he had attendants who
bore the ominous name of Floggers.[2]   So, as Xenophon
grimly remarks, a spirit of discipline and obedience
prevailed at Sparta.   In order that the boys might not
be left without control, even when the Paidonomos was
absent, any citizen who might be passing might order
them to do anything which he liked, and punish them
for any faults which they committed.   The most
sensible and plucky boy in each pack was made a
Prefect over it, and called the Bouâgor, or " Herd-
leader " ; the rest obeyed his orders and endured his
punishments.[3]

---

[1] " Agelai " of young men are mentioned by inscriptions at Miletos and Smurna
[Böckh, 2892, 3326] ; there may have been boarding-schools somewhat resembling
those of Sparta at these towns for young men.

[2] μαστιγόφοροι. Xen. *Constit. of Lak.* ii. 2. Aristotle calls Paidonomoi an aristocratic institution. They existed in Crete, and inscriptions mention them in Karia,
Teos, and many other places.

[3] Plut. *Lukourgos*, 16. Hesychius declares that the Bouâgor was a boy, so the
word cannot mean the Eiren, who was over twenty.

The elder men stirred up quarrels among the boys in order to see who was plucky. Over every school was set one of the young men over twenty who had a good reputation both for courage and for morality.[1] He was called the Eiren. He kept an eye on their battles, and used them as servants at home for his supper; he ordered the bigger boys to bring him firewood, and the smaller to collect vegetables. The only way by which such supplies could be obtained was by stealing them from the gardens and the men's dining-clubs. Apparently, then, the boys dined with him in his house;[2] they were supplied with a scanty meal by their parents to eat there, and were encouraged to make up the deficiency by stealing. "When the Eiren had finished supper, he ordered one of the boys to sing, and to another he propounded some question which needed a thoughtful answer, such as, 'Who is the best of the grown-ups?' For such particular questions are more stimulating than generalities like 'What is virtue?' or 'What is a good citizen?' The answer had to be accompanied by a concise reason; failure was punished by a bite on the hand. Elder men watched, saying nothing at the time, but rebuking the Eiren severely afterwards if he was too strict or too lenient."

Thus we find at Sparta a prefect-system and fagging. But the sense of responsibility produced in the elder boys at English public schools and the practice which they acquire in exercising authority were prevented at Sparta by the perpetual presence of grown men, which made Laconian schools more like French Lycées. There is no class of professional schoolmasters; the Eiren, the

---

[1] Plut. *Lukourgos*, 17; Xen. *Constit. of Lak.* ii. 11.

[2] In which case the Eiren corresponds closely to the Cretan Agelates.

Paidonomos, and any elder who chooses, give the instruction freely and gratuitously. Education, being so
simple, cost nothing at Sparta.

From Plutarch's mention of stealing from the *men's*
dining-clubs it may safely be inferred that boys of this
age dined apart. Whether it was always in the Eiren's
house cannot be ascertained. After the age of sixteen
they must have come into the men's syssitia; for
Xenophon implies that the visitor to Sparta could see
lads of that age at dinner and ask them questions: and
a visitor would certainly not have dined in a dining-
room meant only for boys. Whether the election of
members took place at that age, or whether they still
went to their fathers' clubs, is unknown.

The education was almost entirely physical. Plutarch,
it is true, says that they learnt "letters, because they
were useful." [1] This may have been a later introduction, or perhaps the amount learnt was so little as to
justify Isokrates in saying that the Spartans " do not
even learn their letters, which are the means to a knowledge of the past, as well as of contemporary events "; [2]
he also thought it highly improbable that even "the
most intelligent of them would hear of his speeches,
unless they found some one to read them aloud." [3] They
had, indeed, little reason to learn to read. Their written
laws were very few, and these they learnt by heart, set
to a tune. They had nothing to do with commerce or
even with accounts; very few of them knew how to
count. [4] Hippias, the Sophist, found that all they cared
to listen to, were " genealogies of men and heroes,
foundations of cities, and archæology generally."
Probably, like the Dorian philosopher Pythagoras, and

---

[1] Lukourgos, 16; *Lac. Institutions*, 247.   [2] Isok. *Panath.* 276 D.
[3] *Panath.* 285 C.   [4] Plato, *Hippias Maj.* 285 C.

like Plato, the admirer of all things Dorian, they held
that memory was all-important, and that the use of
writing weakened it.[1] Besides the State-laws set to
music there were songs which praised dead heroes and
derided cowards : the diction was plain and simple, the
subjects grave and moral ; many of them were war-
marches ; all were incentive to pluck and energy.

Rhetoric was, of course, utterly forbidden : a young
man who learnt it abroad and brought it home was
punished by the Ephors.[1] Spartans learned to be silent as
a rule ; when they spoke, their remarks were short and
much to the point, for they thought it wrong to waste
a word.[2] This was definitely taught to the boys, as has
been shown above. " If you converse with quite an
ordinary Laconian," says Plato,[3] " at first he seems a
mere fool ; then suddenly, at the critical point, he flings
forth a pithy saying, and his companions seem no better
than children compared with him." This epigrammatic
wisdom Plato ironically ascribes to the fact that
Laconians really attend Sophists on the sly, and are
greater philosophers than any one knows. Many echoes
of their terse and grim humour have come down to
modern times : such as Leonidas' remark to his troops
at Thermopylae, " Breakfast here : supper in Hades " ;
and the Spartan's description of Athens, " All things
noble there," by which he meant that nothing, however
base, was counted ignoble.

The Spartans must not be regarded as wholly averse
to literature. They knew Homer, and thought him the
best poet of his class, although the manner of life he
inculcated was Ionic, not Doric.[4] Alkman spent his

---

[1] Sext. Empir. *Mathem.* 2, § 21.   [2] Plut. *Lukourgos*, 19-20.

[3] Plato, *Protag.* 342 E.

[4] Plato, *Laws*, 680 D.   Crete repudiated Homer altogether.

life at Sparta, and has left one splendid song for a chorus of Laconian girls. Aristophanes could put a fine chorus into the mouths of Laconians, though its subject is noticeably warlike. For it was war-poems that the Spartans liked. " They care naught for the other poets," says the Athenian orator, Lukourgos, " but for Turtaios they care so exceedingly that they made a law to summon every one to the king's tent, when they are on a campaign, to hear the poems of Turtaios, considering that this would make them most ready to die for their country." [1]

After all, the objects of the Spartan education were not intellectual acuteness and the accumulation of knowledge, but discipline, endurance, and victory in war. Discipline was taught by the perpetual presence of authority, and by very severe punishments. Spartan boys were practically never left to their own devices: perhaps that is the secret of the moral failure of nearly every Spartan who was given a position of authority outside Lakedaimon; for responsibility requires practice. Endurance was taught by their whole mode of life. They went barefooted, with a single garment, played and danced naked under the hot Laconian sun; [2] there were no ointments or luxurious baths for their bodies, only the Eurotas for a swim, and a bundle of reeds for a bed. The food which the boys received was very scanty : often they were turned out into the country in the early morning to provide food for themselves for the whole day by stealing.

This organised stealing was a feature of Spartan education. At an early age, as we have seen, the

---

[1] Luk. *against Leokrates*, 107. The Polemarchos was judge in these singing competitions, and the winner received a bit of meat (Philochoros in Athen. 630 f.).

[2] Plato, *Laws*, 633 E.

small boys were sent out to steal firewood and vegetables for the Eiren who had charge of them.   Later
they were driven out into the country, to forage for
themselves at the expense of the farms.   There was a
definite age at which it was customary to begin stealing.[1]
The articles which might be stolen were fixed by
law, and the legal limits might not be transgressed.[2]
It must be remembered that much property in
Laconia was held in common.   Any one, for instance,
who was belated while hunting might take what food he
pleased from a country house, and even break open seals
to get at provisions.   The Spartans also used one
another's dogs and horses freely, without permission.
It is therefore absurd to say that the system taught the
boys to be dishonest.   If the State agrees to declare certain
articles to be common property, it is no longer stealing
if one citizen removes them from the house of another :
he is no more dishonest than a man who picks black-
berries or buttercups in England.   At one of the English
public schools, tooth-mugs used to be a recognised
article of plunder.   The small fags were expected to
keep their particular dormitory supplied with them, at
the expense of others.   They were punished by the
wronged dormitory if caught in the act of removing
them : but ingenuity in such thefts was regarded as
praiseworthy.   There was a certain number of these
mugs belonging to the whole house ; they were common
property, and could therefore be purloined without
dishonesty.

Moreover, this system of legalised robbery had a
valuable educational object at Sparta.   It was excellent
training in scouting, laying ambushes, and foraging, all
of which it is very important that a future soldier

[1] Plut. *Apoph.*   [2] Xen. *Anab.* iv. 6. 14.

should learn. Xenophon, a soldier himself, notices this, and in the *Anabasis*, when he needs a clever strategist, he selects a Spartan because he has been educated in this way. Since this was the object of the system, the boys, if caught, were flogged, not for stealing, but for stealing clumsily. Isokrates declares that skill in robbery was the road to the highest offices at Sparta. "If any one can show that this is not the branch of education which the Lacedaemonians regard as the most important," he adds, "I admit that I have not spoken a word of truth in my life." [1]

These foraging expeditions of the boys prepared them for the similar, if more arduous, duties of "Secret Service" [2] which awaited them between eighteen and twenty. Young men of this age were sent in bands to the different districts of Laconia for long periods, during which they hid in the woods, slept on the ground, attended to their own wants without a servant, and wandered about the country by day and night. [3] When it appeared good to them or their chiefs they made sudden attacks on the Helots, and slaughtered those who seemed ambitious enough to be dangerous, the Ephors declaring war on their serfs yearly in order that there might be no blood-guiltiness attached to these assassinations. [4] There was a regular officer set over this secret police, who no doubt directed where the particular youths should go. [5] At a critical moment of the Peloponnesian War, 2000 of the bravest and most ambitious Helots suddenly "disappeared," probably by this means. [6] But Plato recognised the educational value of such a

---

[1] Isok. *Panath.* 277.   [2] κρυπτεία, κρυπτή.

[3] Plato, *Laws*, 633 c.

[4] Plut. *Lukourgos*, 28. Isokrates merely mentions that the Ephors could kill as many Helots as they liked (*Panath.* 271 b).

[5] Plut. *Kleom.* 28.   [6] Thuc. iv. 80.

system, if the murders were omitted. In his *Laws*[1]
he institutes a force of κρυπτοί, 720 in number, who
patrol the whole country, taking the twelve districts in
turn, so as to gain a complete acquaintance with it.
They have all the farm-servants and beasts at their disposal, for digging trenches, making fortifications, roads,
embankments, and reservoirs, for irrigation works and
the like. The similarity of name suggests similarity
of functions, but how much of this the κρυπτοί at
Sparta did cannot be fixed. Probably their chief work
was to keep watch over the subject populations,
Perioikoi and Helots, who were otherwise left almost
entirely to their own devices.

In their institutions of the foraging parties and
Secret Service, the Spartans show a clear appreciation of
boy-nature, as well as a keen eye for methods of military
training. Moderns are beginning to realise that the
average boy has so much of the primitive and natural
man in him that, unless he is permitted to "go wild"
and live the savage life at intervals, he is apt to become
riotous and lawless. Hence in recent days the institution of camps for boys in England and "Seton Indians"
in America. The Spartans, alone of Hellenes, fully
recognised this peculiarity of boys, and met it with the
foraging expeditions and secret service. The Athenian
boy was not thus provided for until he became an
ephebos ; hence the Athenian streets were full of
young Hooligans, while the aristocratic lads developed
more refined, if more vicious, methods of giving vent
to their instincts. In these country-expeditions alone
the Spartan boys had an opportunity of escaping from

---

[1] Plato, *Laws*, 763 B. Some have supposed that κρυπτοί is an interpolation. If
so, the resemblance must have been close enough to strike a commentator who knew
Lakedaimon, in spite of the fact that the ages in the two systems are different.

the presence of their elders and developing habits of self-reliance and responsibility. Had Sparta made better use of these opportunities, the fate of her Empire after Aigospotamoi might have been different.

A frequent occupation of all ages at Sparta was hunting. This, too, they recognised to be an excellent training for soldiers, since it involved courage in meeting wild beasts, skill and ingenuity in tracking them, and hardships of all sorts in the forests and on the mountains. Laconia was full of game, and Laconian hounds were famous. The successful huntsman gave what he had killed to enrich the meals of his dining-club, and so won much popularity.

Spartan boys must also have learnt to ride, for they had to go in procession on horseback at the festival of Huakinthos.[1] They were taught to swim, too, by their daily plunge in the Eurotas. A great part of their time was spent in gymnastics, under the close inspection of their elders. Boxing and the pankration were forbidden to the young Spartan, probably because they developed a few particular muscles at the expense of the others.[2] For wrestling no scientific trainers were allowed ; the Spartan type depended solely on strength and activity, not on technical skill ; so a Spartan, when beaten by a wrestler from another country, said his opponent was not a better man, but only a cleverer wrestler.[3] Gladiators, such as those mentioned in Plato's *Laches* as teaching the use of arms, were not permitted at Sparta ; these, however, seem to have been unpractical theorists, quite useless in battle, as General Laches shows by a funny anecdote about one of

---

[1] Polukrates (in Athen. 139 e).   [2] Aristot. *Pol.* viii. 4 ; Plut. *Luk.* 19.

[3] Plut. *Apoph.* 233 E.   Plato adopts the Spartan views about wrestling in the *Laws.*

them.[1] No lounging spectators were permitted in
Spartan gymnasia; the rule was "strip or withdraw."[2]
The eldest man in each gymnasium had to see that
every one took sufficient exercise to work off his food
and prevent him from becoming puffy.[3] The physical
condition of the boys was inspected every ten days by
the Ephors,[4] while the competitions of the epheboi
seem to have been controlled by a special board, the
Bidiaioi, who figure in inscriptions.[5] Aristotle says
of the whole Spartan discipline that it made the boys
"beast-like,"[6] but admits that it did not produce the
one-sided athlete, so common in Hellas, who looked
solely to athletics, and was too much specialised to be
good for anything else. Xenophon[7] says that it would
be hard to find anywhere men with more healthy or
more serviceable bodies than the Spartiatai. The most
beautiful man in the Hellenic army at Plataea was a
Spartan.[8] The Spartan boys' manners were in some
ways surprisingly maidenlike. When they went along
the highway, they kept their hands under their coat,
and walked in silence, keeping their eyes fixed on the
ground before their feet. They spoke as rarely as a
statue and looked about them less than a bronze
figure: they were as modest as a girl. When they
came into the mess-room, you could rarely hear them
even answer a question.[9]

Fighting was encouraged at all ages; there were
organised battles, somewhat resembling football matches,
for the epheboi, in a shady playing-field surrounded by

---

[1] Plato, *Laches*, 183 D, E.   [2] Plato, *Theait.* 162 B and 169 B.

[3] Xen. *Constit. of Lak.* v. 8.

[4] Athen. xii. 550 d. Their dress and bedding was inspected at the same time.

[5] Pausan. iii. 11. 2. βίδεος, Böckh, 1241, 1242; βίδυος, 1254.

[6] Aristot. *Pol.* viii. 4. 1.   [7] Xen. *Constit. of Lak.* v. 9.

[8] Herod. ix. 72.   [9] Xen. *Constit. of Lak.* ii. 4.

rows of plane trees and encircled by streams, access to it being given by two bridges. After a night spent in sacrifice, two teams of epheboi proceeded to this field. When they came near it, they drew lots, and the winners had the choice of bridges by which to enter the ground, selecting no doubt in accordance with the direction of sun and wind, as a modern football captain, who has won the toss, selects the end of the ground from which he will start playing. The epheboi fought with their hands, kicked, bit, and even tore out one another's eyes, in the endeavour to drive the opposing team back into the water.[1]

The grown men were also encouraged to fight by the following device. The Ephors selected three of them, who were called Hippagretai. Each of these three selected one hundred companions, giving a public explanation in each case why he chose one man and rejected the others. So those who had been rejected became foes to those who were selected, and kept a close watch over them for the slightest breach of the accepted code of honour. Each party was always trying to increase its strength or perform some signal service to the State, in order to strengthen its own claims. The rivals also fought with their fists whenever they met.[2]

This systematised pugnaciousness at Sparta presents an interesting parallel to the German University duels and to the fights which used to be almost daily occurrences in the life of an English schoolboy. Most of the older English public schools can still show the special ground which was the recognised scene of these battles.

Floggings were exceedingly common at Sparta.

[1] Paus. iii. 14. 2.   [2] Xen. *Constit. of Lak.* iv.

Any elder man might flog any boy. It was not etiquette for boys to complain to their parents in these cases ; if they did so, they received a second thrashing. But the triumph of this system was the flogging of the " epheboi " yearly at the altar of Artemis Orthia, in substitute for human sacrifice. Entrance for the competition was quite voluntary, but competitors seem always to have been forthcoming even down to Plutarch's days. They began by practice of some sort in the country.[1] The altar was covered with blood ; if the floggers were too lenient to some " ephebos " owing to his beauty or reputation, the statue, according to the legend, performed a miracle in order to show its displeasure.[2] The competitors were often killed on the spot ; but they never uttered a groan.[3] The winner was called the "altar - victor" ($\beta\omega\mu o\nu\acute{\iota}\kappa\eta s$) and an inscription still records such a victory.[4]

The girls at Sparta were also organised into agelai or " packs." [5] They took their meals at home, but otherwise lived a thoroughly outdoor life. They had to train their bodies no less than the boys, in order that they might bear strong children, so they took part in contests of strength as well as of speed.[6] They shared in the gymnasia and in the musical training. Among their sports were wrestling, running, and swimming ; they were exposed to sun and dust and toil.[7] They learned to throw the diskos and the javelin ; [8] they wore only the short Doric " chiton " with split sides.[9]

[1] Hesychius, Φούαξιρ. [2] Paus. iii. 16. 11.
[3] Plut. Lukourgos, 18 ; Cicero, Tusc. Disp. v. 27.
[4] Böckh, 1364.
[5] Pindar, Frag. Hyporch. 8 Λάκαινα παρθένων ἀγέλα.
[6] Xen. Constit. of Lak. i. 4. [7] Cicero, Tusc. Disp. ii. 15.
[8] Plut. Lukourgos, 14.
[9] Whence they were called φαινομήριδες. This chiton may be seen in the conventional statues of Artemis.

They went in procession at festivals like the boys; at
certain festivals they danced and sang in the presence of
the young men, praising the brave among them and
jeering at the cowards.   At the Huakinthia the maidens
raced on horseback.   Theokritos makes a band of 240
maidens, " all playmates together, anoint themselves
like men and race beside the Eurotas." [1]   That passage
also gives wool-work to Laconian maidens (which is
probably untrue, being contradicted by Plato),[2] and
lyre-playing, which is contradicted by a Laconian in
Plutarch, who says that " such rubbish is not Laconian."
The result of all this outdoor training was great
physical perfection : Lampito, the Spartan woman in
Aristophanes' *Lusistrata*, is greatly admired by the
women from other cities for her beauty, her complexion,
and her bodily condition : " she looks as though she
could throttle a bull."   She ascribes it to her gymnastics
and vigorous dancing.[3]   The girls till they married
wore no veil, and mixed freely with the young men ;
in fact, there was one dance where they met in modern
fashion ; first the youth danced some military steps,
and then the maiden danced some of a suitable sort.[4]
Consequently love-matches were far more possible at
Sparta than elsewhere in Hellas.   After marriage
the women had to wear veils, and remained at home ;
gymnastics, dances, and races ceased.

The Spartans were intensely fond of dancing, but it
must be remembered that they often called dancing
what moderns would call drill.   For war was almost a
form of dance ; they marched or charged into battle to

---

[1] Theok. *Idyll* 18. 23.   [2] *Laws*, 806 A.

[3] *Lusistrata*, l. 80 onwards.   In the play Lampito is married.   Aristophanes has
either made a mistake or the gymnastics are meant to be in the past only.

[4] The ὅρμος dance.   Compare the dance at the end of the *Lusistrata*, where
" man stands by woman, and woman by man."

the notes of the flute, crowned and wearing red cloaks.
The march tunes were in frequent use in Sparta, no
doubt at military exercises. Every day the epheboi
were drawn up in ranks, one behind the other, and
went through military evolutions and dancing figures
alternately, while a flutist played to them and beat time
with his foot.[1] This is simply musical drill. The
great national festival of the Gumnopaidia was very
similar. Three great battalions, consisting respectively
of old men, young men, and boys, drawn up in rank
and file, exhibited various movements, chiefly of a
gymnastic sort, singing the songs of Thaletas and
Alkman and Dionusodotos the while and indulging in
impromptu jesting at one another's expense, after the
fashion of a rustic revel-chorus in Attica. Sometimes
the battalions appeared one by one, and were " led out "
like an army, by the Ephors.[2] On other occasions all
three were drawn up in crescent formation side by side,
with the boys in the middle. The festival must have
closely resembled the public parades of the gymnastic
clubs in Switzerland. There were posts of honour and
dishonour, as in battle, cowards usually receiving the
latter. But Agesilaos, the king, once received an
inferior station after his victory at Corinth, and turned
the insult by a jest, " Well thought of, chorus-leader :
that's the way to give honour to the post." [3] Then
there was the war-dance, imitating all the actions of
battle, a sort of manual and bayonet exercise, but
accompanied by much acting and by music. Every
Spartan boy began to learn this as soon as he was five.[4]
It was done in quick time, if we may judge by the
" Pyrrhic " or war-dance foot ($\smile \smile$). There was also

[1] Lucian, *Dancing*, 274.   [2] Xen. *Hellen*. vi. 4. 16.
[3] Xen. *Ag*. ii. 17.   [4] Athen. 630 a.

a wrestling-dance,[1] and most gymnastics were done
to the accompaniment of the flute. In fact, chorus-
dancing was a regular part of the education of Spartans
and Cretans : the only experience of singing which
most of them possessed was acquired in this way.[2] It is
true that elegiacs were sung as solos before the king's
tent on campaigns, and at meals, when the victor got
a particularly good slice of meat ; but probably this
accomplishment was confined to a few. Aristotle asserts
that the Laconians did not learn songs, but claimed
nevertheless to be able to distinguish good from bad.

Such was the Spartan system of education. To an
Englishman their schools have a greater interest than
those of any other ancient State. Sparta produced the
only true boarding-schools of antiquity. The " packs "
of the Spartan boys, like the English public schools,
formed miniature States, to whose corporate interests
and honour each boy learned to make his own wishes
subservient. Spartan boys, too, like our own, had
the smaller traits of individuality rubbed off them by
the publicity and perpetual intercourse with others
involved in the boarding-school system, in order that
the racial characteristics might the more emerge in
them. They, too, learnt endurance by hardship, and
were early trained both to rule and to obey by means
of the institution of prefects and fagging. But here
the resemblance stops short. The Spartans, like most
other nations, were not prepared to pay the price at
which alone an education in responsibility can be
obtained, the price which lies in the possible ruin of
all the boys who are not strong enough to be a law
to themselves. They very rarely left the boys to

[1] Athen. 678 b.   [2] Plato, *Laws*, 666 D.

themselves without grown men to look after them. They were always interfering and supervising, instead of leaving the prefects to exercise their authority. And so, when Spartans were sent abroad to govern cities or command armies, having had no practice in responsibility, they failed shamefully and ignominiously. But this is equally true of the Athenians and of other Hellenes. The Spartans deserve all credit for their experiments with the boarding-school system.

But the system which they adopted had many faults, besides that which has already been noticed. There was no individual attention for the boys. The hardships were excessive and brutalising. While the boys' bodies were developed and trained almost to perfection, their minds were almost entirely neglected : hence the stupidities of Spartan policy and the lack of imagination which their statesmen showed. It was impossible to over-eat or over-drink under the Spartan system, so the young Spartan had no experience in self-restraint.[1] The gymnasia and dining-clubs caused a great deal of quarrelling (which the Spartan authorities welcomed), and of immorality (which was very strictly forbidden) ; the Spartan gymnasia erred less, however, in this latter respect than the Athenian. In war the Spartans were only invincible so long as they were the only trained troops in Hellas ; the rise of professional armies ruined them, for they could not adapt themselves to new circumstances. They produced no art and very little literature, if any. But their whole State was as much a work of art as a Doric temple, and of very much the same order, with its symmetry and regularity, its sacrifice of detail to the whole, its strength and restraint. It was also the

[1] *Laws*, 634-635.

inspiration of at least one great piece of literature, Plato's *Republic*.

If courage was their sole object, as perhaps it was, they succeeded in obtaining it. The coward was a rare, and a most unhappy bird at Sparta. Mothers on several occasions killed sons who returned home from a campaign disgraced. "No one would mess with a coward, or consort with him. When rival teams were chosen for the game of ball, he was omitted. In dances he received the post of dishonour. He was avoided in the streets. No one would sit next to him. He could not find a husband for his daughters or a wife for himself," and was punished for these offences. "He was beaten if he imitated his betters in any way." [1] If the Hellenes were a nation of children, as the old Egyptian called them, the Spartans were at least a manly sort of schoolboy. They deified the schoolboy virtues, pluck and endurance. If we wish to see how far their education, in its best days, enabled them to prove true to their ideals, let us consider those 300 at Thermopylae waiting, with jests on their lips, for the onset of Oriental myriads, and remember that finest of all epitaphs, of which English can give no rendering, written upon their memorial in the pass in honour of their obedience unto death—

> Go tell the Spartans, thou that passest by,
> That here, obedient to their laws, we lie.

The Cretan system of education was very similar in many ways to the Spartan. In both localities the teaching was given by any elder member of the community who chose, not by a professional and paid class of masters. But in Crete education cost the

[1] Xen. *Constit. of Lak.* ix. 5.

parent even less than at Sparta ; for the boys were
fed largely at public cost.[1]   But so was every other
Cretan, male and female alike.   Each community possessed large public estates, cultivated by public serfs.[2]
The revenues thus accruing to the State were applied
to the expenses of government, which were small, and to
the food-supply of all citizens.   Thus men, women,
and children were all fed mainly at public cost.   It
may be noted, however, that there is no question of
providing the children of improvident parents with
meals at the expense of more provident citizens.   Moreover, the heads of families, who each possessed an
allotment, as at Sparta, had to contribute a tenth of the
produce of their estates.

The women-folk took their meals at home,[3] although
the cost of their food was mainly defrayed by the
public revenues.   The men took their meals in dining-
clubs ($\dot{\alpha}\nu\delta\rho\epsilon\hat{\imath}\alpha$).   The whole population of each community was divided into clubs of this sort, apparently
on the family basis, so that two or three families made
up a club between them, to which their children and
descendants would in turn belong.   All the males of
the family attended these meals ; small children, boys,
and young men as well as elders are all mentioned as
being present at the same dinners.[4]   The club is only
an enlarged family party.   The small children sat on the
ground behind their fathers ; they waited on themselves
and on their elders, but the general superintendence of
cooking and attendance was in the hands of a woman
with three or four public slaves and some underlings
in her control.[5]   As they grew older, the sons sat

[1] Aristot. *Pol.* ii. 10. 8.
[2] Additional revenues for the same objects were derived from the taxes paid by
Perioikoi and serfs (Athen. 143 a, b).   [3] Plato, *Laws*, 781 A.
[4] Historians quoted by Athen. 143 e.   [5] *Ibid.*

beside their fathers. Boys ordinarily received half what their parents had ; but orphans were allowed the full quantity at their dead father's club.

Thus the Cretan club was an amalgamation of several families into a sort of clan, whose male members all dined together. All the boys of the clan formed one boarding-school. They all slept in one room, perhaps attached to the dining-hall ; there was always a dormitory attached to each of these buildings for visitors from other cities, so it would be natural to expect a dormitory for the children also. The boys took their meals in the club dining-hall, in the presence of their elders, by whose improving conversations upon politics and morals they were supposed to be educated. These elder members elected one of their number to serve as παιδονόμος or "Super-intendent of the boys" of their club.[1] Under his directions the boys learned letters "in moderation" : they were constantly practised in gymnastics, in the use of arms, especially the bow, which was a great Cretan weapon, and in the war-dances, the Kuretic and Pyrrhic, both indigenous in Crete. They learned the laws of their country set to a sort of tune, in order that their souls might be drawn by the music, and also, that they might more easily remember them. In this way, if they did anything which was forbidden, they had not the excuse of ignorance.[2] Besides this, they were taught hymns to the gods, and praises of good men. The favourite metre for these purposes was the Cretic ($-\cup-$), which was regarded as "severe" and so suitable for teaching courage and restraint.[3] The

---

[1] Strabo, x. 4. 483 (on authority of Ephoros), and Herakleides Pont. iii. (who provide most of the details about Crete).

[2] Aelian, *True History*, ii. 39. [3] Strabo, x. 4. 480.

Pæan was their chief national form of song. Cretan boys were also practised in that terse and somewhat humorous style of speaking which we have already seen at Sparta.[1]

Cretan boys were always fighting either single combats or combined battles against the boys of another club-school. They were taught endurance by many hardships. They wore only a short coat in summer and winter alike. They learnt to despise heat and cold and mountain paths and the blows which they received in gymnasia and in fighting.

They remained in the club-schools till their seventeenth year,[2] when they became epheboi and cele-brated their escape from the garb of childhood by a special festival.[3] Like their contemporaries at Athens, the epheboi took a special oath of allegiance to the State and hatred towards its enemies. A fragment still survives of the oath taken by the epheboi of Dreros, near Knossos.[4] At seventeen the epheboi were collected into " packs " (ἀγέλαι) by private enterprise. A rich and distinguished young ephebos would gather round him as large a pack of his contemporaries as he could ; their numbers no doubt depended partly on his wealth, and still more on his personal popularity. The aristocratic element in this arrangement is very notice-able, as in all the institutions of Crete as contrasted with Sparta. The father of this young chief usually acted as leader of the pack (ἀγελάτης) ; he possessed full authority over them and could punish them as he pleased. He led them out on hunting expeditions and to the " Runs " (δρόμοι), that is, the gymnasia of the

---

[1] Sosikrates (in Athen. 261 e), speaking of Phaistos.

[2] Hesychius, ἀπάγελος.   [3] ἐκδύσια, Antoninus Liberalis, 18.

[4] Mahaffy, p. 81 ; Grasberger, iii. 61.

epheboi. Cretans who had not yet entered a pack of epheboi were excluded from these runs ($\dot{a}\pi\acute{o}\delta\rho o\mu o\iota$) ; when they entered, they were called " members of packs " ($\dot{a}\gamma\acute{\epsilon}\lambda a\sigma\tau o\iota$).[1] The pack-leader could collect his followers where he pleased ;[2] very possibly the epheboi did not attend the club dinners ordinarily, but fed or slept either at their patron's house (whence the need of a rich pack-leader) or in some special room. They thus corresponded closely to the Spartan boys of a younger age under their Eiren. Their food was supplied, like that of all Cretans, largely out of the public revenues. On certain fixed days " pack " joined battle with " pack " to the sound of the lyre and flutes and in regular time, as was the custom in war ; fists, clubs, and even weapons of iron might be used. It was a regular institution, half dance, half field-day, with fixed rules and imposed by law. These battles must have closely resembled the contests of the Spartan epheboi in the shady playing-fields. The life of the boys was surrounded with a military atmosphere throughout. They wore military dress and counted their weapons their most valuable possessions. Young Cretans remained in the packs till after marriage. Then they returned to their homes and the clubs.

Of the practical results of Cretan education nothing can be said. From the day when Idomeneus sets sail from Troy, Crete almost disappears from Hellenic history. Too strong to be attacked by their neighbours, too much weakened by intestine feuds to assume the aggressive, the Cretans remained aloof from their compatriots on the mainland and in the archipelago till the close of the period of Hellenic independence.

[1] Eustathius on *Il.* ix. 518.   [2] Herakl. Pont. iii. 3.

APPENDIX A

SPARTAN SYSSITIA

THESE dining-clubs were organised like "diminutive states."[1] It was enacted who was to recline in the most important place, who in the second, and so on, and who was to sit on the footstool, which was the place of dishonour, usually' assigned only to children. "Each man is given a portion to himself, which he does not share with any one. They have as much barley bread as they like, and there is an earthenware cup of wine standing by each man, for him to put his lips to when he feels disposed. The chief dish is always the same for all, boiled pork. There is plenty of Spartan broth, and some olives, cheese, and figs.[2]

"Each contributes to his mess about 18 gallons of barley meal, 60 or 70 pints of wine, and a small quantity of figs and cheese, and 10 Aeginetan obols for extras." This contribution no doubt covered expenses, for the quantity sent by an absentee king, probably representing the average consumption of an individual, falls well within this estimate (cf. Herod. vi. 57). After the regular meal[3] an ἐπαικλον or extra meal might be served. It would be provided by a member of the mess, consisting either of the results of hunting or the produce of his farm, for nothing might be bought. The ordinary components of such a meal were pigeons, geese, fieldfares, blackbirds, hares, lambs, and kids, and wheaten bread, a welcome change from the usual barley loaves. The cooks proclaimed the name of the giver, so that he might get the credit. ἐπαικλα were often exacted as fines for offences from rich members; the poor had to pay laurel leaves or reeds. There was also a special sort of ἐπαικλον designed for the children, barley meal soaked in olive oil—a sort of porridge, in

---

[1] Persaeus ap. Athen. 140 f.

[2] Dicaearchus ap. Athen. 141 a.

[3] Sphaerus ap. Athen. 141 c, d.; and Molpis, ibid.

fact. According to Nicocles the Laconian, this was swallowed in laurel leaves—which does not sound very inviting.

There were also banquets independent of the messes. These were called κοπίδες.[1] Tents were set up in the sacred enclosure round the temple of the deity in whose honour the feast was given. Heaps of brushwood covered with carpets served for couches. The food consisted of slices of meat, round buns, cheese, slices of sausage, and for dessert dried figs and various beans.

At the Tithenidia, or Nurses' Feast, a κοπίς was given at the temple of Artemis Koruthalia by the stream Tiassos.[2] The nurses brought the boy-babies to it. The sacrifice was a sucking pig, and baked loaves were served. The κοπίδες were evidently a feature of Spartan life : Epilukos makes his " laddie " (κωράλισκος) remark, " I will go to the κοπίς in Amuklai at Appellas' house, where will be buns and loaves and jolly good broth " : which shows that the children's parties at Sparta were regarded as attractive.

The Karneia, the great Spartan festival, was an imitation of camp-life.[3] The sacrificial meal was served in tents, each containing nine men, and everything was done to the word of command.

APPENDIX B

CRETAN SYSSITIA

THE chief authorities for the attendance at these meals are the two historians, Dosiades and Purgion, quoted in Athenaeus (143). Dosiades states that an equal portion is set before each man present, but to the younger members is given a half portion of meat, and they do not touch any of the other things. Purgion says : " To the sons, who sit on lower seats by their fathers' chairs, they give a half portion of what is supplied to the men ; orphans receive a full share." The comparison of the

[1] Polemon *ap.* Athen. 56 a, and 138-139.
[2] Cp. the crèche temples in Plato's *Laws*, 794 A.
[3] Demetrius of Scepsis (*ap.* Athen. 141 e).

two passages shows that the " younger members " mentioned
by Dosiades are what Purgion calls the orphans, and that
they are not yet full-grown men. Thus they must be either
the boys or the epheboi. It is not, however, at all likely
that the epheboi, who were of military age and engaged in
violent exercises, would be given only half rations, so these
younger members are the boys not yet included in the ἀγέλαι.
Dosiades continues : " On each table is set a drinking vessel,
of weak wine. This all who sit at the common table share
equally. The children have a bowl to themselves," that is,
the boys who sat beside their fathers but not at the table.
" After supper first they discuss the political situation, and
then recall feats in battle, and praise those who have distinguished themselves, encouraging the youngers to heroism."
The quotation shows that not merely the small children are
in question, but boys of an age to understand politics and war.

CHAPTER II

ATHENS AND THE REST OF HELLAS :
GENERAL INTRODUCTION

LACONIA and Crete were mainly agricultural countries
that had little concern with trade or manufactures.
Their citizens comprised a landed aristocracy, supported
by estates which were cultivated for them by a subject
population ; there was no necessity, therefore, for them
to prepare their boys for any profession or trade, or
even to instruct them in the principles of agriculture.
The young Spartan or Cretan no more needed professional or technical instruction of any sort than the richer
absentee Irish landlords of the present day. He could
give the whole of his school-time, without any sacrifice
of his financial prospects, to the training of his body
and of his character.

But the rest of Hellas was for the most part the
scene of busy manufactures and extensive trade. It
would be natural to expect that great commercial
peoples, like the Athenians or the Ionians of Asia
Minor, would have set great store by the commercial
elements of education, and to assume that business
methods and utilitarian branches of study would have
occupied a large place in their schools. But this was
very far from being the case. To a Hellene education

meant the training of character and taste, and the symmetrical development of body, mind, and imagination. He would not have included under so honourable a name either any course of instruction in which the pupils mastered their future trade or profession, or any accumulation of knowledge undertaken with the object of making money. Consequently technical training of all sorts was excluded from Hellenic schools and passed over in silence by Hellenic educationalists. Information concerning it must be pieced together from stray facts and casual allusions, and the whole idea of " utilitarian " instruction, in the modern sense of the word, must be carefully put aside during any consideration of Hellenic schools.

For the Hellenes as a nation regarded all forms of handicraft as *bourgeois* (βάναυσος) and contemptible. Herodotos says that they derived this view from the surrounding peoples, who all held it.[1] To do anything in order to extract money from some one else was, in their opinion, vulgar and ungentlemanly. The lyric poets and the Sophists were alike blamed for taking fees. The cheapness and abundance of serf- or slave-labour made it possible for a large proportion of the free population to live in idleness, and devote their time to the development of the body by physical exercises, of the mind by perpetual discussions, and of the imagination by art and music. Citizenship required leisure, in the days before representative government came into vogue. It was owing to this principle that the Athenian received pay for a day's attendance in the Law Courts or the Assembly, for by this means the poorest citizen obtained an artificial leisure for the performance of his duties. Otherwise true citizenship was

---

[1] Herod. ii. 167. Corinth was an exception.

impossible.   Plato regards a tradesman as unfit to be an
acting citizen.[1]   Aristotle rejects as unworthy of a free
man all trades which interfere with bodily development
or take time which ought to be devoted to mental im-
provement.[2]   Xenophon explains the reason of this
attitude.   The discredit which attaches to the *bourgeois*
occupations is quite natural ; for they ruin the physical
condition of those who practise them, compelling them
to sit down and live in the shade, and in some cases to
spend their day by the fire.   The body thus becomes
effeminate, and the character is weakened at the same
time.   Tradesmen, too, have less leisure for serving
their friends and the State.   In some communities,
especially the most warlike, the citizens are not allowed
to practise sedentary trades.[3]   The owner of a factory
or a farm worked by slave-labour was exempt from
corrupting influences : it was only actual work which
was degrading.

A large number, however, from among the poorer
classes were compelled to work with their own hands ;
so these, as well as the slaves, required technical instruction.   Some indications survive as to the manner in
which this was imparted.   Trades were mostly hereditary ; " the sons of the craftsmen learn their fathers'
trade, so far as their fathers and their friends of the
same trade can teach it." [4]   But others might also learn.
Xenophon mentions such cases.   " When you apprentice
a boy to a trade," he says, " you draw up a statement
of what you mean him to be taught," [5] and the fees were
not paid unless this agreement was carried out.   The
Kleitophon [6] mentions as the two functions of the

---

[1] Plato, *Laws*, 846 D.   [2] Arist. *Pol.* viii. 2. 4.
[3] Xen. *Econ.* iv. 3.   Sitting was regarded as a slavish attitude, since the free citizen
mostly stood or lay down.   Xen. *Econ.* iv. 3.   [4] Plato, *Protag.* 328 A.
[5] Xen. *Revenues*, ii. 2.   [6] Plato, *Kleitophon*, 409 B.

builder or the doctor the practising of their profession
and the teaching of pupils. The *Republic*[1] says : " If
owing to poverty a craftsman is unable to provide the
books and other requisites of his calling, his work will
suffer, and his sons and any others whom he may be
teaching will not learn their trade so well." The
teaching of building is mentioned in the *Gorgias*.[2]
In the *Republic*[3] Plato states that the παῖδες of the
potters—a word which will include both sons and
apprentices—act as servants and look on for a long time
before they are allowed to try their hands themselves at
making pots. " To learn pot-making on a wine-jar "
was a proverb for beginning with the most difficult part
of a subject. The pupils of a doctor named Pittalos are
mentioned in the *Acharnians* of Aristophanes.[4] The
comic poets of the early third century contain several
references to cookery-schools. Sosipater makes one
cook say that his pupils must learn astrology, architecture, and strategy before they come to him, just as Plato
had exacted a preliminary knowledge of mathematics
from his disciples. Euphron gives ten months as the
minimum length of a course of cookery. Aristotle
mentions a man at Syracuse who taught slaves how to
wait at table, and perform their household duties : perhaps the play of Pherekrates[5] entitled *The Slave-
Teacher* may have dealt with a similar case. From
these fragments a picture can be drawn of a regular
system of apprenticeship by which the knowledge of the
trades was handed down. Solon, wishing to encourage
Athenian manufactures, had enacted that if a father
did not have his son taught some trade, he could not

---

[1] Plato, *Rep.* 421 E.   [2] Plato, *Gorg.* 514 B.
[3] Plato, *Rep.* 467 A.   [4] Aristoph. *Acharn.* 1032.
[5] The fifth-century comic poet.

legally demand to be supported in his old age.[1] But the general opinion of Hellas still maintained that " technical instruction and all teaching which aimed only at money-making was vulgar and did not deserve the name of education. True education aimed solely at virtue, making the child yearn to be a good citizen, skilled to rule and to obey." [2] For all the gold on the earth and under it, according to Plato, could not pay the price of virtue, or deserve to be given in exchange for a man's soul. Thus the Spartans and Cretans did not stand alone, but had the support of all Hellas, in banishing from their schools any idea of technical or professional instruction.

But in one notable point their idea of education differed from that which was prevalent in most of the Hellenic States. The regular course of education in Athens and in most Hellenic States was for boys alone : no girls need apply. The women lived in almost Oriental seclusion;[3] the duty of an Athenian mother was, according to Perikles,[4] to live so retired a life that her name should never be mentioned among the men either for praise or blame. Listen to the description which an Athenian country gentleman gives of his wife.[5] " What was she likely to know when I married her ? Why, she was not yet fifteen when I introduced her to my house, and she had been brought up always under the strictest super-vision ; as far as could be managed, she had not been allowed to see anything, hear anything, or ask any questions. Don't you think that it was all that could

---

[1] Plutarch, *Solon*, 22.   [2] Plato, *Laws*, 643 E.
[3] Except possibly in Chios and Lokris, and of course in Sparta.
[4] Thuc. ii. 45. 4.   [5] Xen. *Econ.* vii. 5.

be expected of her, if she knew how to take raw wool
and make it into a cloak, and had seen how wool-work
is served out to handmaidens ? " Sokrates, however, to
whom this question is addressed, seems to think that
she might have learnt " from her father and mother the
duties which would belong to her in after life." These,
however, in this case her husband had to teach her.
He explains to her that she must see that everything
has a place to itself and is always put there ; she must
also give out the stores, teach the slaves their duties and
nurse them when they are ill, and tend the young
children. The summary of the explanation is that
Heaven has appointed a fair division of labour between
husband and wife : the wife manages everything indoors
and the husband everything out of doors. A stay-at-
home husband or a gad-about wife equally offend
against respectability. As a rule, apparently, the
women simply sat in the house, " like slaves," as it
seemed to the ordinary athletic Hellene. Xenophon's
model husband suggests that his wife should take exercise by walking about the house to see how the supplies
were given out, to inspect the arrangements of the
cupboards, and to watch the washing and the wringing-
out of the clothes : this exercise will give her health and
an appetite. But Xenophon was an admirer of Spartan
customs and the athletic Spartan women : probably
these ideas would not have occurred to the ordinary
Athenian husband.

Another picture may be quoted from Hellenic
literature to show the extent of education which an
ordinary woman received.[1] A certain Aristarchos
comes to Sokrates in great distress. A number of
female relatives, quite destitute, have been thrown upon

[1] Xen. *Mem.* ii. 7.

his hands owing to various circumstances, and he must support them ; but he has not the requisite means. Sokrates naturally suggests that he should make them work for their living. But they do not know how to, says Aristarchos. However, by dint of questioning, Sokrates elicits the fact that they can make men's and women's garments, and also pastry and bread. These, then, were apparently the accomplishments which an ordinary girl in Hellas, brought up without any idea of having to earn her own living, would acquire. Plato also mentions weaving and cooking as the provinces in which women excel,[1] and describes the women of Attika as " living indoors, managing the household and super-intending the loom and wool-work generally." [2]

Thus the Athenian girl spent her time indoors, learning to be a regular " Hausfrau," skilled in weaving, cooking, and household management. She had her special maid to wait on her,[3] as her brothers had their paidagogos. She would, as a rule, be married young, and would naturally be very shy after such an up-bringing ; the marriage was arranged between the bridegroom and the parents, and, owing to the seclusion of the women at Athens, love-matches were well-nigh impossible. The match was mainly a question of the dowry. Xenophon [4] gives a vivid picture of one of these girl-wives gradually " growing accustomed to her husband and becoming sufficiently tame to hold con-versation with him." To keep their beauty under such conditions they employed rouge and white, and high-heeled shoes. Such mothers would be quite incapable of giving any literary or musical education to their children ; hence the boys went away to school as soon

[1] Plato, *Rep.* 455 c.
[2] Plato, *Laws*, 805 E.
[3] As in Lusias, *ag. Diogeiton*, 32. 28.
[4] In the *Econ.* vii. 10.

as possible. Their school-life usually began when they were about six years old, the exact age being left to the parents' choice.[1] Before this, they learnt in the nursery the various current fables and ballads, and the national mythology.[2] " As soon as the child understands what is said, the nurse and the mother and the paidogogos, yes, and the father himself, strive with one another in improving its character, in every word and deed showing it what is just and what is unjust, what is beautiful and what is ugly, what is holy and what is unholy. It is always ' Do this ' and ' Don't do that.' If a child is disobedient, it is corrected with threats and blows." [3] Besides this purely moral training there might, no doubt, be a certain amount of technical or of literary instruction at home,[4] and bits of poetry might be learnt. Up to this age boys and girls lived together.

The sons of rich parents apparently went to school earliest : their poorer fellow-citizens went later.[5] This was natural. The poor could not keep their sons at school for a long time, for they wanted their services in the shop or on the farm, and the fees were a burden : so they did not send them till they were old enough to pick up instruction quickly. The rich, on the other hand, to whom money was no object, sent their boys to school at an early age, when they could do little more than look on, while their elders worked. Aristotle commends this custom, and imposes two years of such " playing at school " upon the boys of his ideal State.[6]

---

[1] Thus the *Axiochos* (366 D) puts seven years as the age at which grammatistai and paidotribai began. Plato (*Laws*, 794) says six ; Aristotle (*Pol.* vii. 17) about five ; Xenophon (*Constit. of Lak.* ii.) " as soon as the children begin to understand."

[2] Aesop was popular then, as now. This is the μουσική, anterior to γυμναστική, so keenly criticised in the *Republic*.

[3] Plato, *Protag.* 325 c-E.

[4] Xen. *Mem.* ii. 2. 6.

[5] Plato, *Protag.* 326 c.

[6] Aristotle, *Pol.* vii. 17. 7.

The ordinary system of primary education at Athens consisted of three parts, presided over respectively by the " grammatistes," " kitharistes," and " paidotribes." [1] The grammatistes taught reading, writing, and some arithmetic, and made his pupils read and learn by heart the great poets, Homer and Hesiod and others. The kitharistes taught the boys how to play the seven-stringed lyre and sing to it the works of the lyric poets, which they would incidentally have to learn. The paidotribes presided over their physical development in a scientific way ; he taught them wrestling, boxing, the pankration, running, jumping, throwing the diskos and javelin, and various other exercises ; his school-room was the palaistra. To this triple system some boys added drawing and painting ; [2] but this subject seems to have been an extra till late in the fourth century. Literature, music, and athletics composed the ordinary course at Athens.

Which of the three branches of education began first ? Probably they were all taught simultaneously. The order in which they are usually mentioned does not point to a fixed sequence. Letters were naturally mentioned first, because all citizens alike learned this subject. Gymnastics were put last, because, owing to the public gymnasia, these exercises were carried on long after the other schooling had ceased. Moreover, most of the recognised exercises of the palaistra were not taught to small boys ; from the nature of the exercises and from the pictures on the vases it may be

---

[1] The three in this order in Plato, *Protag.* 312 B, 325-326 ; *Charmid.* 159 C ; *Kleitoph.* 407 C ; Xen. *Constit. of Lak.* ii. 1 ; Isok. *Antid.* 267. The first two in this order in *Charmid.* 160 A ; *Lusis,* 209 B ; inverted in *Euthyd.* 276 A. Aristot. (*Pol.* viii. 3) gives γράμματα, γυμναστική, μουσική. Plato in the *Laws* 810 A makes κιθαριστική follow γραμματική ; Aristophanes mentions the paidotribes just after the κιθαριστής.   [2] Aristot. *Pol.* viii. 3. 1.

deduced that the average boy did not learn them till
his twelfth year at the earliest. But physical training
of an easier sort of course commenced much earlier,
and boys seem to have attended a palaistra from their
sixth year onwards to receive it. Both Plato and
Aristotle demand that it should begin several years
before any intellectual instruction ; and Plato, making
athletics such as shooting and riding begin at six, defers
letters till ten and lyre-playing till thirteen. Gymnastics would naturally occupy a part of the day for a
healthy young Hellene during the whole time from
his sixth year till manhood. It is thus that the
Charmides mentions " quite tiny boys " as present in
the palaistra, as well as older lads and young men.

Lyre-playing may have been deferred, as a harder
subject, till the boy had learned letters for several
years ; but the seven-stringed lyre, with the simple
old Hellenic music, was probably not a very difficult
instrument to master. The chief factor which determined the arrangement of subjects in an ordinary
family was no doubt the paidagogos. If there was
only one son, he could go to whatever school his
parents pleased ; but if there were several, elders and
youngers had all to go to the same school at the same
time, for there was only one paidagogos to a whole
family as a rule, and he could never allow any of his
charges to go out of his sight.

That the three subjects were usually taught simultaneously may be inferred from a passage of Xenophon.
" In every part of Hellas except Sparta," he says, " those
who claim to give their sons the best education, as soon
as ever the child understands what is said to him, at
once make one of their servants his paidagogos, and at
once send him off to school to learn letters and music

and the exercises of the Palaistra."¹ The emphasis upon the word "at once" certainly implies that the three subjects began simultaneously.

On the vases letters and music are seen being taught side by side in the same school; this was a convenient and natural arrangement. Writing-tablets and rulers are also seen suspended on the walls of music-schools and palaistrai, and lyres on the walls of letter-schools²; which suggests that the boys went from one building to another in the day, taking their property with them. Plato states that three years apiece was a reasonable time for learning letters and the lyre.³ The eight years between six and fourteen, the ordinary time devoted at Athens in the fourth century to the primary triple course, would give space for these six years, with two years to spare for elaboration. Gymnastics are meant to go on during the whole period in Plato, and so do not require a special allowance of time to themselves.

This system of primary education at Athens may reasonably be traced back to the beginning of the sixth century. Solon is credited with a regulation which made letters compulsory, and with certain moral enactments dealing with existing schools and palaistrai. The much-disputed popularisation of Homer at Athens by Peisistratos was probably connected with the growth of the Schools of Letters. Of the existence of music-schools at this date there is evidence from a sixth-century vase in the British Museum,⁴ which represents a youth amusing himself with a dog, behind a seated man who is playing a lyre. This might not seem very conclusive in itself; but now compare it with the two "amphorai" of the fifth century,⁵ which undoubtedly

---

¹ Xen. *Constit. of Lak*. ii.   ² See Illustr. Plates I. A and I. B.
³ Plato, *Laws*, 810 A.   ⁴ Vase B 192.   ⁵ Vases E 171, 172; see Plates III. and IV.

PLATE I.A.

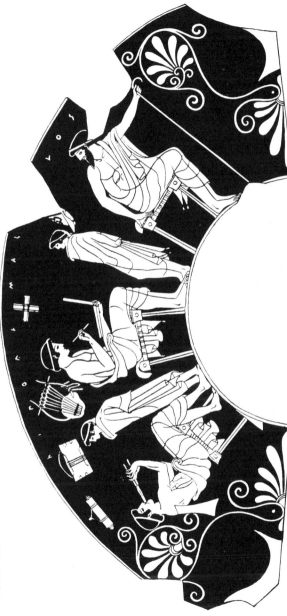

THE FLUTE LESSON, THE WRITING LESSON (ABOVE A WRITING-ROLL, A FOLDED TABLET, A RULING SQUARE, ETC.)

From the Kulix of Douris, now at Berlin (No. 2285).

Monumenti dell' Instituto, ix. Plate 54

PLATE I. B.

THE LYRE LESSON, AND THE POETRY LESSON (ABOVE IS AN ORNAMENTAL MANUSCRIPT BASKET)

From a Kulix by Douris, now in Berlin (No. 2285).

Monumenti dell' Instituto, ix. Plate 54.

represent scenes in a music-school. The situation is
almost identical ; each alike shows the boy playing with
the animal behind his master's chair. Curiously enough,
all three vases come from Kameiros in Rhodes, although
they are of Athenian manufacture. Thus the music-
school may also be traced back well into the sixth
century, in company with the school of letters and the
palaistra ; and the antiquity of the system of Primary
Education is thus established.

In earlier days this primary course had no doubt
sometimes lasted till the boy was eighteen : but towards
the end of the fifth century a secondary stage of education arose, occupying the years immediately preceding
eighteen. This secondary stage is recognised in the
pseudo-Platonic *Axiochos* and in the fragment of
Teles quoted by Stobaeus. More important evidence
is supplied by Plato. In the *Republic* he assigns
an elaborate system of mathematics to the age just
before ἐφηβεία, which he sets at seventeen or eighteen,
the natural age varying with the individual, while the
legal age remained fixed.

When did this Secondary Education begin? Aristotle,
counting back from ἐφηβεία, assigns three years to it.[1]
He has just commended the arrangement of education,
not on hard and fast lines, but in accordance with the
natural growth of the individual: so he must mean his
ἐφηβεία to vary from seventeen to eighteen.[2] Thus he
puts the beginning of secondary education at fourteen
or fifteen, the average age of ἥβη in Hellas, as in Rome.
From ἥβη till twenty-one the young Athenian was a
μειράκιον. Thus in point of age the παῖς of the
primary schools corresponds to the Roman "impubes,"
and the μειράκιον to the "adolescens" ; but μειράκιον

[1] Aristot. *Pol.* viii. 4. 9.   [2] *Ibid.* viii. 1. 2.

and παῖς are used very loosely, and the former word is often replaced by νεανίσκος. We shall, as a rule, call the pupils of the primary schools boys, and those of the secondary lads.

Fourteen did not, however, represent an exact point at which it was compulsory to leave the primary school. Sons of the poor left earlier ; rich or unoccupied Athenians might remain later : Sokrates even attended a lyre-school among the boys when he was middle-aged. The primary schoolmasters started advanced classes in astronomy and mathematics to suit elder pupils.[1] In the palaistrai there were separate classes of boys and lads, who were only supposed to meet on feast-days ;[2] in the *Charmides*, however, grown men, lads, boys, and quite tiny boys are all exercising together.

Many lads, especially in earlier times, did not attend the schools at all, but gave their time to gymnastics and whatever else they pleased.[3] Xenophon relates this as one of the demerits of the Athenian system.[4]

The mental attainments of a lad who is apparently but little over fourteen are sketched in Plato's *Lusis*. The lad Lusis knows how to read and write, and how to string and play the lyre. He recognises a quotation from Homer, and has even come across the " prose treatises of the very wise, who say that like must always be friendly to like ; these are the men who reason and write about the Universe and Nature."[5]

This secondary education, beginning soon after fourteen, was only for the rich : the poor could not afford to keep their sons away from the farm or trade

---

[1] [Plato] *Rivals*, 132 A.   [2] Plato, *Lusis*, 206 D.
[3] Plato, *Laches*, 179 A.   [4] Xen. *Constit. of Lak.* iii.
[5] Plato, *Lusis*, 214 B.

any longer. It might be scattered over the whole of the next six or seven years ; but there was a serious interruption, which usually terminated it. At eighteen the young Athenian became in the eye of the law an ephebos and was called out to undergo two years of military training. During this period of conscription it was no doubt possible, especially in the laxer days of the fourth century, to do some intellectual work ; but Plato is probably only accepting the usual custom when he frees the epheboi of his State from all mental studies and makes them give their whole energies to military and gymnastic training. And when the ephebos returned to civil life, he was a full citizen and was hardly likely to return to school ; he might attend an occasional lecture or so, but that was all.

Thus secondary education usually occupied the years between fourteen and eighteen, although the latter limit was in no way definitely fixed, and the same subjects might be studied at any age. In earlier days no doubt lads spent their time in continuing their musical studies : primary education could be conducted in a more leisurely fashion when there was still little to be learnt, and the lyre may have been deferred till this age, as Plato in similar circumstances defers it in the *Laws*. But in the days of Perikles knowledge began to increase and boys had more to learn. So the lyre was crowded into the first period of education, and a new series of secondary subjects arose. It was these years which were usually devoted to the four years' course which was customary in the school of Isokrates. Before this date the time was, as a rule, spent in attending the lectures of the wandering Sophists or in picking up a smattering of philosophy. Among the subjects which thus formed a part of secondary education were mathematics of various kinds, more advanced literary criticism, a certain amount of natural history and science, a knowledge of the laws and constitution of Athens, a small quantity of philosophy, ethical, political, and metaphysical, and above all, rhetoric. Plato in his *Republic*, developing this Athenian system of secondary education, assigns to the years immediately preceding eighteen the theory of numbers, geometry, plane and solid, kinetics and harmonics, and expressly excludes dialectic as more suitable to a later age ;[1] in the *Laws*, prescribing for the whole population, not for a few selected intellects, he orders practical arithmetic, geometry, and enough astronomy to make the calendar intelligible. The pseudo-Platonic *Axiochos*[2] ascribes to Prodikos the statement that "when a child grows older, he endures the tyranny of mathematicians, teachers of tactics, and 'critics.'" These last are the professors of that curious criticism of poetry which is found, for instance, in the *Protagoras* as a subject of the lectures of that Sophist as well as of Hippias.

At eighteen the young Athenian partially came of age. He then had to submit to a two years' course of military training, of which the first year was spent in Athens and the second in the frontier forts and in camp. During this period he probably had little time for intellectual occupations. But when the military power of Athens collapsed under the Macedonian dominion, the military duties of the epheboi became voluntary, and their training was replaced by regular courses of philosophy and literature. The military system became a University, attended by a few young

---

[1] Rhetoric is, of course, banished from a Platonic state.

[2] [Plato] *Axiochos*, 366 E.

men of wealth and position and a good many foreigners. As the forerunner of the first University, the two years' training of the epheboi may fitly receive the name of Tertiary Education, in spite of the fact that till the third century it involved only military instruction.

Thus we have Athenian education divided into three stages : Primary from six to fourteen, Secondary from fourteen to eighteen, and Tertiary from eighteen to twenty ; while gymnastic training extended over the whole period.

Of these three stages the third alone was compulsory and provided by the State. The second was entirely voluntary, and only the richest and most leisured boys applied themselves to it. Gymnastics of some sort were rendered almost obligatory by the liability of every citizen to military and naval service at a moment's notice ; but they needed little encouragement. Of the primary subjects, letters were probably compulsory by law, and music was almost invariably taught. An old law, ascribed to Solon,[1] enacted that every boy should learn swimming and his letters ; after which, the poorer might turn their attention to trade or farming, while the richer passed on to learn music, riding, gymnastics, hunting, and philosophy. In the *Kriton* of Plato the personified Laws of Athens, recounting to Sokrates the many services which they had done him, mention that they had " charged his father to educate him in Music and Letters." [2] But the Laws in Hellas include the customs, as well as the constitution, of a State. It was certainly customary for nearly every citizen at Athens to

[1] See Petit, *Leges Atticae*, ii. 4, compiled with great ingenuity out of many authors. Hence the proverbs ὁ μήτε νεῖν μήτε γράμματα ἐπιστάμενος, of an utter dunce, and πρῶτον κολυμβᾶν δεύτερον δὲ γράμματα. The spelling-riddles of the tragedians imply a whole nation interested in spelling.   [2] Plato, *Kriton*, 50 D.

learn some music ; but it was not compulsory. We meet no Athenian in literature who is ignorant of his letters ; we meet several who know no music. In Aristophanes, Demosthenes and Nikias are on the look-out for the most vulgar and low-class man in Athens, in order that he may oust Kleon from popular favour, by outdoing him in vulgarity. They find a sausage-seller. But even this man knows his letters, though not very well.[1] Of music, however, he is ignorant, and he has never attended the lessons of a paidotribes,[2] though Kleon seems to expect him to have done so. Kleon, who is represented as an utter boor, is yet said to have attended a lyre-school.[3] In the *Theages*[4] literature and lyre-playing and athletics are mentioned as the ordinary education of a gentleman. In fiercely democratic Athens every parent was eager to bring up his sons as gentlemen, and no doubt sent them through the whole course if he could possibly afford it. But the State attitude towards education, as distinct from the voluntary customs of the citizens, may be summarised in the words of Sokrates to Alkibiades : " No one, so to speak, cares a straw how you or any other Athenian is brought up." [5]

The schoolmasters opened their schools as private enterprises, fixing for themselves the fees and the sub-jects taught. The parents chose what they thought a suitable school, according to their means and the subjects which they wished their sons to learn. Thus Sokrates says to his eldest son, Lamprokles,[6] " When

---

[1] Aristophanes, *Knights*, 189.   [2] *Ibid.* 1235-1239.
[3] *Ibid.* 987-996.   [4] [Plato] *Theages*, 122 E.
[5] Plato, *Alkibiades*, i. 122 B. The Athenian State, however, from the time of Solon onwards, supported and educated at public expense the sons of those who fell in battle. The endowed systems in Teos and at Delphoi belong to the third century ; it is impossible to say whether such existed earlier.
[6] Xen. *Mem.* ii. 2. 6.

boys seem old enough to learn anything, their parents
teach them whatever they themselves know that is
likely to be useful to them ; subjects which they think
others better qualified to teach they send them to
school to learn, spending money upon this object."
This suggests that the poor may frequently have passed
on their own knowledge of letters to their sons without
the expense of a school.   But all this was a private
transaction between parent and teacher.   The State
interfered with the matter only so far as to impose
certain moral regulations on the schools and the
gymnasia, to fix the hours of opening and closing, and
so forth, and to suggest that every boy should be
taught his letters.

The teaching of the elementary stages of Letters,
that is, the three R's, was, as will be shown later on,
cheaply obtained, and was within the reach of the
poorest.   Music and athletics would naturally be more
expensive, for they required much greater study and
talents upon the part of their teachers.   The State
did take some steps to make these branches of education
cheaper, and so throw them open to a larger number.

Gymnasia and palaistrai were built at public expense,[1]
that any one might go and exercise himself without
charge.   These buildings were also open to spectators,
so that any one could acquire at any rate a rudimentary
knowledge of boxing, wrestling, and the other branches
of athletics, by watching his more proficient fellow-
citizens practising them.   The epheboi received instruction in athletic exercises at the cost of the State.   But
the children, so far as they received physical training
in schools, must have received it in private palaistrai ;
their lessons are described as taking place " in the

[1] [Xen.] *Constit. of Athens*, ii. 10.

house of the paidotribes," ἐν παιδοτρίβου—an idiom
which always implies ownership or special rights ; and
the majority of palaistrai were private buildings, called
by their owners' names.   Thus we hear of the palaistrai
of Siburtios, of Taureas,[1] and so forth : Siburtios and
Taureas were no doubt the paidotribai who taught
there.   In a later age, when the boys of different
palaistrai ran torch races against one another, the
palaistra of Timeas is victorious on two occasions, that
of Antigenes once.[2]

By the system of leitourgiai rich citizens were made
chargeable for the expenses of the epheboi of their tribe
who were training for the torch races.   These races
seem to have been the only branch of athletics which
was thus endowed ; however, they were numerous, even
in the smaller country districts, so that many epheboi
must have profited by this free training.[3]   "Leitourgiai"
also provided free instruction in chorus-dancing (which
included singing as well as dancing) for such boys as
were selected for competition.   The rich " choregos "
appointed for the year had to produce a chorus of boys
belonging to his tribe for some festival, paying all the
expenses of teaching and training them himself.[4]   It
is to this free school that the Solonic law refers when
it mentions the "joint attendance of the boys and the
dithyrambic choruses " ; for it goes on to state that
the ordinance with regard to this matter was that the
" choregos " should be over forty.[5]   In Demosthenes,[6]
a certain Mantitheos, who had not been acknowledged
by his father at the usual time, " attended school among

---

[1] Plutarch, *Alkib.* 3 ; Plato, *Charmides*, 153 A.

[2] *C.I.A.* ii. 1. 444, 445, 446.   [3] See Excursus on γυμνασιαρχοί.

[4] He could, and had to, use compulsion in collecting boys. This suggests that a parent could always, if he wished, get this free education for his son.

[5] This rule fell into abeyance.   [6] Dem. *against Boiot.* 1001.

the boys of the Hippothontid tribe to learn chorus-
dancing ": had he been acknowledged, he would have
gone to the Acamantid, his father's tribe.   No doubt,
if the choregos was keen about gaining a victory, he
would give a trial to more than the fifty boys required
for a dithyrambic contest.   In any case, provided that
all the tribes competed, this one contest (and there
were several in the course of a year) gave a free
education to 500 boys.   Xenophon notices that it
was the " demos," the poor majority, who mainly got
the advantage of free training under gumnasiarchoi
and choregoi : [1] the rich naturally preferred to send
their boys to more select schools.[2]

Thus the more elementary stages of letters alone
were compulsory at Athens, but music and gymnastics
were almost universally taught, and the cost of instruction in these subjects was reduced in various ways by
State action : the greater part might be learned for
nothing.   But parents needed little compulsion or
encouragement to get their children taught.   So much
did the Hellenes regard education as a necessity for
their boys, that when the Athenians were driven from
their homes by Xerxes, and their women and children
crossed over to Troizen, the hospitable Troizenians
provided their guests with schoolmasters, so that not
even in such a crisis might the boys be forced to take
a holiday.[3]   And when Mitulene wished to punish her

---

[1] [Xen.] *Constit. of Athens*, i. 13.

[2] On the strength of the passages quoted from the law, and from Demosthenes,
and of Aristophanes, *Clouds*, 964, some have maintained a theory that the Athenian
tribes provided free education in dancing, and perhaps in other subjects, to all free
boys, exclusive of competitions.   But the quotation in Aischines, except for the
actual law, which is a later interpolation, certainly refers only to the choregoi, and
the passage in Demosthenes is concerned only with chorus-dancing for competitions.
In Aristophanes the boys of the same neighbourhood naturally attend the same
school, that is all.   [3] Plut. *Themist.* 10.

revolted allies in the most severe way possible, she prevented them from teaching their children letters and music.[1]

Of State action with regard to education in Hellas elsewhere than in Sparta, Crete, and Athens, little is known. But the Chalcidian cities in Sicily and Italy are said to have provided literary education at public expense and under public supervision.[2] The law enacting this is ascribed to the great lawgiver, Charondas, and, although he is a somewhat shadowy figure,[3] there must have been some foundation for the story, at any rate at a later date. During the Macedonian period kings and other rich men often bequeathed large sums of money to their favourite cities, in order to endow the educational system. We hear of this happening in Teos and at Delphi : in these places the parents, if they paid any fees at all, cannot have paid much. But there is no authority for any such endowments during the period which we are considering.

But if education was neither enforced nor assisted to any considerable degree by the State, it was certainly encouraged by the prizes which were offered. Every city, and probably most villages, had local competitions annually, and in many cases more frequently still, in which some of the "events" were reserved for citizens, while others were open to all comers. There were separate prizes for different ages ; the ordinary division was into boys and grown men, an intermediate class of "the beardless" being sometimes added. But in some Attic inscriptions the boys are divided into

[1] Ael. *Var. Hist.* vii. 15.   [2] Diod. Sic. xii. 42.
[3] Probably lived *circa* 500 B.C.

three groups, and in Chios the epheboi were so distributed.

These competitions were no doubt largely athletic. But music was usually provided for as well, and in many places there were literary competitions also. At Athens the different φρατρίαι seem to have offered prizes annually on the Koureotis day of the Apatouria to the boys who recited best, the piece for recitation being chosen by each competitor. Kritias took part in the competition when ten years old.[1] From Teos we have a list of prizemen, belonging, it is true, to a later date ; but it may be quoted, to give some idea of what the subjects might be.[2]

Senior Class (by age).

For rhapsody, Zoïlos, son of Zoïlos.

For reading, Zoïlos, son of Zoïlos.

Middle Class.

For rhapsody, Metrodoros, son of Attalos.

For reading, Dionusikles, son of Metrodoros.

For general knowledge, Athenaios, son of Apollodoros.

For painting, Dionusios, son of Dionusios.

Junior Class.

For rhapsody, Herakles.

For reading.

For caligraphy.

For torch race.

For playing lyre with fingers.

For playing lyre with plektron.

For singing to lyre.

For reciting tragic verse (tragedy).

For reciting comedy.

For reciting lyric verse.

From Chios we have the following [3] :—

When Hermesileos, Dinos, and Nikias were gumnasiarchoi, the following boys and epheboi were victorious in the competitions and offered libations to the Muses and Herakles from the sums which were given to them in accordance with the decree of the people, when Lusias was taster of the offerings :—

---

[1] Plato, *Tim.* 21 B.   [2] Böckh, 3088.
[3] *Ibid.* 2214. I have omitted patronymics.

For reading, Agathokles.

For rhapsody, Miltiades.

For playing lyre with fingers, Xenon.

For playing lyre, Kleoites.

Long Distance Race (varied from 2¼ miles to about ¾ mile).

Boys	. . .	Asklepiades.
Junior epheboi		Dionusios.
Middle	,,	Timokles.
Senior	,,	Moschion.
Men	,,	Aischrion.

Stadion (200 yards).

Boys	. . .	*Athenikon.*
Junior epheboi		Hestiaios.
Middle	,,	*Apollonios.*
Senior	,,	Artemon.
Men	,,	Metrodoros.

Diaulos (400 yards).

Boys .	. .	*Athenikon.*
Junior epheboi		Hubristos.
Middle	,,	Melantes.
Senior	,,	*Apollonios.*
Men	,,	Menis.

(Apollonios seems to have been so good that, though a middle ephebos, he competed in and won the senior ephebos' race here, unless there were two boys of the same name.)

Wrestling.

Boys	. . .	*Athenikon.*
Junior epheboi		Demetrios.
Middle	,,	Moschos.
Senior	,,	Theodotos.
Men	,,	Apellas.

Boxing.

Boys . . . . Herakleides.

(The rest is wanting.)

(Notice the three victories of the boy Athenikon.)

At Thespiai in Boiotia [1] there were prizes for senior and junior boys in the various races, and in boxing, wrestling, pankration, and pentathlon, besides open prizes for poetry and music of all kinds. Attic inscriptions arrange the events thus [2] :—

Stadion.		*Diaulos.*		*Fighting in Heavy Arms.*	
Junior	Boys.	Junior	Boys.	Junior	Boys.
Middle	Boys.	Middle	Boys.	Middle	Boys.
Senior	Boys.	Senior	Boys.	Senior	Boys.
Boys	Open.	Boys	Open.	Epheboi.	
Men.		Men.			

---

[1] *C.I.G. Boeot.* 1760-1766.   [2] Böckh, 232, 245.

The Olympian and Pythian festivals, however, had only a single series of contests for boys :—

Olympia.

Boys. Stadion (Pind. *Ol.* xiv.).
Boxing (Pind. *Ol.* x., xi.).
Wrestling (Pind. *Ol.* viii.).
(only in 628 B.C.) Pentathlon.
(not till 200 B.C.) Pankration.

Pythia.

Boys. Long Distance Race.
Diaulos (400 yards) (Pind. *Puth.* x.).
Stadion (200 yards) (Pind. *Puth.* xi.).
Boxing.
Wrestling (Bacchul. xi.).
Pankration (not till 346 B.C.).

But at Nemea both pentathlon[1] and pankration[2] for boys had already been established by Pindar's time, as well as the more usual contests.[3]

How far individual schoolmasters, as distinct from the State, gave prizes to their pupils, is little known ; an epigram in the *Anthology* supplies the only evidence, by narrating that "Konnaros received eighty knuckle-bones because he wrote beautifully, better than the other boys."[4] But probably as a general rule the task of rewarding merit was left to the public contests.

Thus the State did much to encourage, if it did little to assist or enforce, education. With such splendid rewards before them, boys were probably quite eager to attend school, or at any rate the palaistra. As soon as they were old enough to go to school,[5] they

---

[1] Pind. *Nem.* vii.   [2] Bacchul. xiii., Pind. *Nem.* v.
[3] Wrestling, Pind. *Nem.* iv., vi.   [4] *Anthol.* ed. Jacobs, vi. 308.
[5] Sometimes earlier. Plato, *Protag.* 325 c.

were entrusted to an elderly slave,[1] who had to follow
his master's boys about wherever they went and never
let them go out of his sight.[2]   This was the paidagogos
—a mixture of nurse, footman, chaperon, and tutor—
who is so prominent a figure on the vases and in the
literature of classical Hellas.   There was only one for
the family, so that all the boys had to go about together
and to attend the same schools and the same palaistrai
at the same time.[3]   He waited on them in the house,
carried their books or lyres to school, sat and watched
them in the schoolroom, and kept a strict eye upon
their manners and morality in the streets and the
gymnasia.   Thus, for instance, in Plato, Lusis and
Menexenos have their paidagogoi in attendance at the
palaistra, who come and force them away from the
absorbing conversation of Sokrates, when it is time for
them to go home.[4]   On a vase these attendants may
be seen sitting on stools behind their charges, in the
schools of letters and music, with long and suggestive
canes in their hands.[5]   A careful parent would, of
course, see that a slave who was to occupy so responsible a position was worthy of it : but great carelessness
seems often to have been shown in this matter.   The
paidagogoi of Lusis and Menexenos, boys of rank and
position, had a bad accent, and on a festival day, it is
true, were slightly intoxicated.[6]   Plutarch notices that

[1] Elderly, as in the picture of Medeia and her children given in Smith's *Smaller
Classical Dictionary* under " Medea," and on Douris' Kulix, Plates I. A and I. B (if
those are paidagogoi), and on other vases.

[2] So Fabius Cunctator was called Hannibal's paidagogos, because he followed
him about everywhere.

[3] There is only one for Lusis and his brothers (Plato, *Lus.* 223 A), for Medeia's
two children (Eur. *Med.*), for two boys in *Lusis,* 223 A, and for Themistocles'
children (Herod. viii. 75).

[4] Plato, *Lus.* 208 c.   He is referred to as ὅδε, showing that he is present.

[5] Illustr. Plates I. A and I. B.   Perhaps only the walking-stick carried by all
Athenians.   [6] Plato, *Lus.* 223 A.

in his time parents often selected for this office slaves
who were of no use for any other purpose.[1] Xenophon,
feeling the demerits of the Athenian custom, commends
the Spartans, who entrust the boys not to slaves, but
to public officials of the highest rank.[2] But in well-
regulated households the paidagogos was often a most
worthy and valuable servant. Sikinnos, who attended
the children of Themistokles in this capacity, was
entrusted by his master with the famous message to
Xerxes, which brought on the battle of Salamis ; he
was afterwards rewarded with his freedom, the citizenship of Thespiai, and a substantial sum of money.[3]
The custom of employing these male-nurses dated back
to early times at Athens : for Solon made regulations
about them.[4]

Boys were entrusted to paidagogoi as soon as they
went to school at six. This tutelage might last till
the boy was eighteen[5] and came of age ; but more
frequently it stopped earlier. Xenophon,[6] in his wish
to disparage everything not Spartan, declares that in
all other States the boys were set free from paidagogoi
and schoolmasters as soon as they became μειράκια,
i.e. at about fourteen or fifteen. The conjunction of
schoolmasters suggests the explanation of the variations
in age. When an elder brother ceased to attend
school, and his younger brothers were still pursuing
their studies, there being only one paidagogos, he had
to be left unattended. But in cases where there was
only one son, or where the eldest of several stayed on

---

[1] Plut. *Education of Boys.*   [2] Xen. *Constit. of Lak.* ii. 2.
[3] Herod. viii. 75.   [4] Aischin. *ag. Timarch.* 35. 10.
[5] In the guardian's accounts given by Lusias, *ag. Diogeiton*, 32. 28, a paidagogos is
paid for till the boy is eighteen ; but there was a younger brother, for whom he may
have been required, so the elder may have been free earlier. In Plautus (*Bacch.* 138)
we find a paidogogos in attendance till his charge was twenty.
[6] Xen. *Constit. of Lak.* iii. 1.

at school until he came of age, he would have the
paidagogos to attend him until he was his own master.

The life of such an attendant must have been an
anxious one in many cases. Plato compares his relations towards his charges with the relations of an
invalid towards his health : " He has to follow the
disease wherever it leads, being unable to cure it, and
he spends his life in perpetual anxiety with no time for
anything else." [1] With unruly boys of different ages,
and consequently of different tastes and desires, the
slave must have been often in a difficult position.
He had, however, the right of inflicting corporal
punishment.

The chief object of the paidagogos was to safeguard
the morals of his charges. Boys were expected to be
as modest and quiet in their whole behaviour, and as
carefully chaperoned, as young girls. Parents told
the schoolmasters to bestow much more attention upon
the boy's behaviour than upon his letters and music.[2]
This attitude was characteristic of Athens from
the first. The school laws of Solon, as quoted by
Aischines, deal wholly with morality. He gives the
following account of them [3] :—

" The old lawgivers stated expressly what sort of
life the free boy ought to lead and how he ought to
be brought up ; they also dealt with the manners of
lads and men of other ages." " In the case of the
schoolmasters, to whom we are compelled to entrust
our children, although their livelihood depends upon
their good character, and bad behaviour is ruinous to
them, yet the lawgiver obviously distrusts them. For
he expressly states, first, the hour at which the free

[1] Plato, *Rep.* 406 A.   [2] Plato, *Protag.* 325 D.
[3] Aischin. *ag. Timarch.* 9.

boy ought to go to school ; secondly, how many other boys are to be present in the school ; and then at what hour he is to leave. He forbids the schoolmasters to open their schools and the paidotribai their palaistrai before sunrise, and orders them to close before sunset, being very suspicious of the empty streets and of the darkness. Then he dealt with the boys who attended schools, as to who they should be and of what ages ; and with the official who is to oversee these matters. He dealt too with the regulation of the paidagogoi, and with the festival of the Muses in the schools and of Hermes in the palaistrai. Finally, he laid down regulations about the joint attendance of the boys and the round of dithyrambic dances ; for he directed that the Choregos should be over forty."

" No one over the age of boyhood might enter while the boys were in school, except the son, brother, or son-in-law of the master : the penalty of infringing this regulation was death. At the festival of Hermes the person in charge of the gymnasium [1] was not to allow any one over age to accompany the boys in any way : unless he excluded such persons from the gymnasium, he was to come under the law of corrupting free boys."

It will be noticed that these regulations are entirely concerned with morality : they safeguard an existing system. They prescribe neither the methods nor the subjects of education ; for with such matters the Athenian government did not interfere. But over the question of morals it becomes unexpectedly tyrannous, and makes the most minute regulations worthy of the strictest bureaucracy. It interfered on

---

[1] γυμνασιαρχής.   See Excursus on γυμνασιαρχοί.   This law was totally neglected in Socratic Athens. See Plato's *Lusis*.

this point in other ways also. The solemn council on
the Areiopagos had a special supervision over the
young, from Solon's time onward ; this was partially
taken away from it by Ephialtes and Perikles, but
the *Axiochos* shows that, though in abeyance, it continued to exist ; in the middle of the fourth century,
however, Isokrates laments that it had fallen into disuse.

The *Axiochos* also states that the ten Sophronistai,
elected to guard the morals of the epheboi, exercised
control over lads also. These officials probably took
their rise in the days of Solon : the regulation that
they must be over forty harmonises with the other
enactments of those days ; and, although they died out
at the end of the fourth century, they were revived under
the Roman Empire. Now it is most unlikely that
the archaistic legislators of imperial times would have
revived an office which had only existed during the
closing decades of the fourth century. Solon is known
to have appointed a magistracy specially to deal with
the children ;[1] and, if these magistrates were not the
Sophronistai, all trace of his creation has been lost,
which is most unlikely to have happened. So the
Sophronistai probably date from early times. Their
duty was a general supervision of the morals of the
young ; their chief function would be to prosecute,
on behalf of the State, parents and schoolmasters
who infringed Solon's moral regulations. But such
prosecutions would usually be undertaken by private
individuals concerned in the case, and so this magistracy
tended to become a sinecure. It may even have ceased
to exist after the fall of the Areiopagos. But it
seems to have revived under the restored democracy

---

[1] Aischin. *ag. Timarch.* 10. The word σωφρονιστής, in a general sense, occurs
three times in Thucydides.

PLATE II.

THE FLUTE LESSON—THE BOY'S TURN
Wiener Vorlegeblätter, Series C, Plate 4.
From a Kulix by Hieron, now at Vienna.

for a while (if the *Axiochos* belongs to Aischines the Sokratic), to sink again in the middle of the century. At the close of the century it revives once more with the changes in the ephebic system, and finally perishes when the epheboi became too few to need ten officers to supervise their morals. An account of the Sophronistai of this later period will be given in connection with the epheboi.

The strategoi [1] exercised a superintendence over the epheboi during their two years' training as recruits, as would naturally be expected. Late in the fourth century they appear also to have been connected with the local schools in Attica ; an inscription at Eleusis, which Girard assigns to 320 B.C., thanks the strategos Derkulos for the diligence which he had shown in supervising the education of the children there.[2] Whether they exercised such functions in the days when their military duties were more important, is more than doubtful. But any Athenian magistrate could interest himself in the schools, no doubt, and intervene to check abuses.[3]

In the period of juvenile emancipation and increasing luxury and indulgence for children which marked the closing decades of the fifth century, it became customary for conservative thinkers to look back with longing, and no doubt idealising, eyes to the "good old times." The sixth and early fifth centuries came, probably unjustly, to be regarded as the ideal age of education, when children learned obedience and morality, and were not pampered and depraved ; when they were

---

[1] Deinarchos, *ag. Philokles*, 15.

[2] Girard, *L'Éducation Athénienne*, pp. 51, 52.

[3] The Archon Eponumos had the control of orphans and probably intervened if their education was neglected.

beautiful and healthy, not pale-faced, stunted, and over-educated.

Listen to Aristophanes,[1] yearning for " the good old style of education, in the days when Justice still prevailed over Rhetoric, and good morals were still in fashion. Then children were seen and not heard ; then the boys of each hamlet and ward walked in orderly procession along the roads on their way to the lyre-school,—no overcoats, though it snowed cats and dogs. Then, while they stood up square—no lounging—the master taught them a fine old patriotic song like ' Pallas, city-sacker dread,'[2] or ' A cry that echoes afar,'[3] set to a good old-fashioned tune. If any one tried any vulgar trills and twiddles and odes where the metre varies, such as Phrunis and Co. use nowadays, he got a tremendous thrashing for disrespect to the Muses." While being taught by the paidotribes, too, they behaved modestly, and did not spend their time ogling their admirers. " At meals children were not allowed to grab up the dainties or giggle or cross their feet." " This was the education which produced the heroes of Marathon. . . . This taught the boys to avoid the Agora, keep away from the Baths, be ashamed at what is disgraceful, be courteous to elders, honour their parents, and be an impersonation of Modesty—instead of running after ballet-girls. They passed their days in the gymnasia, keeping their bodies in good condition, not mouthing quibbles in the Agora. Each spent his time with some well-mannered lad of his own age, running races in the Akademeia under the sacred olives, amid a fragrance of smilax and leisure and white poplar, rejoicing in the springtide when plane-tree and

---

[1] Aristoph. *Clouds*, 960 ff.   [2] By Lamprokles (476 B.C.).
[3] By Kudides (? = Kudias.   Smyth, *Melic Poets*, p. 347).

elm whisper together." All the voices of generations of boys, bound down to indoor studies when wood and field and river are calling them, the complaint of ages of fevered hurry and bustle, looking back with regret on the days of " leisure " and " springtide," seem to echo in Aristophanes' lament for the ways that were no more.

" This education," he goes on, " produced a good chest, sound complexion, broad shoulders, small tongue ; the new style produces pale faces, small shoulders, narrow chest, and long tongue, and makes the boy confuse Honour with Dishonour : it fills the Baths, empties the Palaistra."

The next witness to be called is Isokrates. He is somewhat prejudiced by his dream of restoring the Areiopagos to its old power, but he is an educational expert and his evidence is supported by that of many others. In the days when the Areiopagos had the superintendence of morals, he says,[1] " the young did not spend their time in the gambling dens, and with flute-girls and company of that sort, as they do now, but they remained true to the manner of life which was laid down for them. . . . They avoided the Agora so much, that, if ever they were compelled to pass through it, they did so with obvious modesty and self-control. To contradict or insult an elder was at that time considered a worse offence than ill-treatment of parents is considered now. To eat or drink in a tavern was a thing that not even a self-respecting servant would think of doing then ; for they practised good manners, not vulgarity."

Call Plato next.[2] " In a democratic state the schoolmaster is afraid of his pupils and flatters them, and the pupils despise both schoolmaster and paidagogos. The

[1] Isok. *Areiop.* 149 C, D. [2] Plato, *Rep.* 563 A.

young expect the same treatment as the old, and contradict them and quarrel with them. In fact, seniors have to flatter their juniors, in order not to be thought morose old dotards."

The counts of the indictment are luxury, bad manners, contempt for authority, disrespect to elders, and a love for chatter in place of exercise. The old regime had strictly forbidden luxury. Warm baths had been regarded as unmanly, and were even coupled with drunkenness by Hermippos.[1] The boys had only worn a single garment, the sleeveless chiton, a custom which survived till late times in Sparta and Crete ; but at Athens they began to wear the ἱμάτιον or overcoat as well. Xenophon, blaming parents "in the rest of Hellas" (*i.e.* elsewhere than in Sparta), says : " They make their boy's feet soft by giving him shoes, and pamper his body with changes of clothes ; they also allow him as much food as his stomach can contain." [2] Children began to be the tyrants, not the slaves, of their households. They no longer rose from their seats when an elder entered the room ; they contradicted their parents, chattered before company, gobbled up the dainties at table, and committed various offences against Hellenic tastes, such as crossing their legs. They tyrannised over the paidagogoi and schoolmasters. Alkibiades even smacked a literature-master. A similar change came over the position of children in England during the latter half of the nineteenth century. If Maria Edgeworth could have met a modern child, she would have uttered quite Aristophanic diatribes against the decay of good manners.

With this change went a more serious matter, a change of tone. Whether the old days were as moral

---

[1] *Floruit* 432 B.C. (in Athen. 18 c).   [2] Xen. *Constit. of Lak.* ii. 1.

as the conservatives supposed, may be doubted ; but the atmosphere of Periclean and Socratic Athens, as represented by all its literary lights, was certainly most unsuitable for the young. Perhaps general morality was no worse, but the immorality was no longer concealed from the children. The old laws which had excluded unsuitable company from the schools and palaistrai were neglected, and these educational buildings became the resort of all the fashionable loungers of Athens.

The preference given to conversation over exercise was a feature of the age. In part, it was a preference for intellectual as against purely physical education. The free discussion with children of ethical subjects probably ceased with the death of Sokrates ; this can hardly be regretted, if Plato's evidence as to the nature of Socratic dialogues is to be believed. From the importance which Plato gives to gymnastics as a corrective to exclusive μουσική even in the education of his highly intellectual Philosopher-Kings, we may suspect that the revolt against excessive athletics at Athens, of which Euripides had been the leader, had gone too far, and that a reaction was needed. Certainly the Athenians do not distinguish themselves for pluck or energy in the fourth century : in Platonic phrase, the temper of their resolution had been melted away by their exclusive devotion to intellectual and artistic pursuits.

Let me close this subject, however, with a more pleasing picture of that αἰδώς or modesty at which the older education had aimed. It is taken·from the midst of that brilliant but corrupt Socratic Athens.[1] Young Autolukos had won the boys' contest for the pankration at the great Panathenaic festival. As a treat,

[1] Xen. *Banquet*, iii. 13.

Kallias, a friend of his father, had taken him to the horse-races, and afterwards invited him out to dinner with his father Lukon : such a dignity was rarely accorded to an Athenian boy.

The boy sits at table, while the grown men recline. Some one asked him what he was most proud of—" Your victory, I suppose ? " He blushed and said, " No, I'm not." Every one was delighted to hear his voice, for he had not said a word so far. " Of what then ? " some one asked. " Of my father," replied the boy, and cuddled up against him.

These shy, blushing boys were a feature of the age. The stricter parents, knowing the dangers which surrounded their sons, tried to keep them entirely from any knowledge or experience of the world.

As far as can be discovered from the somewhat fragmentary evidence, the Athenian type of education was prevalent throughout the civilised Hellenic world, with the exception of Crete and Lakedaimon, which had systems of their own. Xenophon, in praising the Spartan system and contrasting it with that which was prevalent in neighbouring countries, ascribes to what he calls "the rest of Hellas" educational customs and arrangements exactly similar to those which are found to have existed at Athens. His statement is borne out by other evidence. Chios certainly had a School of Letters before 494 B.C. ; for a building of this sort collapsed in that year, destroying all but one of the 120 pupils.[1] Boiotia, byword for stupidity, had schools even in the smaller towns. A small place like Mukalessos had more than one ; for a detachment of wild Thracian mercenaries in the pay of Athens fell

[1] Herod. vi. 27.

upon the town at daybreak one morning during the Peloponnesian War, and entering " the largest school in the place," killed all the boys.[1] Arkadia had an equally bad reputation ; yet, according to Polubios,[2] in every Arcadian town the boys were compelled by law to learn to sing. Troizen must have had schools in 480, when she provided them for her Athenian guests. Aelian vouches for schools in Lesbos,[3] Pausanias[4] for a school of sixty boys in Astupalaia in 496 B.C. The poet Sophocles dined with a master of letters whose school was either in Eretria or Eruthrai.[5] The inscriptions show that before the third century there were flourishing schools in most of the islands.

Gymnastic education must have gone on in every Hellenic city, for the athletic victors at the great games come from every part. Musical training too was required for the dancing and singing which were universal throughout Hellas ; but how far the lyre was taught must remain doubtful. In Boiotia the flute replaced the lyre in the schools. But it may be taken for granted that letters, some sort of music, and gymnastics were taught in every part of civilised Hellas, with the possible exception that letters may not have been taught at Sparta.

Secondary Education, as long as it was supplied by the Sophists, reached every village in the Hellenic world ; later, it had a tendency to be confined to the large towns. The Tertiary system of military training and special gymnastics for the epheboi would seem, from the scanty evidence of the inscriptions, to have been well-nigh universal.

I will now proceed to give a more detailed account

---

[1] Thuc. vii. 29. [2] Pol. iv. 20. 7. [3] Ael. *Var. Hist.* 7. 15.
[4] Pausan. vi. 9. 6. [5] Athen. 604 a-b.

of the several branches of this widespread educational system. As the evidence comes almost entirely from Athens, my description will deal in the main with Athenian education ; but, as the same type prevailed throughout the greater part of Hellas, the description may be taken as applying to the other cities also.

CHAPTER III

WE have seen that Primary Education in Hellas consisted of letters and music, with a contemporary training
in gymnastics ; to which triple course was added, late in
the fourth century, drawing and painting. How the day
was divided between mental and physical training is
unknown—probably, like everything else, this varied
with the taste of the individual—but the following
sketch from Lucian,[1] although it belongs to a much
later date, may perhaps give some idea of a schoolboy's
day :—

"He gets up at dawn, washes the sleep from his
eyes, and puts on his cloak. Then he goes out from
his father's house, with his eyes fixed upon the ground,
not looking at any one who meets him. Behind him
follow attendants and paidagogoi, bearing in their hands
the implements of virtue, writing-tablets or books containing the great deeds of old, or, if he is going to a
music-school, his well-tuned lyre.

"When he has laboured diligently at intellectual
studies, and his mind is sated with the benefits of the
school curriculum, he exercises his body in liberal

[1] Lucian, *Loves*, 44-45.

pursuits, riding or hurling the javelin or spear. Then
the wrestling-school with its sleek, oiled pupils, labours
under the mid-day sun, and sweats in the regular athletic
contests. Then a bath, not too prolonged ; then a
meal, not too large, in view of afternoon school. For
the schoolmasters are waiting for him again, and the
books which openly or by allegory teach him who was
a great hero, who was a lover of justice and purity.
With the contemplation of such virtues he waters the
garden of his young soul. When evening sets a limit
to his work, he pays the necessary tribute to his stomach
and retires to rest, to sleep sweetly after his busy day."

The school hours were naturally arranged to suit the
times of Hellenic meals, for which the boys returned
home. The ordinary arrangement was a light breakfast
at daybreak, a solid meal at mid-day, and supper at
sunset. So the schools opened at sunrise.[1] Solon
enacted that they should not open earlier. They closed
in time to allow the boys to return home to lunch,[2]
opened again in the afternoon, and closed before sunset.[3]
How many of the intermediate hours were spent in
work,[4] and what intervals there were, is unknown.
There was, of course, no weekly rest on Sundays ; but
festivals, which were whole holidays, were numerous
throughout Hellas, and, in Alexandria at any rate, on
the 7th and 20th of every month the schools were closed,
these days being sacred to Apollo.[5] There were also
special school festivals, such as that of the Muses, and

[1] Aischin. *ag. Timarch.* 12 ; Thuc. vii. 29 ; Plato, *Laws.*

[2] Lucian, *Parasite*, 61.   [3] Aischin. *ag. Timarch.* 12.

[4] *Anthol. Palat.* x. 43 has been quoted as evidence that six hours' work a day
was a maximum. The epigram runs : " Six hours suffice for work ; rest of the day,
expressed in numerals, says ζῆθι, 'enjoy life.' " But the point is the joke that the
numerals for 7, 8, 9, 10, the later hours of the day, are ζ', η', θ', ι', which spells
ζῆθι. The epigram does not mean to state a fact ; the joke is its only *raison d'être.*
In any case schools are not mentioned.   [5] Herondas, *Schoolmaster* (iii.) 53.

holidays in commemoration of benefactors; thus Anaxagoras left a bequest to Klazomenai, on condition that
the day of his death should be celebrated annually by a
holiday in the schools.[1] It must also be remembered
that one of the three branches of Primary Education in
Hellas would be called play in England : an afternoon
spent in running races, jumping, wrestling, or riding
would not be regarded as work by an English schoolboy.
Music, too, is usually learned during play-hours in an
English school. Even Letters, when the elementary
stage was past, meant reciting, reading, or learning by
heart the literature of the boy's own language, and most
of it not stiff literature by any means, but such fascinating fairy-tales as are found in Homer. There is little
trace of Hellenic boys creeping unwillingly to school :
their lessons were made eminently attractive.

Of the fees which were paid to schoolmasters little
is known. An amusing passage in Lucian,[2] dealing
with the under-world, describes those who had been
kings or satraps upon earth as reduced in the future
state " to beggary, and compelled by poverty either to
sell kippers or to teach the elements of reading and
writing." From this it may be inferred that elementary schoolmasters did not make much money by
their fees. This inference is supported by the fact that
even the poorest Athenians managed to send their sons
to such schools. Plato in the Laws reserves the
profession for foreigners, thus suggesting that it was
neither well paid nor highly esteemed. To call a man
a schoolmaster was almost an insult ; Demosthenes,
abusing Aischines, says, " You taught letters, I went
to school." [3] The weakness of the masters' position may

---

[1] Mahaffy, Greek Education, p. 54.   [2] Lucian, Nekuom. 17.
[3] Dem. de Cor. 315.

be seen too from the extreme contempt with which their pupils seem to have treated them. The boys bring their pets—cats and dogs and leopards—into school, and play with them under the master's chair. Theophrastos,[1] in describing the characteristics of the mean man, says that " he does not send his children to school all the month of Anthesterion " (that is, from the middle of February to the middle of March) " on account of the number of feasts." The school-bills were paid by the month, and, since boys did not go to school on the great festivals, and Anthesterion contained many such days, the mean parent thought he would not get his money's worth for this particular month, and so withdrew his boys while it lasted.

Mean parents also deducted from the fees in proportion, if their sons were absent from school owing to ill-health for a day or two ;[2] but this was not usually done. The bills were paid on the 30th of each month.[3] Schoolmasters apparently had some difficulty in getting their bills paid at all ; according to Demosthenes' statement, his bills were never paid, owing to the fraudulent behaviour of his guardian Aphobos.[4]

No doubt the fees varied according to the merits of the school, for the schools at Athens seem to have differed greatly. Demosthenes, when boasting of his career, in his speech *On the Crown*, says that he went as a boy to the *respectable* schools ;[5] the quality and quantity of the teaching must have been varied to suit the parent's pocket. For the poor there would probably be schools where only the elements of reading

[1] Theoph. *Char*. 30.   [2] *Ibid*. 30.
[3] Herondas, iii. 3.   [4] Demos. *ag. Aphobos*, i. 828.
              [5] Demos. *Crown*, 312.

and writing were taught.   In the higher class of school
these elements would be taught by under-masters,
frequently slaves ; but free citizens might also be
reduced by poverty to take such a post.   This may be
seen from the case of the father of Aischines, the
orator.[1]   Impoverished and exiled like many democrats
by the Thirty Tyrants, he returned with the Restoration
a ruined man.   To earn his living, he became an usher
at the school of one Elpias, close to the Theseion,
and taught letters : his son Aischines seems to have
begun his life by assisting his father in this occupation.
His opponent, Demosthenes, takes advantage of the
contempt with which these ushers were regarded to
declare that the father was a slave of Elpias,[2] " wearing
big fetters and a collar," and the son was employed in
" grinding the ink and sponging the forms and sweeping
out the schoolroom ($\pi\alpha\iota\delta\alpha\gamma\omega\gamma\epsilon\hat{\iota}o\nu$), the work of a
servant, not of a free boy."

No doubt letters and music were often taught at
the same school, in different rooms.   Such an arrangement would be natural and convenient.   The vases
suggest it, but their evidence is uncertain.   The school
buildings seem often to have been surrounded by playgrounds.   A passage in Aelian[3] shows us the boys,
just let out of school, playing at tug-of-war.   No
doubt in these places they played with their hoops
and tops, and amused themselves with pick-a-back and
the stone- and dice-games which corresponded to our
marbles.   In villages these playgrounds probably did
duty as palaistrai.

The headmaster of the school sat on a chair with a

[1] Demos. *Crown*, 270.   This is the most probable restoration of the facts from
the statements of the opposing orators.

[2] *Ibid.* 313.

[3] Aelian, *Var. Hist.* xii. 9 (at Klazomenai).

high back ; under-masters and boys had stools without
backs, but cushions were provided. For lessons in
class there were benches.[1] There was a high reading-
desk for recitations. Round the walls hung writing-
tablets, rulers, and baskets or cases containing manuscript
rolls labelled with the author's name, composing the
school library ; the rolls might also hang by themselves.[2]
Masters were expected to possess at any rate a copy of
Homer—Alkibiades thrashed one who did not. Sometimes they emended their edition themselves.[3] In the
music-schools hung lyres and flutes and flute-cases.
The παιδαγωγεῖον mentioned by Demosthenes may have
been an anteroom where the paidagogoi sat, but more
probably the word is only a rhetorical variant for
" schoolroom." There were often busts of the Muses
round the walls,[4] which were also decorated with vases,
serving for domestic purposes, and, perhaps, illustrating
with their pictures the books which the boys were
reading. At a later date, at any rate, a series of
cartoons, illustrating scenes in the *Iliad* and *Odyssey*,
were sometimes hung upon the walls : the " Tabula
Iliaca," now in the Capitoline Museum, has been
recognised as a fragment of such a series.

The first stage was to learn to read and write.
Instead of a slate, boys in Hellas had tablets of wax,
usually made in two halves, so as to fold on a hinge
in the middle, the waxen surfaces coming inwards and
so being protected. Sometimes there were three pieces,
forming a triptych, or even more. For pencil, they

---

[1] Benches do not appear on vases, because a row of boys involves elaborate perspective ; the artist preferred to take single boys on stools, as a sort of section of a
class, just as he gave the stools only two legs. Xen. *Banquet*, 4. 27, shows two
boys sitting side by side. It is not necessary to reject benches, with Girard.

[2] Alexis, *Linos* (in Athen. 164 B.C.). See Illustr. Plates I. A and I. B.

[3] Plut. *Alkib.* 7.   [4] Herondas, iii. 83. 96.

had an instrument with a sharp point at one end, suitable for making marks on the wax, and a flat surface at the other, which was used to erase what had been written, and so make the tablets ready for future use. These tablets are shown in the school-scenes on the fifth-century vases.[1] At a later period, when parchment and papyrus became more common, these materials were used in the schools. Lines could be ruled with a lump of lead, and writing done either with ink and a reed pen or with lead ; for erasures a sponge was employed.

The early stages of learning to write are described in the *Protagoras* of Plato.[2] "When a boy is not yet clever at writing, the masters first draw lines, and then give him the tablet and make him write as the lines direct." The passage has been variously interpreted. Some regard the master as merely writing a series of letters which the boy is to copy underneath. The word used in Greek for the master's writing is ὑπογράψαντες, and it is significant that the word for a "copy" in this sense is a derivative of this word, ὑπογραμμός. Such a copy, corresponding to the phrases like "England exports engines" or "Germany grows grapes," which are employed in English schools for this purpose, is extant.[3] It is a nonsense sentence designed to contain all the letters of the alphabet μάρπτε σφὶγξ κλὼψ ζβυχθηδόν. If this rendering is correct, the master wrote a sentence of this sort on the tablets, and the boy copied it underneath. Others interpret the lines which the master draws on the tablet as parallel straight lines, within which the boy

---

[1] See Illustr. Plate No. I. A.   [2] Plato, *Protag.* 326 D.

[3] In Clement of Alexandria, who gives two others.   *Strom.* v. 8 (p. 675, Potter). A writing copy set by a master, though not of the alphabetical kind described by Clement, is actually extant on a wax tablet in the British Museum (Add. MS. 34,186). It consists of two lines of verse written out by the master and copied twice by a pupil.

had to write. Just such a device is often employed
in English copy-books. The word used for "lines,"
γραμμαί, usually means "straight lines," which supports
this interpretation. But ὑπογραφή, on the other hand,
a derivative of ὑπογράφειν, is used for irregular traces,
e.g. a footstep,[1] and ὑπογράφειν itself is a technical
term in Hellenic art for "sketching in" what is afterwards to be finished in detail. Consequently a third
rendering of the passage makes the master draw a
faint, rough outline of the various letters, and the boy
has to go over them with his pen, marking the grooves
in the wax deeper and filling in the details. For
example, in England, the master might draw | · | and
the boy go over the two vertical lines and draw in
the other two, M. Thus all three interpretations are
sensible and rest on good authority. But surely the
master may be regarded as adopting all three processes,
according to the intelligence of the pupils. For the
beginner he would outline the whole letter, and leave
him only the task of going over it again. Then he
would gradually give less and less help, till the boy was
capable of writing the letters with the assistance of the
parallel lines alone. Finally these would be withdrawn,
and the boy would be left to write his imitation of the
copy without assistance. The phrase in Plato is purposely vague, and will include the whole of this process.

The letters were written in lines horizontal and
vertical, so that they fell beneath one another. No
stops or accents were inserted, and no spaces were left
between words. The writing-master probably ruled
both the horizontal and the vertical lines on the tablet
for his pupil. On the Vase of Douris,[2] an under-
master is represented as writing with his pen on

---

[1] Aeschylus, *Choeph.* 209.   [2] Illustr. Plate I. A.

a wax tablet, while a boy stands in front of him. He
is probably meant either to be writing a copy or else
correcting his pupil's exercise. Over his head hangs a
ruler, for marking out the guiding lines on the tablet.
Behind the boy sits a bearded man with a staff, who is
probably the paidagogos. The boys in the class are
clearly coming up one by one to receive their copies or
have their exercises corrected, while the rest are doing
their writing. It will be noticed that there is no desk
or table : the Hellenes wrote with their tablets on their
knees.

As soon as the boy had acquired a certain facility in
writing, he entered the dictation class. The master read
out something, and the boys wrote it down.[1]   At first,
of course, very simple words would be dictated, and
there would not be much to write. But, later on, the
boys would write at his dictation passages of the poets
and other authors. For this purpose, ink and parchment may sometimes have been employed : Aischines
seems to have " ground ink "[2] for a writing-school.
Various " elaborations in the way of speed and beauty "
of writing seem to have been customary in the case of
more advanced pupils.[3]   Possibly they learnt to make
flourishes and ornamental letters. Speed would naturally
be taught, for it was usual to take notes at the lectures
of Sophists and Philosophers, and speed is required
for this purpose. This must have involved the use
of the cursive letters, which otherwise were not needed,
for the Hellene had not very much writing to do,
unless he became a clerk to a public body.

Learning to read must have been a difficult business
in Hellas, for books were written in capitals at this

[1] Xen. *Econ.* xv. 5.   [2] Demosth. *de Cor.* 313.
[3] Plato, *Laws*, 810 A (cp. the prizes for calligraphy in Teos).

time.   There were no spaces between the words, and no
stops were inserted.   Thus, the reader had to exercise
much ingenuity before he could arrive at the meaning
of a sentence.   Still more difficult for the boys to grasp
was the Attic accent, upon which the masters set a great
importance.   So difficult was it, that few foreigners
ever acquired it, and a born Athenian, if he went abroad
for a few years, often lost the power of speaking with
the Attic intonation.   The first step in learning to read
is to acquire the alphabet.   The Hellenes, wishing, as
usual, to make learning as easy as possible, seem to have
put the alphabet into verse.   A metrical alphabet,
ascribed to Kallias, a contemporary of Perikles, is still
extant, but in a mutilated form, which has been restored
in several not very convincing ways.   Probably it has
been adapted to suit different alphabets, for there were
several current in different parts of Hellas.   The following is a conjectural restoration :—

> ἔστ' ἄλφα, βῆτα, γάμμα, δέλτα τ', εἶ τε, καί
> ζῆτ', ἦτα, θῆτ', ἰῶτα, κάππα, λάβδα, μῦ,
> νῦ, ξεῖ, τὸ οὖ, πεῖ, ῥῶ, τὸ σίγμα, ταῦ, τὸ ὖ,
> πάροντα φεῖ τε χεῖ τε τῷ ψεῖ εἰς τὸ ὦ.[1]

This complete alphabet of twenty-four letters, which
appears in modern Greek Grammars, was not adopted
for official purposes at Athens till 403 B.C., "but it is
clear that it was in ordinary use at Athens consider-
ably earlier." [2]

This metrical alphabet formed the prologue to what
may be called a spelling-drama, in which the whole
process of learning to spell was expressed either in
iambic lines or in choral songs.   Since its author,
Kallias, is coupled with Strattis, the comic poet,[3] it

---

[1] Athen. 453 d.   [2] Giles' *Manual of Comparative Philology*, § 604.
                    [3] Athen. 453 c, d.

may be inferred that the play was a comedy, not a tragedy ; the chorus would then be twenty-four in number. Each member of the chorus represented one of the twenty-four letters. In the first choric song the letters were put together in pairs, in the fashion of a spelling class. The first strophé runs as follows :—

Beta	Alpha	BA
Beta	Ei	BĔ
Beta	Eta	BĒ
Beta	Iota	BI
Beta	Ou	BŎ
Beta	U	BU
Beta	O	BŌ [1]

In the corresponding antistrophé Gamma was similarly coupled with the seven vowels, and so on apparently through the alphabet. During the song, which was set to excellent music, the members of the chorus, dressed to represent the letters quite clearly, and no doubt posturing in the right attitude, would form themselves into the required pairs. Thus, during the first line Beta and Alpha would come together, during the second Beta and Ei, and so on. After this song came a lecture on the vowels, in iambic verse, the chorus being told to repeat them one by one after the speaker. There seems to have been a plot of some sort in this extraordinary drama, but the main interest was, no doubt, the spelling. Opportunities were also taken for describing the shapes of the letters, the audience having to guess what letter was intended. This kind of alphabetical puzzle seems to have caught the popular fancy at Athens, for Euripides,

[1] A fragment of terra-cotta has been found at Athens, containing on it :

αρ βαρ γαρ δαρ
ερ βερ γερ δερ

which must have belonged to some spelling-book—perhaps the brick formed part of the wall of a schoolroom.—Quoted by Girard, p. 131.

Agathon, and Theodektes all employed it. In each case the concealed word was " Theseus."

Euripides' description, if it be his, may be rendered thus :—

> First, such a circle as is measured out
> By compasses, a clear mark in the midst.
> The second letter is two upright lines,
> Another joining them across their middles.
> The third is like a curl of hair. The fourth,
> One upright line and three crosswise infixed.
> The fifth is hard to tell : from several points
> Two lines run down to form one pedestal.
> The last is with the third identical.

In the same spirit, Sophocles, in his satyric drama *Amphiaraos*, introduced an actor who represented the shapes of the letters by his dancing.[1] Periclean Athens seems to have taken a very keen interest in matters of spelling : the audience must all have known their letters, or such devices could never have become so popular.

Kallias' play is the ancestor of such books as *Reading without Tears*. His dramatic presentation of the process of spelling must have caught the imagination and impressed the memory of many Athenian boys. It may even be suspected that his method was adopted in enterprising schools, and spelling lessons were conducted to a tune, perhaps even accompanied by dancing.[2] The tunes of Kallias were highly praised, and were, no doubt, very different from the monotonous drone which announces to the outside world the presence of a Board School.

[1] Athen. 454 f.

[2] This is by no means inconceivable, when it is remembered that the Hellenes often set even the laws to music, in order to make them easier to learn and remember.

To return to more prosaic methods. Plato gives an interesting sketch [1] of a reading class. " When boys have just learnt their letters, they recognise any of them readily enough in the shortest and easiest syllables, and are able to give a correct answer about them. But in the longer and more difficult syllables they are not certain, but form a wrong opinion and answer wrongly. Then the best way is to take them back to the syllables in which they recognise the same letters and then compare them with those in which they made mistakes, and, putting them side by side, show that in both combinations the same letters have the same meaning."

Take an English example. The master writes SCRAPE on the blackboard and asks the boys to tell him what letters it contains. The class fail to recognise the letters : the word is too long and difficult. The master then writes beside it consecutively APE, RAPE, CAPE, in all of which the boys recognise the letters correctly. Then CRAPE and SCRAP. From these he passes on to SCRAPE, which they now recognise by analogy from the words which they know already. " Finally, they learn always to give the same name to the same letter whenever it comes." [2]

The methods by which boys learn to spell are the same in all ages. " When boys come together to learn their letters, they are asked what letters there are in some word or other." [3] A certain amount of mental arithmetic seems to have been included in this stage of spelling : the pupils were asked *how many* letters there were in a word, as well as the order in which they were arranged.[4] But this will be discussed later.

[1] Plato, *Polit.* 278 A, B. [2] *Ibid.*
[3] *Ibid.* 285 C. [4] Xen. *Econ.* viii. 14.

While the boys were still unable to read, and often afterwards owing to the comparative scarcity of books, the master dictated to them the poetry which he intended them to learn by heart, and they repeated it after him.

The Kulix of Douris gives an interesting picture of either a reading or a repetition lesson.[1] On a high-backed chair sits an elderly master, holding a roll in his hand. On it is inscribed what is clearly meant to be an hexameter line from some epic poet, but Douris was not very well educated, and so the line is misspelt and will not scan. In front of the master stands a boy, behind whom sits an elderly man who is probably, as in the writing scene, a paidagogos. The master may be dictating the poem while the boy learns it by heart after him, or he may be hearing him say it. But very possibly the scene represents a reading-lesson. The attitudes of boy and master are not very convenient, if both are reading out of the same book ; but this was unavoidable, for, owing to the canons of vase-painting, the figures could only be full-faced or in profile, and the front of the manuscript had to be turned in such a way as to be legible.

On the walls of the school hang a manuscript rolled up and tied with a string, and an ornamental basket. These baskets were used as bookcases, to hold the manuscript rolls. They may sometimes be seen on vases suspended over the heads of reading figures, as in the British Museum vase,[2] which represents a woman reading a scroll. The paidagogos, we may notice, is revealing his humble origin by crossing his feet, a serious offence against good manners in Hellas.

" When the boys knew their letters and were

beginning to understand what was written, the masters put beside them on the benches the works of good poets for them to read, and made them learn them by heart. They chose for this purpose poets that contained many moral precepts, and narratives and praises of the heroes of old, in order that the boy might admire them and imitate them and desire to become such a man himself." [1] It is noteworthy that Hellenic boys began at once with the very best literature to be found in their language : there was no preliminary course of childish tales.   Grammar, when invented, was taught at a later stage : the boys plunged straight into literature.

The schoolmasters at Athens differed as to which was the best way of introducing boys to their national literature.   The great majority held that a properly educated boy ought to be saturated in all poetry, comic and serious, hearing much of it in the reading class, and learning much of it—in fact, whole poets—by heart.[2] A minority would pick out the leading passages,[3] the " purple patches," and certain whole speeches,[4] and put them together and have them committed to memory. Plato argued in favour of expurgated editions of passages carefully selected according to a very strict standard, since much in literature was good and much bad.[5]

Homer, of course, played the largest part in these literary studies ; from early times " he was given an honourable place in the teaching of the young." [6]   Vast

---

[1] Plato, *Protag.* 325 E.   [2] Plato, *Laws*, 811.

[3] τὰ κεφάλαια—a phrase used in later times for " commonplaces," " topics," which suggests that these selections were of that sort.

[4] As the great speeches are picked out from Shakespeare for " repetition " nowadays.

[5] Plato, *Laws*, 802, 811.

[6] Isokrates (*Paneg.* 74 A).   He says the object was to make the boys hate the barbarians ; as, *e.g.*, English boys might learn *Henry V.* in order to dislike the French !

quantities of the *Iliad* and *Odyssey* were learnt by heart. Nikeratos, in Xenophon,[1] says : " My father, wishing me to grow up into a good man, made me learn all the lines of Homer ; and now I can repeat the whole of the *Iliad* and *Odyssey* from memory." Such prodigious feats were, no doubt, assisted by the rhapsodes, who could be heard at Athens declaiming Homer " nearly every day." [2] The Hellenes did not let their greatest poet lie neglected, to be " revived " at long intervals. Homer was supposed to teach everything, especially soldiering and good morals. " I suppose you know," continues Nikeratos,[3] " that Homer, the wisest of men, has written about all human matters. So whoever of you wishes to excel as a householder or public speaker or general, or desires to become like Achilles or Aias or Nestor or Odusseus, let him come to me." Then he proceeds to show how, for example, the poet gives full directions about the proper way to drive a chariot in a race. Aristophanes[4] makes the shade of Aeschylus say, " Whence did divine Homer win his honour and renown, save from this, that he taught drill, courage, the arming of troops ? Many a man of valour he trained, and our own dead hero, Lamachos. I took my print from him, and represented many deeds of valour done by a Patroklos or lion-hearted Teukros, to rouse my countrymen to model themselves upon such men, when they heard the trumpet sound."

The great poet does not seem to have been taught pedantically ; the attention of the boys was not concentrated simply on the difficulties of the Homeric vocabulary. In fact, probably they were little troubled with such points ; the sense, the rhythm, and the beauty

[1] Xen. *Banquet*, iii. 5.   [2] *Ibid.*
[3] *Ibid.* iv. 6.   [4] Aristoph. *Frogs*, 1035.

of the original do not depend upon an exact understanding of every word, as many a modern reader has
discovered.   In a fragment of Aristophanes,[1] a father
asks his son the meaning of some hard words in Homer,
such as ἀμένηνα κάρηνα and κόρυμβα ; the son is quite
unable to translate them, at any rate when separated
from their context, and can only retort by asking his
father to interpret some archaic phrases in Solon's laws.
A later comic poet [2] introduced a cook who insisted on
using Homeric language, just as a modern *chef* writes
his *menu* in French ; the man who has hired him is
ludicrously unable to understand his phrases, and has to
go in search of a commentary.

Explanations and interpretations of supposed moral
allegories in Homer, and lessons drawn from a close
study of his characters, were very popular in Hellas,
and no doubt figured in the schools.

If Homer occupied the first place in literary education, other leading authors were not neglected.   All
the great poets were made useful.   " Orpheus taught
ceremonial rites and abstinence from bloodshed, and
Mousaios medicine and oracles, and Hesiod the tillage
of land, the seasons of fruits and ploughing." [3]   Hesiod
probably served more as a theological handbook than as
a manual of agriculture ; the moral precepts to Perses
in the *Works and Days* probably also found favour
with schoolmasters.   The fourth-century comic poet
Alexis gives an interesting catalogue of a school
library.[4]   Besides Orpheus, Hesiod, and Homer, who
have been mentioned already, there are Epicharmos,
Choirilos, the author of an epic poem on the Persian
war, and what is called vaguely " tragedy," probably

---

[1] From the *Banqueters*.
[2] Straton (in Athen. 382, 383).
[3] Aristoph. *Frogs*, 1032.
[4] Athen. 164.

meaning a selection from the great tragedians. We can see from Plato's attacks that Aeschylus and Euripides must have been important in the schools, and we know that Athenian gentlemen were expected to be able to recite them at dinner-parties, and must therefore have learnt them by heart. The vague words " tragedy " and " comedy " are similarly used of the recitations of the boys at Teos. Various editions of moral precepts were also popular. Among these were *The Precepts of Cheiron*, or Cheironeia, supposed to have been given by the wise Centaur to his pupil Achilles and put into verse by Hesiod ; on a vase at Berlin three boys are seen reading this work with apparent interest. The extant lines of Theognis are often supposed to represent a school edition of the poet's works, containing the more improving portions. The lyric poets were taught at the lyre-school, and I shall discuss them later.

Alexis also mentions " all sorts of prose works " in the school library. The only one of these to which he gives a more definite name is a cookery-book by Simos. But that is only introduced for the sake of a joke ; such a work would not, of course, figure in an Athenian school. Aesop may have been a prose work read in schools ; it was considered the sign of an ignoramus " not to have thumbed Aesop," or to be able to quote him.[1] Such moral works as Prodikos' *Choice of Herakles* were probably popular in schools. The case of Lusis in Plato suggests that some of the old nature-philosophers may have been read. No doubt the school library varied according to the taste of the master, and his freedom of choice may have led to some curious selections. But on the whole prose works very

[1] Aristoph. *Birds*, 471 ; *Wasps*, 1446. 1401.

rarely figured in the elementary schools, partly because they were usually too technical, still more because the artistic and literary sense of the Hellenes regarded poetry, if only because of its greater beauty and its imaginative value, as better for educational purposes than prose.

It must be remembered that when boys recited Homer or Aeschylus or Euripides, they acted them, delivering even the narrative with a great deal of gesture, and dramatising the speeches as fully as they could. The almost daily recitations of the rhapsodes, and the frequent dramatic performances in the theatres, gave them plenty of examples of the way to act. The Hellenes were extremely sensitive and sympathetic : they were a nation of actors. The rhapsode Ion tells Plato that, when he recited Homer, his eyes watered and his hair stood on end. This may give the modern reader some idea of what his repetition-lesson meant to a boy at Athens. More may be gathered from Plato's vehement denunciations of dramatisation in poetry intended for use in schools ; he believed that this continuous acting exerted an evil influence upon character. But this question will be discussed elsewhere.

The schoolrooms were used as the scene of lectures, to which grown-up men were invited ; probably the lectures would be given to the boys at a different time. The wandering teacher, Hippias of Elis, meeting Sokrates one day, invited him to such a lecture, which, from its subject, was clearly meant mainly for the young.[1] After the fall of Troy, according to the story which Hippias invented for the occasion, Neoptolemos asked the wise old Nestor what was good and honourable conduct and what manner of life would cause a

[1] Plato, *Hipp. Maj.* 286 B.

young man to win renown. Given this convenient opening, Nestor replied by suggesting many excellent rules of conduct. Hippias had delivered this lecture at Sparta, where it had won great applause. He now proposes, he says, "to deliver it the day after to-morrow in the schoolroom of Pheidostratos, and to impart much other valuable information at the same time, at the request of Eudikos son of Apemantos. Mind you come and bring any friends who will be capable of appreciating what I say." No doubt it was a very excellent little sermon on the duties of life, closely analogous to Prodikos' famous *Choice of Herakles*, and most improving for the pupils of Pheidostratos, if they were allowed to attend.

One charming picture of two Athenian school friends,[1] in their sleeveless tunics, is extant. "I saw you, Sokrates," says a guest at a dinner-party, "when you and Kritoboulos at the School of Letters were both looking for something in the same book, putting your head against his, and your bare shoulder against his shoulder."

It is also recorded that the Athenians were great hands at nicknames :[2] it may be inferred that this peculiarity extended also to their schoolboys.

A vivid picture of school life has recently come to light in the third Mime of Herondas. It belongs to the Alexandrian period in point of date, but many of its details will, no doubt, suit the Athenian schools just as well ; it is, however, quite inconceivable that gags and fetters were used as punishments at Athens in the schools.

A mother, Metrotimé, brings her truant boy,

---

[1] Xen. *Banquet*, iv. 27. School friendships are also mentioned in Aristot. *Eth.* viii. 12 ; Aristoph. *Clouds*, 1006.　　　　[2] Athen. 242 d.

Kottalos, to his schoolmaster Lampriskos to receive a flogging.

> METROTIMÉ.   Flog him, Lampriskos,[1]
> Across the shoulders, till his wicked soul
> Is all but out of him. He's spent my all
> In playing odd and even : knucklebones
> Are nothing to him. Why, he hardly knows
> The door o' the Letter School. And yet the thirtieth
> Comes round and I must pay—tears no excuse.
> His writing-tablet, which I take the trouble
> To wax anew each month, lies unregarded
> I' the corner. If by chance he deigns to touch it,
> He scowls like Hades, then puts nothing right
> But smears it out and out. He doesn't know
> A letter, till you scream it twenty times.
> The other day his father made him spell
> MARON ; the rascal made it SIMON ; dolt
> I thought myself to send him to a school :
> Ass-tending is his trade. Another time
> We set him to recite some childish piece ;
> He sifts it out like water through a crack,
> " Apollo," pause, then " hunter."

The poor mother goes on to say that it is useless to scold the boy ; for, if she does, he promptly runs away from home to sponge upon his grandmother, or sits up on the roof out of the way, like an ape, breaking the tiles, which is expensive for his parents.

>   Yet he knows
> The seventh and the twentieth of the month,
> Whole holidays, as if he read the stars.
> He lies awake o' nights adreaming of them.
> But, so may yonder Muses prosper you,
> Give him in stripes no less than——
>   LAMPRISKOS.   Right you are.
> Here, Euthias, Kokkalos, and Phillos, hoist him
> Upon your backs.[2] I like your goings on,

---

[1] The translation is free, and I omit a good deal that is less relevant.
[2] For a picture of such a flogging see p. 599 of Bury's *Roman Empire*.

My boy. I'll teach you manners. Where's my strap,
The stinging cow's-tail!

 KOTTALOS.   By the Muses, Sir,
Not with the stinger.

 LAMP.   Then you shouldn't be
So naughty.

 KOTT. O, how many will you give me?

 LAMP. Your mother fixes that.

 KOTT.   How many, mother?

 METR. As many as your wicked hide can bear.

 KOTT. Stop, that's enough, stop.

 LAMP.   You should stop your ways.

 KOTT. I'll never do it more, I promise you.

 LAMP. Don't talk so much, or else I'll bring a gag.

 KOTT. I won't talk, only do not kill me, please.

 LAMP. Let him down, boys.

 METR.   No, leather him till sunset.

 LAMP. Why, he's as mottled as a water-snake.

 METR. Well, when he's done his reading, good or bad,
Give him a trifle more, say twenty strokes.

 KOTT. Yah!

 METR. I'll go home and get a pair of fetters.
Our Lady Muses, whom he scorned, shall see
Their scorner hobble here with shackled feet.

The exact age at which arithmetic was taught to
boys at Athens involves a somewhat complicated inquiry.
The arrangements which Plato makes in the *Republic*
and *Laws* defer this subject till the age of sixteen. In
the *Laws*[1] he says : " It remains to discuss, first the
question of Letters, and secondly that of the Lyre and
practical arithmetic—by which I mean so much as is
necessary for purposes of war and household management and the work of government." His citizens will
also require, he thinks, enough astronomy to make the
calendar intelligible to them. In this passage he distinctly couples practical arithmetic with music ; and

[1] Plato, *Laws*, 809 c.

when he proceeds to detail, he makes the study of the
lyre last from thirteen to sixteen, and then deals with
arithmetic, the weights and measures, and the astrono-
mical calendar, studies which terminate with the seventeenth year. This course is designed for all the free
boys in his State : it is to be noticed that it is eminently
practical, elementary, and concrete. In the *Republic*
he is educating a few picked boys : before they are
eighteen they are to have gone through a course of
abstract and theoretical mathematics, the Theory of
Numbers, Plane and Solid Geometry, Kinetics and
Harmonics. Thus he mentions two sorts of mathematics, the one practical and concrete, called by the
Hellenes λογιστική,[1] whose object is mainly mercantile,
and the other theoretical and abstract, which they called
ἀριθμητική. Both sorts are to be learned in the period
next before the eighteenth year.

But it must not be assumed that this was the case
at Athens. The philosopher is dealing with an ideal
State, where education can be arranged in the theoretically best way, not with the real Athens, where the boy
might be called away to the counting-house or the
farm at any moment, and many did not stay at school
after they had once learned to read and write. Moreover Plato, as a good Pythagorean, saw a peculiar
appropriateness in making numbers follow music, and
his Dorian sympathies made him divide up education
into clearly marked periods, in each of which only one
subject was taught. This arrangement, I have already
shown, did not find favour at Athens.

His system must, then, be received with caution.

---

[1] The distinction between λογιστική, reckoning up and comparing numbers,
chiefly in bills and the like, practical arithmetic, and ἀριθμητική, theory of numbers,
is noted in Plato, *Gorg.* 451 B.

It is inherently far more probable that the simpler, practical arithmetic would be taught at the elementary schools of letters, which all citizens, including future tradesmen and artisans, attended, not at some later date in a separate school. But can any evidence be found for such an arrangement? Yes, Plato himself in the *Laws*[1] declares that the future builder ought to play with toy bricks and learn weights and measurements when he is a child. His builder, at any rate, cannot wait to learn arithmetic till he is sixteen. Then, in the same work, he quotes the instance of Egypt, where "a very large number of children learn practical arithmetic *simultaneously with their letters*," and he goes on to commend the methods by which it was taught. Now Egypt in the *Laws* is represented as the home of ideal education, a sort of Utopia. Again, in Plato[2] Protagoras blames his brother Sophists for "leading their pupils *back*, much against their wish, and casting them *again* into the sciences from which they have escaped, practical arithmetic and astronomy and geometry and music." How could the Sophists[3] be described as "leading them back and casting them again" into studies from which they had escaped? Where had they learnt these subjects before they were fourteen? It could only have been at school. But what the Sophists taught must have been new to the boys, or they would not have paid to learn it. It was new, because the Sophists taught the advanced and theoretical stages, which appear in the *Republic*, and the elementary schoolmasters taught the simpler and con- crete elements of arithmetic, weights and measures, and the calendar, described in the *Laws*, which were

[1] Plato, *Laws*, 643 B.C.   [2] Plato, *Protag.* 318 D.
[3] So Theodoros in the *Theaitetos*.

necessary to every Athenian citizen. From all this it may be assumed that the Athenian boys, like Plato's Egyptian boys, learnt simple arithmetic, weights and measures, and perhaps the calendar, "simultaneously with their letters."

Now there are two passages in Xenophon which seem to suit this view. They are not conclusive in themselves, but they give a valuable hint. In the first [1] it is stated that any one who knows his letters could say *how many* letters there are in "Sokrates," and in what order they occur. In the second,[2] in the course of an argument, two illustrations are used, in close connection with one another. The passage runs :—
"Take the case of Letters. Suppose some one asks you how many letters there are in 'Sokrates,' and which are they ? . . . Or take the case of Numbers. Suppose some one asks what is twice five ? " These two quotations certainly make simple counting a part of learning letters, with which study the second passage also closely connects the multiplication table. It would seem that it was part of a spelling lesson to answer such questions as " How many letters in 'Sokrates' ? " Answer, " Eight." " Where does R come ? " Answer, " Fourth." It may be noticed also that the symbols of the numerals in ancient Hellas were, with one or two exceptions, identical with the current alphabet. The games with cubic dice and knucklebones, to which the boys were much addicted, must also have needed some arithmetical skill. The natural conclusion is that simple arithmetic, with, probably, the weights and measures, and the outlines of the calendar, were taught by the letter-master: the practice of music by the music-master : while the theory of numbers, of

---

[1] Xen. *Econ.* viii. 14.   [2] Xen. *Mem.* iv. 4. 7.

astronomy, and of music were taught by the Sophists
to μειράκια.

Simple counting was done on the fingers. " Reckon
on your fingers," says a character in Aristophanes,[1]
" not with pebbles." A common word for counting
was πεμπάζειν, " to reckon on the five fingers " ; the
division of the month into three periods of ten days
can be traced to the same custom. But by various
devices it was possible to count up to very large

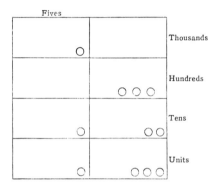

numbers on the fingers. Pebbles were also employed
to assist in arithmetic. In the case of complicated
accounts a reckoning board (ἄβακος or ἄβαξ) was used,
on which the pebbles varied in value according to their
position. Such boards go back to early days at Athens,
for Solon compared the life of a courtier to a pebble
upon them, since he was now worth much and now
little.[2] A character in a fourth-century comedy[3] sends
for an abacus and pebbles, in order that he may do his
accounts. The pebbles were arranged in grooves,

[1] Aristoph. *Wasps*, 656.   [2] In Diogenes Laertius, i. 2. 10.
[3] Alexis (in Athen. 117 e).

MUSIC-SCHOOL SCENES

From a Hudria in the British Museum (E 171).

being worth one or ten or a hundred and so forth,
according to the groove in which they were placed.
If they were put on the left-hand side of the board,
their value was multiplied by five.[1] The various
games of πεσσοί, which somewhat resembled chess, were
played on a somewhat similar board to this, and these
chess-boards were known as ἄβακες. Now the art of
playing with πεσσοί is more than once coupled by
Plato with arithmetic or mathematics generally in such
a way as to show that the game must have involved
mathematical skill.[2] As was usual in Athens, instruction went hand in hand with amusement, and, in
playing games, the boys learned arithmetic willingly.
A similar value seems to have attached to the game of
knucklebones, which the boys in the *Lusis* are found
playing during their whole holiday. Each boy carried
a large basket of knucklebones, and the loser in each
game paid so many of them over to the winner. The
art of playing this game is also coupled with mathematics by Plato;[3] so it must at any rate have
encouraged the study of arithmetic, in his opinion. In
the school scene of the British Museum amphora, a
little bag, usually supposed to contain knucklebones, is
figured : so they may even have been used in schools
for teaching arithmetic. In another school scene this
bag is present with a lyre and ruler ; so it was evidently
part of the school furniture.

After such revelations of Hellenic educational
methods, it is natural to suppose that the ingenious

---

[1] An abacus of a very similar sort is still in use in China and Japan, even in
banks. The " pebbles " are pushed to and fro, not in grooves, but on wires passing
through the middle of them. Calculations can be made by this means with
marvellous rapidity.

[2] e.g. *Polit.* 299 D.   πεττείαν ἢ ξύμπασαν ἀριθμητικήν.

[3] Plato, *Phaid.* 274.

devices by which the "Egyptians," [1] according to Plato, "make simple arithmetic into a game" for their children, were really used in Attica. One of these devices [2] was as follows. The master took, say, sixty apples. First he divided them among two boys, who were made to count their share, thirty each ; then among three boys, twenty each ; then among four, fifteen each ; then among five, twelve each ; and then among six, ten each. This would teach the system of factors. Then, again, a real or imaginary competition in boxing or wrestling [3] was arranged, say in a class of nine. The boys would work out, by actual experiment, how many fights would be necessary, if each boy had to fight all the others one by one, and how many if a system of rounds and byes was introduced. This might even teach Permutations and Combinations.

In another case a number of bowls, some containing mixed coins, gold, silver, and bronze, some all of one sort, would be handed round the class. The boys would have to count them, add and subtract them, and so on. Thus they would learn addition and subtraction of money, and would also gain a clear knowledge of the national coinage.

Plato was immensely impressed with the educational value of Arithmetic. "Those who are born with a talent for it," he says, "are quick at all learning ; while even those who are slow at it, have their general intelligence much increased by studying it." [4]   "No branch of education is so valuable a preparation for household management and politics, and all arts and

---

[1] Plato, *Laws*, 819 B.

[2] The restoration of this process rests on Athen. 671 ; the other two are purely conjectural.

[3] Suggests at once Hellenic, not Egyptian customs.

[4] Plato, *Rep.* 526 B.

crafts, sciences and professions, as arithmetic ; best of all, by some divine art, it arouses the dull and sleepy brain, and makes it studious, mindful, and sharp." [1]

The question of the more advanced stages of Mathematics, which were taught to older boys, may be left for the chapter on Secondary Education.

The chief and often the sole instrument taught in the music school was the seven-stringed lyre,[2] with a large sounding-board originally made of a tortoise's shell.[3] It might be played either with the hand or else with the " plektron " or striker ; the boy Lusis had learnt to do either.[4] The boys were also taught how to tighten and relax the strings by turning the pegs till the proper degree of tension was obtained. They brought their own lyre with them from home, the paidagogos carrying it behind his charge. This was a wise regulation from the master's point of view ; for the boys seem to have usually ruined these instruments by their early efforts.[5] Like the piano, the lyre required great delicacy of touch and very agile fingers, and these qualities could only be obtained by continual practice.[6]

As would naturally be expected, individual tuition was usual in the lyre-school ; instrumental music cannot be learnt in class. The vases make this point quite clear. The master has a single boy seated in front of him ; both hold lyres in their hands, to which they are singing, the words of the song being some-

---

[1] Plato, Laws, 747.

[2] Technically speaking, this was the λύρα, the κιθάρα being a professional instrument which was not taught at school.   [3] Illustr. Plate I. B.

[4] Plato, Lusis, 209 B. On Inscriptions there are separate prizes for the two methods.   [5] Xen. Econ. ii. 13.

[6] Ibid. xvii. 7.

times represented by a string of little dots. In Plate IV., on the left of this group, a boy is coming up to take his turn, lyre in hand, while behind him stands his paidagogos, leaning on a reading-desk and following his charge with his eyes. On the right is a boy just taking up his flute-case and preparing to depart, while another sits in the corner, wrapped in his cloak, waiting for his turn to take a lesson. In Plate III.,[1] the master is playing a barbitos and apparently singing, while the pupil plays the flute. On the left is a flute-master playing, and a pupil just leaving him, flute in hand. Another pupil, with a lyre, is waiting to take a lesson from the master in the centre, and is amusing himself meanwhile by playing with an animal that is probably a leopard,[1] like that which figures in Plate IV. Another pet, a dog, is howling in disgust at the music. On the right, a pupil with a flute is advancing to take a lesson from the flute-master in front of him. Behind him follows a young man, who may be an elder brother replacing the customary paidagogos for the nonce, or an admirer. In the background sits a small child, sucking his thumb, probably the younger brother of one of the pupils, who has come, in accordance with Aristotle's advice, to look on, although still too young to learn.

As soon as his pupils knew how to play, the master taught them the works of the great lyric poets,[2] which were not taught in the school of letters. These were set to music, and the boys sang them and played the accompaniment. Every gentleman at Athens was expected to be able to sing and play in this manner when he went out to a dinner-party. The custom,

---

[1] Cp. British Museum Vase E 57, on which a man is leading a leopard by a string.

[2] Plato, *Protag.* 326 B.

PLATE IV.

IN A LYRE-SCHOOL

From a *Hudria* in the British Museum (E 172).

however, began to become unfashionable during the
Peloponnesian War. When old Strepsiades, in the
Clouds,[1] asked Pheidippides to take the lyre and sing a
song of Simonides, his new-fashioned son replies that
playing the lyre was quite out of date, and singing over
the wine was only fit for a slave-woman at the grind-
stone. Whether this state of feeling continued and
whether it had a prejudicial effect on the music-schools
cannot be decided. Sometimes the guests brought
their boys to sing to the company : in the *Peace* the
son of the hero Lamachos is going to sing Homer, while
the coward Kleonumos' boy has a song of Archilochos
ready. Alkaios and Anakreon were also favourites ;[2]
the lyric portions of Kratinos' comedies, too, are
mentioned as sung at banquets :[3] no doubt, the same
was true of the other great comedians. As the iambic
parts of Aeschylus and Euripides were recited at the
dinner-table, it is natural to suppose that their songs
were also sung. The aged Dikasts in the *Wasps* sing
the choruses from Phrunichos' *Sidonians*. Old songs
like Lamprokles' " Pallas, dread sacker of cities " and
Kudides' " A cry that echoes afar " were popular in
earlier times. No doubt there was plenty of variety
in accordance with the master's taste. At the music
school, too, may have been taught the metrical version,
set to music, of the Athenian laws, which was ascribed
to Solon,[4] and that of the legislation of Charondas,
which Athenian gentlemen sang over their wine.[5]
Athenian boys were expected to know the laws by the
time that they were epheboi, and may well have been
taught them in this convenient and attractive way at

---

[1] Aristoph. *Clouds*, 1356.
[2] Aristoph. fragment of *Banqueters*.
[3] Aristoph. *Knights*, 526.
[4] Plut. *Solon*, iii.
[5] Hermippos (in Athen. 619 b).

the lyre-master's. To know how to play the lyre became the mark of a liberal education, since every one learned letters, but the poorest did not enter the music-school. "He doesn't know the way to play the lyre," became a proverb for an uneducated person, who had not had so many opportunities in life as his wealthier fellow-citizens. So, as a plea for a defendant we find—

> He may have stolen. But acquit him, for
> He doesn't know the way to play the lyre.[1]

To this the Dikast retorts that he has not learnt the lyre either, so he must be forgiven if he is so stupid as to condemn the accused.[2]

At the beginning of the fifth century the Hellenes were stimulated, according to Aristotle,[3] by their growing wealth and importance to make many educational experiments, especially in music. All manner of musical instruments were tried in the music-schools, but were rejected on trial, when the moral effects could be better appreciated. Among the instruments thus found wanting was the flute. At one time the flute became so popular at Athens that the majority of the free citizens could play it. But its moral effect proved to be unsatisfactory ; it was the instrument which belonged to wild religious orgies, and it aroused that hysterical and almost lunatic excitement[4] which the Hellenes regarded as a useful medicine, when taken at long intervals of time, for giving an outlet to such feelings and working them off the system, in order that a long period of calm might follow. But such a medicine was most unsuitable to be the daily food of boys. The

---

[1] Aristoph. *Wasps*, 959.   [2] *Ibid.* 989.   [3] Aristot. *Pol.* viii. 6. 11.

[4] For this reason it was opposed to *Dorian* influences by Pratinas. It was excluded from the Pythian games (Pausan. 10. vii. 5). Pratinas bids it be content to "lead drunk young men in their carousals and brawls."

flute had two other disadvantages. It distorted the
face sufficiently to horrify a sensitive Hellene.[1] It also
prevented the use of the voice : the boys could not
sing to it, as they sang to the lyre. So Athena, in the
old legend, had been quite right in throwing the
instrument away in disgust : it was only suitable for a
Phrygian Satyr, for it made no appeal to the intellect,
but only to the passions.[2]

This is Aristotle's account. It may be objected
that the vases which represent scenes in the music-
schools show the flute and the lyre being taught side
by side, and apparently equally popular. But these
vases can mostly be traced more or less certainly to
the first half of the fifth century, and so they bear out
Aristotle's statement. Moreover, the flute did not, of
course, die out in Hellas by any means ; it only became
an extra, instead of the regular instrument in schools.
The most notable Athenians, Kallias and Kritias and
Alkibiades, are said to have played it.[3] It always
remained popular at Thebes. But at Athens, in the
banquets, while the guests usually played the lyre
themselves, the flute was as a rule only played by
professional flute-girls,[4] although on the vases the guests
are sometimes found performing on this instrument
also.[5] Probably the Athenian attitude may be summed
up in the " ancient proverb " :[6]

> A flutist's brains can never stay :
> He puffs his flute, they're puffed away.

---

[1] Telestes, in his defence of the flute, could only retort that Athena, being condemned to eternal spinsterhood, ought not to be particular about her looks
(Athen. 617).   [2] Aristot. *Pol.* viii. 6. 11.
    [3] Athen. 184 d. Plutarch, however, says that when Alkibiades' masters tried to
make him learn the flute, he refused, declaring that it was unfit for gentlemen
(*Alk.* ii. 5).   [4] Not a respected profession at Athens.
    [5] Brit. Mus. E 495, 64, 71.   [6] Athen. 337 f.

It was usual to play on two flutes at the same time. Such a pair has been found,[1] together with a lyre, in a tomb at Athens. The flutes are somewhat over a foot in length, and have five holes on the upper and one on the lower side. Each has a separate mouthpiece. Besides this, flute-players sometimes wore a sort of leathern muzzle[2] over their mouths; but this does not appear in the schools. The pair of flutes were carried in a double case, made of some spotted skin; it had a pocket on one side, to hold the mouthpieces,[3] and a cord attached by which it could be hung up when not in use. The two flutes seem to have corresponded to treble and bass, "male" and "female" as Herodotos calls them. The treble was on the right, the bass on the left.[4] Flutes could be set to different harmonies, apparently by some rearrangement of stops. In the case of the flute, as in the case of the lyre, individual tuition was the rule. First the master played an air, and then the boy had to repeat it, while the master criticised.[5] Or the master played the air on a barbitos and sang to it, while the pupil accompanied him on the flute. This method had two advantages. The master was able to play at the same time as the boy, and give him instruction while playing, which the flute prevented him from doing. The song, too, which he was enabled to sing obviated one of the chief disadvantages of the flute: for the Hellenes objected to instrumental music as meaningless, unless it was accompanied by words.

There seem to have been music-schools scattered throughout Attica, besides those established in the capital: the description of the village boys marching off

---

[1] Smith's *Dictionary of Antiquities*.   [2] φορβεία. It belonged to professionals.
[3] γλωσσοκομεῖον.

[4] See the "Inscription" of the *Andria* and other plays of Terence.
[5] See Illustr. Plate II.

to the lyre-master's in a snow-storm without overcoats has already been quoted. The names of a few masters are extant. Lampros taught Sophocles the poet.[1] Sokrates[2] recommends Nikias to send his son to the famous Damon, who "is not merely a first-class musician, but also just the man to be with boys like this." But whether these musicians kept regular schools cannot be ascertained. Sokrates himself in his later years attended the music-school of Konnos, and learned among the boys. "I am disgracing Konnos the music-master," he says, "who is still teaching me to play the lyre. The boys who are my schoolfellows laugh at me and call Konnos the 'Greybeard teacher.'"[3] The same Konnos adopted the common but iniquitous custom of bestowing his chief attention on his more promising pupils, while neglecting the backward.[4] Aristophanes caricatures Kleon's school-days as follows : "The boys who went to school with Kleon say he would often set his lyre to the Dorian (= Gift-ian) harmony alone. Finally, the lyre-master lost his temper and told the paidagogos to take him away, saying, "This boy can't learn anything but the Briberian (Dorodokisti) mode."[5]

The attitude of the philosophers towards music will be discussed elsewhere. Plato's view may be summed up in the words which he puts in the mouth of Protagoras the Sophist.[6] "The music-master makes rhythm and harmony familiar to the souls of the boys, and they become gentler and more refined, and having more rhythm and harmony in them, they become more efficient in speech and in action. The whole life of Man stands in need of good harmony and good rhythm."

---

[1] Athen. 20 f.

[2] Plato, *Laches*, 180 D.

[3] Plato, *Euthud.* 272 C.

[4] *Ibid.* 295 D.

[5] Aristoph. *Knights*, 987-996.

[6] Plato, *Protag.* 326 B.

Aristotle's attitude is briefly this. "Music is neither a necessary nor a useful accomplishment in the sense in which Letters are useful, but it provides a noble and worthy means of occupying leisure-time." [1]

Aristotle mentions that in his day some added drawing and painting to the three parts of the course. [2]   It was not universal, like these, and it does not seem to have started till the fourth century. In the *Republic* and *Laws* Plato does not attack and criticise it among the other educational subjects ; but it plays so prominent a part in the *Republic* that it is obvious that the philosopher regarded it as a dangerous enemy to the views which he wished to spread. It is noticeable that the discussion of Art comes in as an after-thought, in Book X. May it not be inferred that when Plato wrote the earlier books, drawing and painting were not yet in vogue in the schools, but they became popular before he had finished his great work ?

In Periclean Athens the possibilities of artistic training had certainly existed. In the *Protagoras*, [3] as an instance in some argument, it is suggested that the lad Hippokrates might "go to this young fellow who has been in Athens of late, Zeuxippos of Heraklea. Every day that he was with him he would improve as an artist." Earlier in the same dialogue Sokrates remarks that his friend might go to Polukleitos or Pheidias, and pay to be taught sculpture. [4]   The large numbers of boys who became apprentices to the potters at Athens must have learned line-drawing and designing and painting from the earliest times. But art probably did not become a usual part of a liberal, as distinct from

[1] Aristot. *Pol.* viii. 3. 7.

[2] *Ibid.* viii. 3. 1.

[3] Plato, *Protag.* 318 B.

[4] *Ibid.* 311 C.

a technical, education till the middle of the fourth century.

This date is fixed by a passage in Pliny.[1] According to him, its introduction was due to Pamphilos the Macedonian. At his instance, first at Sikuon, where he lived, and afterwards in the rest of Hellas, free boys were taught before everything painting on boxwood, and this art was included in the first rank of the liberal arts. Now Pamphilos' picture of the Herakleidai is mentioned in the *Ploutos* of Aristophanes, which appeared in 388 B.C. Apelles, his pupil, began to come into prominence about 350 : Pamphilos himself seems to have lived on till the close of the century. The introduction of painting into the schools at Sikuon may therefore be dated, roughly, about 360 B.C., and from there the custom spread over Hellas. By 300 B.C. no doubt art had become a regular part of the educational curriculum ; for the philosopher Teles,[2] who probably lived about that time, mentions the gymnastic trainer, the letter-master, the musician, and the painter as the four chief burdens of boys. A trace of the new art-schools, with their technical vocabulary, is found in the *Laws*, the work of Plato's old age :[3] " paint in or shade off," he says, " or whatever the artists' boys call it."

Of the methods used in drawing and painting in Hellas little trace is left. Polugnotos and his contemporaries had produced idealised pictures, taking points from many beautiful men and women and uniting them to make one perfect man or woman. When Idealism gave way to Realism in Hellas, the change affected painting also. The artists tried to create a real

[1] Plin. *Hist. Nat.* 35.   [2] Stob. *Floril.* 98, p. 535.

[3] Plato, *Laws*, 769 B.

illusion in their works, taking subjects like chairs or tables and making the spectator believe them to be real. They were helped by the developments of perspective and foreshortening, which were discovered at this time. It is against this exaggerated realism and the choice of homely subjects that Plato's attack is directed : he hates such illusions as shams.[1] In the diatribes of the *Republic* the possibility of idealised painting seems to be forgotten. Whether the boys in the art-schools also suffered by this change and were condemned to draw chairs and tables only cannot be decided.

The pupils, of course, did not have paper to draw and paint upon, nor was canvas employed. Ordinarily they used white wood, boxwood for preference, owing to its smoothness. Lead or charcoal would serve for drawing ; for erasures, instead of india-rubber a sponge was used.[2] They may, perhaps, have practised on their wax tablets. One process was σκιαγραφία, " shadow-drawing," which produced rough sketches in light and shade : these seem to have been only intelligible when considered from a distance. Plato regarded them with distrust, as a sort of conjuring.[3]

In ordinary painting, which might be either water-colour or encaustic,[4] the first thing was to sketch in the outline (ὑπογράφειν, περιγραφή) ; the artist then filled in (ἀπεργάζεσθαι) the picture with his colours, with perpetual glances, now to the original, now to the copy, mixing his paints the while. Beginners would, no doubt, rub out (ἐξαλείφειν) frequently, and paint in again.

---

[1] See *Rep.* x. 596 E, 605 A, etc. In the *Sophist*, 235 D, 266 D, etc., Plato reserves his denunciation for φανταστική which creates illusions ; he almost approves of εἰκαστική. Idealised painting is hinted at in *Rep.* 472 D, 484 C.

[2] Aeschylus, *Agamemnon*, 1329.   [3] Plato, *Theait.* 208 E.

[4] The modern oil process was not employed till late on in the Renaissance. Fresco was common.

Aristotle,[1] in discussing artistic education, notices that it gave boys a good eye for appreciating art, and enabled them to exercise good taste in buying furniture, pottery, and other household requisites, which, to judge from the scanty relics, must have been masterpieces of beauty in the house of a cultivated Athenian. But still more important, it gave them "an eye for bodily beauty" :[2] which suggests that the human form, especially its proportions, formed the chief study of the art-schools. Proportion was the essence of Hellenic art ; the great sculptors, as is well known, spent much time in drawing up a canon of perfect proportions for the human body. The boys may well have used their companions in the palaistrai for models, and the canons of physical proportion which they were taught by the art-master would serve to stimulate them with a desire to attain to such a perfection of body by their own athletic exercises.

---

[1] Aristot. *Pol.* viii. 3. 12.

[2] θεωρητικὸν τοῦ περὶ τὰ σώματα κάλλους.

CHAPTER IV

It is well known that the Hellenes attached an enormous importance to physical exercise. This was partly, no doubt, due to their intense appreciation of bodily beauty, which it was the endeavour of their gymnastic training to produce. But it must be remembered that to be in "good condition" was essential to them. Any morning an Hellenic citizen might find himself called upon to take the field against an invader, or might be despatched to ravage an enemy's territory. Only the most cogent excuses were accepted. Plato[1] has left a vivid picture of a rich man, who has lived in idleness and luxury, suddenly called out to serve his country. Unhappy Dives marches along panting and perspiring, he is ill on board ship, and in battle when he has to charge or fight vigorously, he has no wind and is in a state of hopeless misery ; while his poorer or wiser companions, who are " lean and wiry, and have lived in the open air," mock at him and despise him. Sokrates points out to young Epigenes,[2] who has neglected his physical condition, what risks he runs. In battle, when a

[1] Plato, *Rep.* 556 B-D.   [2] Xen. *Mem.* iii. 12. 1.

retreat is sounded, he will be left behind by his companions, and be either killed or taken prisoner by the foe ; and the lot of the captive was frequently slavery for life, unless his friends ransomed him.   But there were also intellectual and moral risks.   "Bodily debility," says Sokrates, "frequently causes a loss of memory, and low spirits, and a peevish temper, and even madness, to invade a man, so as to make even intellectual pursuits impossible."   To be a good citizen and to be a good thinker a man must always be in good physical condition.   It became a duty to oneself and to the State " to live in the open air and accustom oneself to manly toils and sweat, avoiding the shade and unmanly ways of life." [1]   By divine ordinance, " Sweat was the doorstep of manly virtue," as old Hesiod had sung. [2]

This addiction to gymnastic exercises of all kinds was characteristic of the Hellenic peoples from the days of Homer.   The original object had been symmetrical development of the body, health, speed, strength, and agility.   But, as the Egyptian sage remarked, the Hellenes were a nation of children—it is just that which gives to them their charm and interest —and children usually and naturally care most for the body.   Consequently athletics were carried too far : they became an end in themselves, instead of being merely a means of attaining physical activity and health. The professional athlete became a sort of spoilt child, fed at public expense, [3] courted by crowds of admirers, and all the time he was quite useless for everything except his own particular sort of contest, boxing or

[1] Plato, *Phaidr.* 239 c.   [2] Hesiod, *Works and Days,* 289.

[3] Solon reduced this endowment to 500 drachmai for an Olympian victor, 100 for an Isthmian (Plut. *Solon,* 23).

wrestling or the like. The tendency was ruinous : the Hellenes preferred to be good gymnasts rather than good soldiers.[1] The competitor, boy or man, who entered for one of the great prizes had to live in complete idleness from other pursuits.[2] Such professionals " slept all the day long, and if they departed from their prescribed system of training in the very slightest degree, they were seized with serious diseases."[3] Consequently they were useless as soldiers, since in war it is necessary to be wide awake, not torpid, and to be able to stand vicissitudes of heat and cold, and not to be made ill by changes of diet. Specialisation even led to deformity. The long-distance runner developed thick legs and narrow shoulders, the boxer broad shoulders and thin legs.[4] It is to this specialisation that Galen[5] attributes the decline in utility of Hellenic athletics. Philostratos even notes that only in the good old days was the health of athletes not actually impaired by their exercises. In those times, he says, they grew old late, and took part in eight or nine Olympic contests—retained, that is, their efficiency for thirty years or more ; moreover, they were as good soldiers as they were athletes. Later, these habits changed, and athletes became averse to war, torpid, effeminate, luxurious in their diet. The medical profession took upon itself to advise them—a good thing in its way, but unsuitable for athletes ; for it told them to sit still after meals before taking exercise, and introduced them to elaborate cookery. Bribery also

---

[1] Plut. *Quaest. Rom.* 40.   [2] Plato, *Laws*, 807 c.

[3] For this their vast appetites were partly responsible. Milo and Theagenes each ate a whole ox in a single day (Athen. 412 f). Astuanax the pankratiast ate what was meant for nine guests (*ibid.* 413 b).

[4] Xen. *Banquet*, ii. 17.

[5] Galen, *On Medic. and Gym.* § 33 (ed. Kühn. v. 870).

PLATE V. A.

SCENES IN A PALAISTRA

Archaeologische Zeitung, 1878, Plate II. From a Kulix at Munich, attributed to Euphronios.

PLATE V. B.

SCENE IN A PALAISTRA—A BOY WITH HALTERES, A BOY WITH JAVELIN, AND TWO PAIDOTRIBAI

Archaeologische Zeitung, 1878, Plate 11. From a Kulix at Munich, attributed to Euphronios,

came into vogue among the professionals ; usurers began to enter the training schools on purpose to lend them money for bribing their opponents.[1] The first recorded instance of this was early in the fourth century.[2]

Critics of this exaggerated athleticism were not wanting, even in the earliest times. The attack begins with Xenophanes of Kolophon. In an elegiac poem he writes : " If a man wins a victory at Olympia . . . either by speed of foot or in the pentathlon, or by wrestling, or competing in painful boxing, or in the dread contest called the pankration, his countrymen will look upon him with admiration, and he will receive a front seat in the games, and eat his dinners at the public cost, and be presented with some gift that he will treasure. All this he will get, even if he only win a horse race. Yet he is not as worthy as I ; for my wisdom is better than the strength of men and steeds. Nay, this custom is foolish, and it is not right to honour strength more than the excellence of wisdom. Not by good boxing, not by the pentathlon, nor by wrestling, nor yet by speed of foot, which is the most honoured in the contests of all the feats of human strength—not so would a city be well governed. Small joy would it get from a victory at Olympia : such things do not fatten the dark corners of a city."

Pass straight from this to the works of Pindar, in order to see whether Xenophanes' attack was justified. To Pindar the world holds nothing better than an Olympian victory. Be the descendant of athletes and be an athlete yourself—that is the summit of human attainment and bliss. His gods are either athletes themselves or founders of athletic contests. A man's true desires may usually be best traced in the conception

---

[1] Philos. *On Gymnastics*, 54.   [2] Pausan. v. 21. 10.

which he forms of the future state : Pindar's portrait of Elysium is characteristic.   First the scenery, a magnificent description in his best manner :

> In that Underworld the sun shines in his might
> > Through our night.
> Round that city through the dewy meadow-ways
> > Roses blaze.
> Through the fragrant shadows, bright with golden gleams,
> > Fruitage teems. . . .
> Every flower of joyance blooms nor withers there.[1]

And in this Paradise how are the shades of the departed occupying themselves ?   " Some take their joy in horses, some in gymnasia, some in draughts." [2]   That is the highest bliss conceivable, in Pindar's opinion.

But Euripides did not agree with him.   He denounces the athletic life with much vigour.[3]   " Of countless ills in Hellas, the race of athletes is quite the worst. . . . They are slaves of their jaw and worshippers of their belly. . . . In youth they go about in splendour, the admiration of their city, but when bitter old age comes upon them, they are cast aside like worn-out coats.   I blame the custom of the Hellenes, who gather together to watch these men, honouring a useless pleasure.[4]   Who ever helped his fatherland by winning a crown for wrestling, or speed of foot, or flinging the quoit, or giving a good blow on the jaw?   Will they fight the foe with quoits, or smite their fists through shields ?   Garlands should be kept for the wise and good, and for him who best rules the city by his temperance and justice, or by his words drives away evil deeds, preventing strife and sedition."

---

[1] Pind. *Olymp.*   [2] Pindar, frag.

[3] Fragment of *Autolukos.*

[4] A very bold attack on the Olympian games, which must have caused a sensation in the theatre.

In return for this, the athlete-loving populace, finding their voice in the popular poet Aristophanes,
denounced Euripides and his Sophist friends for empty-
ing the gymnasia and making the boys desire only a
good tongue, instead of a sound body, turning them
into pale-faced, indoor pedants, fit for nothing but
jabbering nonsense. The attitude of the poet in the
Clouds and *Frogs* is just that of an average schoolboy
discussing a student.

Plato has already been quoted as an authority against
the athlete of his day. In the *Laws* he rejects every
kind of gymnastics which is not strictly conducive to
military efficiency, and, like the Spartans, condemns the
pankration and boxing. Races in the ideal State are to
be run in full armour, and the javelin and spear are to
replace the quoit. It is exactly the position of some
moderns, who would substitute shooting and field-days
for cricket and football. The case against the athletes
may be closed with Aristotle's testimony : he also condemns the specialisation of the trained professional.[1]

But these denunciations of athletes do not apply so
much to Athens as to the other States of Hellas. The
Athenian Agora was full of the statues of generals and
patriots, not, as was the usual custom, of athletes.[2]
The author of the treatise on the Athenian constitution,[3]
writing in the early days of the Peloponnesian War,
notices that the democracy had driven gymnastics out
of fashion.[4] He writes as one of the aristocrats who,
like Pindar and his princely friends, cared mainly for
the body and the outward beauties of life : the democracy
was vulgar, for it could not spend all its time in bodily

[1] Aristot. *Pol.* vii. 16. 13.   [2] Lukourg. *ag. Leok.* 51.

[3] [Xen.] *Constit. of Athens*, i. 13.

[4] κατέλυσε must mean this, as in [Andok.] *ag. Alkibiades*, where that gentleman
is said to be καταλύων τὰ γυμνάσια by his bad example.

exercises and musical banquets. No doubt at that period in Athens, as can be seen in Aristophanes, there was a reaction in favour of intellectual pursuits against the exclusive athleticism of the preceding age : the time of the citizens in a great democracy was also largely monopolised by State duties, whether in the Assembly or in the Law Courts or in fighting by sea or land. But athletics still remained quite sufficiently popular even at Athens, and athletic " shop " remained one of the chief topics of conversation at a dinner-party.[1]

Gymnastic exercises centred round two sorts of buildings which are often confused, the " gymnasium " and the " palaistra." The former may be said to correspond to the whole series of fields and buildings intended for games, which surround a modern public school, including football and cricket grounds, running track and jumping pit, fives courts, and so forth. The " palaistra " often resembled little more than the play-ground of a village school : it only demanded a sandy floor, and sufficient privacy to protect the exercises from intrusion : such buildings could be run up at private expense in the smallest villages, and were often attached to private houses. A " gymnasium," on the other hand, must have cost a vast sum to erect : even a great capital like Athens only possessed three in the fourth century ; small towns must have been unable to afford them at all. But the gymnasia were public buildings, open to all ; they were always full of citizens of all ages, practising or watching others practise ; they were a fashionable place of resort, where Sophists lectured in the big halls, and philosophers taught in the shady gardens. For the trainer who wished to instruct his

[1] See end of Aristoph. *Wasps*.

class of boys they were wholly unsuitable ; besides, any casual stranger could stand by and get a lesson for nothing. Consequently, even at Athens, the boys were taught in palaistrai which could be closed to the public :[1] in the towns and villages there was no other place.

It is quite true that boys went to the gymnasia. Aristophanes[2] talks of " a nice little boy on his way home from the gymnasium." In Antiphon,[3] some older boys are practising the javelin in a gymnasium ; a younger boy, who had been standing among the spectators, being called by his paidotribes, runs across the course and is killed. If the reading " paidotribes," for which K. F. Hermann would substitute " paidagogos," is correct, we find a paidotribes and his class of younger boys present in a gymnasium, probably to practise javelin-throwing, which must have demanded a larger space than the palaistra often afforded. The elder boys are probably not under his tuition, for they are using real javelins, not the unpointed shafts which were employed at school. Paidotribai with small palaistrai may often have taken their classes to the free public gymnasia to practise the diskos, the javelin, and running, which required a large space. But none the less the palaistra was the usual scene of the teaching of boys.[4] It must not, however, be supposed that a palaistra was always reserved for boys. The " many palaistrai," which the democracy built for itself,[5] were doubtless as much public buildings, open to all ages, as the Akademeia or Lukeion. The palaistrai owned or

---

[1] As shown by the beginning of Plato, *Lusis*, 203 B.

[2] Aristoph. *Birds*, 141.   [3] Antiphon, *Second Tetralogy.*

[4] The law quoted in Aischines *ag. Timarchos* is spurious, being a later interpolation ; it cannot therefore be used as evidence.

[5] [Xen.] *Constit. of Athens*, ii. 10.

hired by private teachers must have been open to adults
when the boys were not present; that which is the
scene of the *Lusis* was apparently attended by two
classes, one of boys and the other of youths, who only
met there on festival days.   In the palaistra of Taureas,
however, mentioned in the *Charmides*, the different
classes seem all to meet in the undressing-room ; but
on that occasion the building may have been open for
general practice, not for teaching.   Some such arrangement into classes must have taken place in the village
palaistrai.[1]   The master who taught the boys in the
palaistra was called the paidotribes, "boy-rubber" :
he must have owed his name to the great part which
rubbing, whether with oil or with various sorts of dust,
played in athletics.[2]   He was expected to be scientific.
He had to know what exercises would suit what con-
stitutions : [3] he is often coupled with the doctor.[4]   His
object was to prevent, the doctor's to cure, diseases.
He even prescribed diet.   Besides health, he was
expected to aim at beauty and strength.[5]   His training,
in Plato's opinion, also served to produce firmness of
character and strength of will : he must therefore know
how much training to administer to each boy, for too
much would cause excess of these qualities and lead
to savage brutality, and too little would result in
effeminacy.[6]

[1] The division of the boys into classes by age in the contests points to such a
usage. Cp. the ἡλικίαι at Teos.

[2] Later, this was done by a special official, the ἀλειπτής.

[3] Aristot. *Pol.* iv. 1. 1.

[4] *e.g.* Plato, *Gorg.* 504 A ; *Protag.* 313 D ; Aristot. *Pol.* iii. 16. 8.

[5] Plato, *Gorg.* 452 B.

[6] The paidotribes is distinguished from the gumnastes as the schoolmaster
from the crammer. The gumnastes coached pupils chiefly for the great games,
while the paidotribes presided over physical training generally, especially of boys,
but sometimes of epheboi. See the elaborate discussion in Grasberger, i. 263-
268.

Since so much science was demanded of the paido-tribes, parents exercised much forethought in choosing a gymnastic school for their boys :[1] they would " call upon their friends and relations to give advice, and deliberate for many days," in order to find a trainer whose instructions would " make their son's body a useful servant to his mind, not likely by its bad condition to compel him to shirk his duty in war or elsewhere." [2] This at Athens, no doubt : in the smaller towns and villages there could have been little choice : parents must have taken what they could get.

On arriving at the chosen palaistra with his paida-gogos the boy would find a class assembling. He would first go into the undressing-room [3] and strip. For all the exercises were performed naked. This no doubt gave the trainer a good opportunity of watching which muscles most required development, and what constitutional weaknesses, if any, must be treated cir-cumspectly. Passing into the palaistra proper, the boy would find an enclosure surrounded, in the case of the more expensive schools, with pillars. There would be no roof. Hellenic custom maintained that it was healthy to expose the naked body to the open air and the mid-day sun : a white skin was regarded as a sign of effeminacy.[4] If the sun became dangerously hot, little caps were worn, which at other times hung on the walls of the palaistra. The floor was sand. Before wrestling or practising the pankration or jumping, the boys had to break up the soil with pickaxes [5] in order to make it soft : these pickaxes were also suspended on the walls. Beside them would

---

[1] Plato, *Protag.* 313 A.   [2] *Ibid.* 326 C.   [3] ἀποδυτήριον.
[4] See Thompson, Plato, *Phaedr.* 239 C., and Eur. *Bacch.* 456.
[5] Illustr. Plate VI. A.

be also *kôrukoi* or punch-balls, *haltêres* (a sort of dumb-bell, used for jumping and other exercises), the scrapers with which the dirt and sweat were removed, bags to hold the cords which were used as boxing-gloves, and spare javelins. Grown-up men were not allowed to enter during the lessons, but could apparently, if they wished, watch " from outside," that is, probably, from the dressing-room, where we often find Sokrates conversing with the pupils, boys and lads: he could not, probably, penetrate further.

The symbol of office which marked the paidotribes was a long forked stick depicted in the vases.[1] This was probably derived from the branch which the umpires at the games held in their hands. The two symbols are so much alike when represented on the vases[2] that it is often hard to distinguish them. There were generally several under-masters in the palaistra. The more proficient boys also were employed in teaching backward schoolfellows; these " pupil-teachers " appear on vases,[3] holding the stick of office like the grown-up masters. No doubt, poor boys managed to get instruction in this manner from their richer friends in the public gymnasia and palaistrai, without attending a school at all.

The staff of a palaistra also included professional flute-players, for most of the exercises[4] were performed to the sound of a flute, in order that good time might be preserved in the various movements. The player in these cases wore the φορβεία or mouth-band.[5]

As I have pointed out in Chapter II., although the literary authorities make gymnastic training of a sort

---

[1] Illustr. Plates VI. A and VI. B.

[2] See especially the Panathenaic vases in the British Museum.

[3] *e.g.* Brit. Mus. E 288.

[4] Brit. Mus. B 361, E 427, E 288.

[5] Illustr. Plate VIII.

PLATE VI. A

IN THE PALAISTRA : WRESTLERS, PAIDOTRIBES, BOY PREPARING GROUND

Gerhard's *Auserlesene Vasenbilder*, cclxxi. Fig. 2.

PLATE VI. B.

IN THE PALAISTRA : BOY PUTTING ON BOXING-THONG, A PANKRATION LESSON, AND A PAIDOTRIBES

Gerhard's *Auserlesene Vasenbilder*, cclxxi. Fig. 1.

begin with the seventh year, it is not at all probable that the more recognised exercises, such as boxing and wrestling, began till a good many years later. The vases suggest that these subjects were taught some years after letters and music had begun, for they represent only older boys as learning them. Aristotle seems to vouch for a graduated course of gymnastic exercises during boyhood.[1]

What did the boys learn at the palaistra in the meantime ? Deportment and easy exercises. A passage in Aristophanes informs us that they were taught the most graceful way to sit down and get up.[2] Vases represent boys learning how to stand straight. There were also all sorts of exercises in which the unpointed javelin played the part of a training-rod and the halteres the part of dumb-bells. The paidotribes might also try to strengthen particular muscles in particular boys. In an epigram,[3] a trainer is exercising a boy's middle by bending him over his knee, and then, while holding his feet fast, swinging him over backwards.

No doubt what was known as "gesticulation" ($\tau\grave{o}$ $\chi\epsilon\iota\rho o\nu o\mu\epsilon\hat{\iota}\nu$) played a large part in this earlier training. "Gesticulation" meant a scientific series of gestures and movements of all the limbs, somewhat like the modern systems of physical education taught by Sandow and others. It was chiefly an exercise for the arms, as the name implies, but on a celebrated occasion Hippokleides the Athenian stood on his head on a table and "gesticulated" with his feet.[4] The particular movements were very carefully designed, and were all intended to be beautiful and gentlemanly.[5] Gesticulation served as a preparation for various dancing - systems, but was

---

[1] Aristot. *Pol.* viii. 4.   [2] Aristoph. *Clouds*, 973.
[3] *Anthol. Palat.* xii. 222.   [4] Herod. vi. 127-129.   [5] Athen. 629 B.

distinct from dancing, for Charmides was able to ges-
ticulate but unable to dance.[1] It was also preparatory
to gymnastics, for it resembled the movements of a
boxer sparring at the air for lack of an opponent.[2]
The halteres were possibly often employed, for they
played a part in many gymnastic exercises.[3] This
" gesticulation," then, being a preliminary to gymnastics
and dancing, would be the natural thing for the small
boys to learn in the palaistra. Other early exercises
were rope-climbing[4] and a sort of leap-frog.[5] The
various kinds of ball-game,[6] mostly designed to exercise
the body scientifically, may also have been employed.
Of the regular exercises of the palaistra, which I am
about to discuss, running and jumping would suit quite
small boys ; the diskos and javelin could also be begun
at an early age, for smaller sizes were made for children.

The age at which the recognised exercises were first
taught no doubt varied with individual taste and
physical capacity : no strict line can be drawn. These
exercises were wrestling, boxing, the pankration, jumping, running, throwing the diskos and the javelin.

Wrestling (πάλη) was probably regarded as the most
important of these subjects, for it gave its name to the
Palaistra. For this exercise the soil was broken up
with the pickaxe and watered : the bodies of the
combatants were oiled beforehand. By these means
the Hellenes prevented their boys from disfiguring their
bodies with bumps and bruises, and the slipperiness of
the ground and of the antagonist's body made the
exercise more difficult and therefore more valuable.

---

[1] Xen. *Banquet*, ii. 19.
[2] Plato, *Laws*, 830 c.
[3] Philostratus, *On Gymnastics*, 55.
[4] Galen, *De sanit. tuend*. ii. 8.
[5] Grasberger, i. 154.
[6] Described at length, Grasberger, i. 84-98.

Three throws were necessary for victory. There were two sorts of wrestling. In one the victor had to throw his antagonist without coming to the ground himself; this was a matter of ingenious twists and turns somewhat like the Japanese jiu-jitsu. In the other both combatants rolled over and over on the ground : this was less scientific. The leading paidotribai had their own favourite systems of wrestling, with various openings, as in chess, and various ways of meeting them. "What style of wrestling did you learn at the Palaistra?" Kleon asks the sausage-seller.[1] When two boys were set to wrestle in school, they were not allowed to contend as they pleased with a view to victory, but had to carry out the directions of the paidotribes.[2] A fragment of a system of wrestling has been unearthed at Oxurhunchos.[3]

Suppose there are two boys, Charmides and Glaukon. The paidotribes sets them to wrestle, while the rest of the class watch. He holds a long forked stick in his hand. Pointing with it to Charmides, he says, "You put your right hand between his legs and grip him." Then to Glaukon, "Close your legs on it, and thrust your left side against his side." To Charmides, "Throw him off with your left hand." To Glaukon, "Shift your ground, and engage." Each group of directions, or figure ($\sigma\chi\hat{\eta}\mu a$), as it was called, closes with the word "Engage" ($\pi\lambda\acute{\epsilon}\xi o\nu$). At this point, probably, the two boys were allowed to wrestle at will, the result, however, being foreseen and inevitable owing to the previous moves.

An epigram in the *Anthology* represents instruction

---

[1] Aristoph. *Knights*, 1238.

[2] See Illustr. Plate VI. A for a wrestling lesson. Lucian, *Ass.* 8-11.

[3] Oxyrhynchus Papyri, Grenfell and Hunt, Part III. No. 466 (1903). The papyrus is of the second century.

of this sort being given : the boy retorts in the middle,
" I can't possibly do it, Diophantos ; that's not the
way boys wrestle." [1]

But, to use a parallel given by Isokrates, a pupil is
not yet a complete orator, when he knows how to
create pathos, irony, and so forth, and has been taught
the parts of a speech : he has still to learn when and
where and in what order to employ these several
artifices. So with wrestling. A boy who knows his
" figures " is not yet a wrestler : he has got to learn
when is the right moment to employ each of them in
an actual contest with a real antagonist. " When the
paidotribes has taught his pupils the ' figures ' invented
for bodily training and practised them and made them
perfect in these, he makes the boys go through their
exercises again and accustoms them to physical toil, and
compels them to string together one by one the figures
which they have learnt, that they may have a firmer
grasp of them and get a clearer comprehension of the
right occasions for using them : for it is impossible to
comprehend these in an exact science." [2] The boys
have to judge for themselves, in the heat of the
contest, which figure it will be expedient to use : the
trainer cannot fix that beforehand. But they will best
be able to judge, if by long practice they have
discovered which figures suit them best and which
prove fatal to a particular type of opponent.

Boxing was similarly taught by a series of " figures."
The boys used the light gloves, consisting of strings
wound round the hands, not the heavy, metal-weighted
gloves which professional athletes wore. The *pankration* [3]
was a mixture of boxing and wrestling : the boys

---

[1] *Anthol. Palat.* xii. 206.   [2] Isok. *Antid.* 184.
[3] See Illustr. Plate VI. B for a pankration lesson.

PLATE VII.

Photo by Mr. R. Coupland.

STADION AT DELPHI FROM THE FORTIFICATIONS OF PHILOMELOS.
Length about 220 yards.

Photo by Mr. R. Coupland.

STADION AT DELPHI FROM THE EAST END.

usually wore similar gloves for this but left the fingers
unfastened, only the wrists and knuckles being protected : sometimes they fought with bare hands.   For
both these exercises it was usual to wear dogskin
caps, in order to protect the ears from injury.   The
pankration seems to have been regarded as an unsatisfactory game for boys : so it was excluded from both
Olympian and Pythian games till a comparatively
late date.   For one thing, it was dangerous, and
the exercise was very severe.   But in the palaistra,
carefully regulated by the paidotribes and stopped
when the fighting became dangerous, no doubt it was
harmless enough.   Alkibiades, however, once succeeded
in biting an opponent who was pressing him hard, being
ready to do anything rather than be beaten.   " You
bite like a girl, Alkibiades ! " exclaimed the indignant
boy.   " No, like a lion," answered Alkibiades.[1]

Running needs no comment : the methods are much
the same in all ages.   The chief distances for races in
Hellas were the Stadion or 200 yards,[2] the Diaulos or
quarter-mile, and the Long-distance race, which varied
from three-quarter mile to about three miles.   The
race in armour was not taught to boys.   Races were
often run over soft sand, where the runners sank in,
just as long-distance races in England often include a
ploughed field or two.   The sand made running both
a more severe exercise (so that a shorter distance
sufficed) and also a better training for war.

For the *long jump* the Hellenes used the " halteres "
or light dumb-bells, to assist their momentum.[3]   Even
in competitions, a flute-player stood by, to give the
competitors the assistance of his music : no doubt it

---

[1] Plut. *Alkib.* ii. 3.   [2] See Illustr. Plate VII.

[3] See Illustr. Plate V. B.

helped them to manage their steps so as to "take off" on the right spot. They alighted into a large sandy pit, dug up by the ever-present pickaxe: the jump was only measured if they came down on to this evenly, leaving a clear trace of their foot.

The *diskos* was a flat circle of polished bronze or other metal.[1] The specimen in the British Museum is between 8 and 9 inches in diameter, and is inscribed with athletic pictures on either side. It was flung with either hand. A great many attitudes were necessary before the diskos was launched, and every muscle of the body must have been well exercised in the process. The time was given, in the palaistra, by a flute-player. In competitions both the distance and the direction of the throw were taken into consideration.

Boys learnt to throw the *javelin and spear* by practising with long unpointed rods, which were also used for a variety of physical exercises. The mark seems to have been a sort of croquet-hoop or pair of compasses, fixed into the ground: other targets were also employed.[2] The vases which represent this pursuit often show the paidotribes carrying this hoop or fixing it into the ground. It was planted at a fixed distance which was stepped out.

It may be mentioned, before we leave the "paidotribes," that his fee for his whole course seems to have been a μνᾶ, about £4:[3] this enabled the pupil to attend his lectures "for ever," that is, perhaps till the course was finished. Or perhaps this sum made a pupil a life-member of a particular private palaistra.

Let us now look into one of the gymnasia at Athens, the Akademeia or Lukeion. We will suppose

---

[1] Illustr. Plate V. A.   [2] Illustr. Plate V. B.
[3] Athen. 584 c, referring to about 320 B.C.

that it is late in the afternoon, for this was a favourite time for taking exercise : the Athenians liked to get a good appetite for their evening meal. Outside, a troop of young men who intend to be enrolled in the State-cavalry are practising their evolutions, mounting, in the absence of stirrups, by a leaping-pole, and charging in squadrons. On another side a body of heavy infantry with spear and shield are assembling for a night march into the Megarid ;[1] they are packing their supplies, onions and dried fish, perhaps, into their knapsacks as they fall in, and are grumbling at having to leave Athens just when a festival is coming ; a burly countryman is complaining to his general that it is not his turn to serve, as he took part in the raid into Boiotia last week, and his general is threatening him with a prosecution for insubordination if he becomes abusive. After paying our respects to the patron deities, Herakles and Hermes and Eros,[2] and having muttered a curse on all tyrants suggested by the statue of Eros which Charmos the father-in-law of Hippias the Peisistratid set up,[3] we enter the gymnasium.

The first room which we come to is the undressing-room.[4] On the benches round the walls a row of men are sitting discussing the exact nature of Self-control : an extremely ugly person, to whom they all pay great respect, is stating that it is an exact science, and, if only they can discover this science, the whole world will become virtuous. Lads and men are stripping all about the room, and passing off to take their exercises elsewhere ; others keep coming in and dressing and listening to the discussion for a minute or two. A handsome young fellow comes in : the ugly man makes

---

[1] Aristoph. *Peace*, 357.   [2] Zeno in Athen. 561 c.
[3] Athen. 609 D.   [4] ἀποδυτήριον. See Plato, *Charmides*, 153 ff.

room for him with great energy, and his friends who
are sitting at the end of the bench are pushed off
suddenly on to the floor. A shout of laughter,
mingled with some strong Attic abuse, arises. Not
wishing to be involved as witnesses in an interminable
lawsuit, we hurry out through the further door into a
great cloister.[1] In the centre of this is a large open
space, with no roof. Here we meet a well-known
mathematician from Kurene,[2] who is walking round the
cloister with a crowd of pupils : he is explaining to
them that famous theorem about right-angled triangles,
whose proof is so neat that Pythagoras the vegetarian
sacrificed a hundred oxen when he discovered it. At
intervals the mathematician stops and draws a diagram
in the dust with his stick. As we follow him, we can
look into the rooms which surround the cloister. In
one, a crowd of men are anointing themselves with oil.[3]
The rubbing, which is so good for all bodily ills, and
the oil, even if not followed by any further exercise, are
regarded as an excellent thing. An Athenian gentleman
is expected to carry about a certain fragrance of this
oil,[4] and his skin must always be sleek with it ; but as
a rule the anointing is a prelude to exercise, and is
meant to make the joints supple and the body slippery
enough to elude a wrestler's grip.[5] A slave or an
attendant stands by many of the men, holding one of
those dainty oil-flasks which make so great a feature in
modern Museums of Archæology. Through the next

---

[1] κατάστεγος δρόμος. Plato, *Euthud.* 273 A.

[2] Theodoros (Plato, *Theait.*).

[3] This was often done outside (Plato, *Theait.* 144 c). The oil-room (ἐλαιοθέσιον)
of Vitruvius may be a later invention. This preliminary anointing was called
ξηραλοιφεῖν. After the baths they rubbed themselves with a mixture of oil and
water ; this was χυτλοῦσθαι.

[4] See Xen. *Banquet*, I. 7.   [5] Aristoph. *Knights*, 492.

door we see the "dusting-room." Various sorts of
dust were used for rubbing the body. They served
to clean it of sweat after exercise, to open the pores, to
warm it when cold, and to soften the skin. A yellow
dust was particularly popular; for it made the body
glisten so as to be pleasant to look at, as a good body
in good condition ought to be.[1] Next perhaps will be
the bathing-room—a popular place in the evening, for
it was usual to take a bath before dinner.[2] The
bathers either splash themselves out of great bowls
which stand upon pedestals, or receive a shower bath
by getting a companion or an attendant to pour a
pitcher of water over them. Tanks capable of receiving the whole body at once were not usual, though
known to Homer.[3] Then we see the room of the
korukos, or punch-ball, which will present a very curious
appearance.[4] The *korukos* is a large sack hanging
from the ceiling by a rope. The lighter *korukoi* are
filled with fig seeds or meal, the heavier with sand.
They hang at about the height of a man's waist. You
push one of them gently at first, and more and more
violently as you gain experience; having pushed it,
you plant yourself in the way of the rebound, and try
to stop the sack with your hands or your chest or your
back or your head. If you are not strong enough, you
will be knocked over, and the room will laugh. This
will practise you in standing steady, and make all parts
of your body firm and muscular. The *korukos* can
also be used as a punch-ball, to strengthen the boxer's
arms and shoulders. This exercise is especially recommended for boxers and pankratiasts: the latter

[1] Philostratus, *On Gymnastics*, 56.   It was usual to be dusted before wrestling.
[2] Xen. *Banquet*.
[3] For a good bathing scene, see Brit. Mus. Vase E 83.   Also E 32.
[4] Philostratus, *On Gymnastics*, 57.

ought to use the heavier variety. Perhaps there will also be some lay-figures hanging up round the walls, for these also were used for practising. Here, too, some unlucky individuals who, from unpopularity or other causes, are unable to find an antagonist, will be exercising their fists on thin air. But both these expedients were regarded as ridiculous.[1]

There were a large number of other rooms round the cloister, some intended for exercises in wet weather, for, if possible, exercise was always taken out of doors ; for it was regarded as a great object to make the skin brown and hard by exposure to the sun. So King Agesilaos put his Asiatic captives up for sale in his camp naked, in order that his Hellenic soldiers, seeing their pale, soft flesh, unused to exposure, might despise their enemy. But as most of these rooms were furnished with seats, they were largely used as lecture-halls by wandering Sophists,[2] who gave free lectures in them to any passer-by who might care to listen, in order to attract regular, paying pupils. So we can take our pick and hear lectures on poetry or metaphysics, music or rhetoric, geography or history, at our pleasure.

After this, we can turn our attention to the great central courtyard,[3] which is surrounded by the cloister, or to the racecourse and open spaces which lie beyond it. In one part will be the wrestling arena.[4] Pairs of oiled, naked combatants will be struggling together, amid a crowd of cheering spec-

[1] Plato, *Laws*, 830 c.

[2] Particular Sophists attached themselves to particular gymnasia and palaistrai which they came to regard as their schools. Mikkos has already occupied the newly-built palaistra in the *Lusis*, 204 A. Cp. Plato's position at the Akademeia and Aristotle's at the Lukeion.

[3] αὐλή (Plato, *Lusis*, 206 E).   [4] κονίστρα.

tators, and perhaps the trainer will be standing by, giving them directions. One group attracts especial attention : for the pair are going to represent Athens at Olympia next year. Elsewhere the pankratiasts are contending, some sparring at arm's length, others joined in a deadly grapple, rolling over and over on the ground and pummelling one another's heads with their gloved knuckles. They are covered with clotted dust and oil and will need much scraping. Then there are the boxers, bearing either the light gloves, or, if they intend to take part in a big competition, the heavy iron balls padded over with leather which were used in the great Games.[1] There are races too in progress, lap by lap round the great Stadion. Some of the runners are naked, others are wearing helmet and shield, since they are practising for the Race in Armour. Friends run beside them for a little way, pacing them and encouraging them. Others are jumping, with the halteres in their hands, into the pit, while their friends mark the point where their heels have left a mark in the sand. A professional flute-player, with his mouth-band on, sets the time. Each is, no doubt, hoping to beat Phaüllos' great jump of 55 feet—the world's record. Everywhere are crowds of spectators,[2] and everywhere eager trainers giving advice, hoping, if their pupil gains a prize at some great Games, to make a name for themselves, and attract a crowd of lads to their paid lessons : perhaps they will even be immortalised by some contemporary Pindar in a song in honour of their pupil's victory.

In another corner, it may be, there will be teams

---

[1] Plato, *Laws*, 830 B.

[2] For the excitement of the spectators and their shouts of encouragement see Isok. *Euag.* 32.

practising together. A regiment of epheboi may be
undergoing their gymnastic training before service
on the frontier : [1] or a team of them may be training, watched by the rich "gumnasiarchos," for the
torch-race at the festival of Hephaistos, or for the
race from the Temple of Dionusos to that of Athena
of the Sunshades, where the winner will receive a large
bowl containing wine and honey and cheese and meat
and olive oil—not all mixed together, let us hope.[2]
There may also be teams practising wrestling and other
bodily exercises together. Their trainer, "thinking it
impossible to lay down separate regulations for each
individual, orders roughly what suits the majority. So
every one of the team takes an equal amount of exercise,
and they all start and all stop running, or wrestling, or
whatever it may be, at the same moment." [3]

In the larger open spaces we shall find Athenians
throwing the diskos, like Muron's celebrated figure, or
practising archery, or flinging the spear or javelin.
In watching these care must be exercised: unwary spectators may be killed or injured. Mythology is full of
unfortunates killed in this way. Was not the fair
Huakinthos slain by Apollo's quoit? Antiphon, too,
in his new book on speech-writing, takes as one of his
themes a boy killed by a comrade's javelin accidentally.
We can also take a lesson in the use of spear and shield
from the teacher of arms : a pair of Sophists, who
specialise in this subject, have just come to Athens, and
will doubtless be exhibiting their skill here. We remember, though, that the warlike Spartans ridicule these
professors, and General Laches regards them as quite

---

[1] Some gymnasia provided a large "Room of the Epheboi." So in Vitruvius'
model.

[2] Athen. 495-6.   [3] Plato, *Polit.* 294 D, E.

useless for military purposes, as we heard him telling
Sokrates the other day.[1]   So we will pass on.

The vast majority of people in the gymnasium
confine themselves to walking about.   The colonnades
and the gardens are convenient and attractive, and
there is plenty to watch everywhere.   The "xustos,"
or covered cloister,[2] where athletes exercise in bad
weather, is particularly popular among the walkers.
And while they walk, they talk.   There is a group of
philosophical students arguing about the Supreme Good
or constructing an ideal State.   There is a party of
inquirers who are discussing the nature of plants, or
the varieties of crustaceans.   Yonder, a half-naked,
unkempt enthusiast is declaiming against luxury.
" Man," he cries, " is independent of circumstances."
Everywhere, walkers and spectators and talkers, but
walkers above all.

For the average Athenian spent all his time upon
his legs: to sit down was the mark of a slave.[3]   He
walked nearly all day : the distance which he covered
in five or six days would easily stretch from Athens to
Olympia.   He took a walk before breakfast, another
before lunch, another before dinner, and another between
dinner and bed.[4]

Games of ball are going on in the ball-court yonder.[5]
We may remember that the poet Sophocles was a
famous player.[6]   But the shadow on the great sun-dial
has nearly reached the ten-foot mark which announces
dinner-time to the Athenian world.   The crowds who
have been exercising themselves are scraping off the

---

[1] But by the end of the fourth century the teacher of arms becomes an
important individual in the training of the epheboi.

[2] Plato, *Euthyd.* 273 A.   [3] Xen. *Econ.* iii. 13.

[4] Xen. *Econ.* xi. 18 ; *Banquet*, i. 7, ix. 1.   [5] σφαιριστήριον.

[6] Athen. 20 f.

sweat and dirt with the στλεγγίς or scraper,[1] or else
hurrying to the bath-rooms. After the bath comes
another anointing, with oil and water this time.[2]   Then
away through the nearest gate into the city, while the
great buildings on the Akropolis grow misty in the
twilight and Athena's guardian Spear catches the last
rays of the setting sun.

All this was open to the poorest Athenian : there
was no fee for entrance.   The only expenses were those
incurred in buying an oil-flask and scraper, which the
State did not as a rule provide, and any fees that might
be paid to a trainer for special " coaching."   The poor
could learn as much as they required from watching
those who were proficient.   It was usual to tip the man
in the public baths who poured cold water over the
bathers and assisted them generally : but this probably
did not apply to the bath-rooms in the gymnasia.   The
State certainly made it easy for every citizen to take as
much exercise as he pleased.

Women were wholly excluded from athletics at
Athens.   In Sparta girls exercised themselves as much
as the boys.   In other Dorian States feminine athletics
were encouraged to a less degree.   At Argos there
were foot-races for girls.   In Chios they could be seen
wrestling in the gymnasia.[3]

But the gymnasia and palaistrai, though they provided so many different kinds of exercises, did not
supply the Hellenes with their sole opportunities for
keeping the body in good condition.   Hunting was a
popular employment at Sparta and no doubt elsewhere :
Xenophon, who was devoted to it, would have liked

---

[1] Brit. Mus. E 83, for a picture of this in use.

[2] χυτλοῦσθαι.   [3] Athen. 566 e.

to make it more popular in Attica,[1] where it languished, perhaps from lack of game. Swimming and rowing were usual accomplishments. Riding was compulsory for rich citizens at Athens, for they had to serve in the cavalry ; it was also popular in Thessaly, the land of horses. Military service provided both an incentive to physical exercise and a frequent means of obtaining it. Dancing was universal throughout the Hellenic world and played a larger part in Hellenic education than is usually recognised. At Sparta it was of paramount importance. At Athens it was taught free to large numbers of boys under the system of leitourgiai. Plato divides physical education into dancing and wrestling.[2] Aristophanes[3] brackets dancing between the palaistra and music, when he wishes to give the three elements of a gentleman's education. Choral dancing to a Hellene was at once the ritual of religion, the ordinary accompaniment of a festival or public holiday, the highest form of music, and the most perfect system of physical exercise then discovered.

The modern reader finds it very hard to realise why Hellenic philosophers attach so much educational importance to the various kinds of dance. This is because modern dancing differs from its ancient proto-type in two very important particulars : it is not connected with religion and it is not dramatic. In the East dancing was, and is, the language of religion. David, to show his fervour, danced before the Ark with all his might. In Hellas, dancing accompanied every rite and every mystery.[4] The choral dance afforded the outlet to religious enthusiasm which else-

---

[1] *Hunting with Hounds*, passim.   So Plato in the *Laws*, with reservations.
[2] Plato, *Laws*, 795 E.   [3] Aristoph. *Frogs*, 729.
[4] Lucian, *On Dancing*, 15.

where is provided by services : any change in its characteristics was a change in ritual and in the inexpressible sentiments and moral attitudes which become so closely bound up with habitual religious observances. And, since it was the usual ritual of worship, dancing became all-important in education, as providing the forms through which the highest aspirations of the children were accustomed to find expression.

The boy who danced in honour of Dionusos was trying to assimilate himself to the god, whose history and personality would be brought home to him vividly by the vineyards around him : they would serve him for a parable. The vine that came so mysteriously out of the earth, lived its short life in the rain and sunshine, and was crushed and killed at the harvest, to rise again in the strange juice which thrilled him with such wondrous power—there was plenty of parable for him there. And while he felt the god's history so vividly, he was acting it, for acting was the very essence of Hellenic dancing. He would act the sorrows of Dionusos, his persecution from city to city, and his final conquest ; he would match each incident in the story with suitable inward feelings and outward gestures of sorrow and triumph. Thus his dancing came to be a keenly religious observance, accompanied by more vivid acting than is possible on a modern stage ; such dancing, it must be remembered, was the parent of Attic Drama. The dramatic power of such acting became enormous ; one dancer, it is said, could make the whole philosophic system of Pythagoras intelligible without speaking a word, simply by his gestures and attitudes.[1]

In such dramatic dancing the subject or plot was important. Here the weakness of the old Hellenic

[1] Athen. 20 d.

mythology became fatal. For it was the old myths
that supplied the motives of religious dances as well
as of the drama, and many of them were morally
unsatisfactory. When a chorus of boys danced the
Birth-pangs of Semelé, the most famous dithyramb
of Timotheos, not unnaturally objections were raised.
The new school of musicians and poets, which arose
towards the end of the fifth century, tried to represent
everything and anything in the most realistic way
possible : their dancers had to imitate with voice and
gesture " blacksmiths at the forge, craftsmen at work,
sailors rowing and boatswains giving them orders,
horses neighing, bulls bellowing," [1] and so forth. They
chose the commonest and coarsest scenes, just like
Dutch painters. In their hands, dancing became something vulgar, as well as morally risky, though still under
a semi-religious sanction. It is this charge which
justified Plato's denunciations of the dramatic element
in poetry and music. It must be remembered that the
choregos at Athens, who collected the boys from his
tribe to dance these dithyrambs, could use compulsion
if fathers refused to allow their sons to join his chorus.[2]
Yet the advantages of learning to dance were great,
quite apart from the religious aspects. Dancing was a
scientifically designed system of physical training, which
exercised every part of the body symmetrically.[3] The
different masters invented systems of their own, just
as the paidotribai invented systems of wrestling ; in
both cases the teaching began with a series of figures,
which were afterwards fitted together. Different
localities also had their own particular figures.[4]

[1] Plato, *Rep.* 396 A, B.
[2] Antiphon, *The Choreutes*, 11.   [3] Xen. *Banquet*, ii. 17.
[4] Lakonian and Attic (Herod. vi. 129); Persian (Xen. *Anab.* vi. 1. 10); Troizenian
Epizephurian Lokrian, Cretan, Ionian, Mantinean in Lucian, *On Dancing*, 22.

The solo dance was used for private exercise. It also made its way into the drama. Sometimes, too, in the choral performances one or two of the best dancers were singled out to perform more elaborate evolutions expressing the dramatic course of the subject. But the choral dance was universal throughout Hellas. Its motives ranged from the solemn religious questionings of Aeschylus to the drunken buffoonery of the vine-festivals. The dance might be the act of worship of a whole people, as in the great festivals at Delos. It might, like the Gumnopaidia at Sparta, be designed to exhibit the physical perfection and practise the military evolutions of a nation in arms. It might celebrate the triumphant return of an Olympian victor to his native city, as did many of the dances which accompanied the extant odes of Pindar. The chorus-songs of Tragedy and Comedy were set to dances of a sort ; but from these last boys seem to have been excluded.

For educational purposes, besides the dithuramboi already mentioned, the two most important classes were the War-dance and the Naked-dance (γυμνοπαιδία).[1] In the War-dance the performers, clad in arms, imitated all the ways in which blows and spears might be avoided, now bending to one side, now drawing back, now leaping in the air, now crouching down : then, again, they acted as though they were hurling javelins and spears and dealing all manner of blows at close quarters.[2] The Kuretic dance in Crete was very similar ; the dancers "in full armour beat their swords against their shields and leaped in an inspired and warlike manner."[3] The field-days, when teams of boys and "packs" of epheboi fought one another to the sound of music, were

---

[1] Not necessarily nude, for γυμνός only represents the absence of the armour used in the War-dance.   [2] Plato, *Laws*, 815 A.   [3] Lucian, *On Dancing*, 8.

only a more warlike sort of dance. In fact, war and
the war-dance were as closely connected in Hellas as
war and drill in Modern Europe. The Thessalians
called their heroes "dancers"; Lucian quotes an
inscription that "the people set up this statue to
Eilation, who danced the battle well": "chief dancer"
(προορχηστήρ)[1] was a dignified title. The same author
observes that in warlike Sparta the young men learn
to dance as much as to fight, and that their military
and gymnastic exercises alike were inextricably mixed
up with dancing.[1]

The "Naked-dance" was to gymnastics what the war-
dance was to war.[2] It represented the movements of
the palaistra set to music, accompanied by some singing.[3]
The style was solemn, like that of the ἐμμέλεια, or
dance of Tragedy. It was performed in the main by
boys, as the name γυμνοπαιδία implies; but grown men
also took part, as at Sparta, where practically the whole
male population danced it at once. Plato seems to
mean a similar type by his "peace-dance" (in the
Laws), which is to be a thanksgiving for past mercies
or a prayer for continued prosperity.

In the regular system of education at Athens, it
is true, the boys learned only to sing and play, not
to dance. But owing to the perpetual demand for
boys from each of the ten tribes to compete at the great
festivals in war-dances and dithyrambs, dancing must
have been a common accomplishment. These competitors also attracted and encouraged a large number
of dancing-masters. Any boy who showed promise

---

[1] Lucian, On Dancing, 8.

[2] The dance known as γυμνοπαιδική is described in Athen. 631 b, as including
representations of wrestling. In 678 b, c, the festival of the Γυμνοπαιδίαι, and the
dances in it are referred to, but no mention is there made of wrestling.

[3] Athen. 630 d.

as a dancer, or perhaps even as a singer only, would be singled out by the agents who collected choroi for the choregoi.

Some rich man, let us call him Tisias,[1] has just been appointed choregos of the Erechtheid tribe for the war-dance of boys at the Panathenaic festival, or a boy-chorus in dithyrambs at the Thargelia. After drawing lots with the choregoi of other tribes, he gets Pantakles assigned to him as his poet and music-master, to teach the boys : he might, if he wished, hire at his own expense extra dancing- and music-masters.[2] Tisias then sends for Amunias, whom the Erechtheid tribe have chosen to collect their choroi and keep an eye on them while they are being trained. If Tisias bears a bad name or is unpopular with his tribe, he and his agent will have trouble in collecting the boys ; for the fathers will refuse to give them up, and there will be fines imposed and securities taken, before the chorus assembles. But as a rule the parents will accept gladly ; it is a chance of a free education for a month or so, for Tisias will pay all expenses, even of meals, and the State supplies the teacher ; it is a chance, too, for the boy to distinguish himself.

Meanwhile, Tisias will have provided a suitable schoolroom, in his own house, if possible ; rich men, to whom the post of choregos was a frequent burden, would keep an apartment for the purpose. If he himself is busy, he will depute friends, who can be trusted to swear in his favour before the Courts, to watch the teaching ; the agent will also be present.[3] For sometimes accidents occurred. Once a boy was

---

[1] This sketch is drawn chiefly from Antiphon, *The Choreutes.*

[2] Demos. *ag. Midias*, 533.

[3] Rivals sometimes tried to interrupt the lessons or bribe the teacher (Demos. *Mid.* 535).

given a dose to drink, to improve his voice, and it killed him.[1]

When the day of the competition came, the chorus would be suitably dressed at Tisias' expense ; he might perhaps allow them gold crowns.[2] There might be nine other choroi entering for the prize, but in the time of Demosthenes this was not common. The whole Athenian people and many foreigners would be present at the contest, and it would be an anxious day for choregos, boys, and parents. The State gave the prizes,[3] usually a tripod, which went to the winning choregos, who would set it up in some public place with an appropriate inscription, such as—

The Oeneid tribe was victorious ; a choros of boys. Eureimenes, son of Meleteon, was choregos. Nikostratos taught.[4]

Or—

Lusikrates, son of Lusitheides of Kikunna, was choregos. The boys of the Acamantid tribe won. Theon played the flute. Lusiades taught. Euainetos led.[5]

We pass to the position which riding held in Athenian education. The two richest classes in the State were liable to service in the cavalry. They had to supply their own horses, which were examined and, if unfit, rejected ; but the State paid them a sum of £8 annually for maintenance and arms in time of peace. As, however, the number of the citizen cavalry never rose above 1000, the whole of these two classes can never have been so employed at once : the remainder served in the heavy infantry. The two Hipparchoi elected for the year, and their subordinates, the ten Phularchoi,

---

[1] The situation of Antiphon's speech.   [2] Demos. *Mid.* 520.
[3] Xen. *Hiero*, ix. 4.   [4] Böckh, 212.   [5] *Ibid.* 221.

who each commanded a tribal contingent, on coming
into their office, would note how many of the thousand
who had served in the former year were no longer
liable to service owing to age, and would fill up the
vacancies ; they would also make good those gaps
which occurred from time to time during their term of
office owing to wounds or death or sudden poverty.
To secure a recruit, they had only to go to some
rich and active young man who was not already
serving ; if he refused to be enrolled, they could
prosecute him. The training often began before
eighteen, for Xenophon speaks of persuading the
recruit's guardians,[1] from whom he would be free at
that age. So Teles mentions the horse-breaker as
among the teachers of the lad in the secondary stage
of education. No doubt it took some training to
make an efficient cavalryman, and the Hipparchoi
liked to take the recruits young ; but to keep a stud
was the favourite amusement of a rich young Athenian,
and many would learn to ride without any view to
military efficiency. As the Hellenes rode without
stirrups, mounting was one of the great difficulties of
the young rider, and figures chiefly on the vases.
Often they used the long cavalry-spear as a vaulting-
pole.[2] Otherwise a groom or the master gave the
pupil a leg up : on a vase[3] in the British Museum
the master is seen simply pushing the boy into his
seat. A comic poet,[4] who has left us a picture of
the young recruits learning to ride under the eye
of their Phularchoi, speaks only of mounting and
dismounting.[5] " Go to the Agora," says the speaker to

---

[1] Xen. *Hipparch.* i. 11.   [2] Illustr. Plate IX.
[3] Brit. Mus. E 485.   [4] Mnesimachos, *Hippotrophos* (Athen. 402 f).
[5] See Illustr. Plates X. A, X. B and the Frontispiece for scenes in a riding-school.

his slave, "to the Hermai, where the phularchoi keep coming, and to the pretty disciples whom Pheidon is teaching to mount their steeds and to get down again." Xenophon, among much sound advice to the young rider about buying, training, and keeping his horse, gives the Hipparchos the following suggestions :—

"Persuade the younger men to vault on to their horses. It will be best if you supply the teacher for this. The older men may be put up by some one else in the Persian way. To practise the men in keeping their seats over difficult country, frequent riding expeditions are a good thing, but will be unpopular. So tell your men to practise by themselves whenever they are in the open country. But take them out yourself occasionally and test them over all sorts of ground. Give them sham fights in different kinds of country. In order to make them keen about throwing the javelin from horseback,[1] stir up rivalry between the different squadrons and give prizes for this and for good riding and the like. Above all make yourself and your attendant gallopers as smart as possible." [2]

There were frequent reviews under the eyes of the Boule. In the race-course at the Lukeion there was a sham fight, each hipparchos commanding five squadrons which pursued one another, and then charged front to front, passing through the gaps in one another's lines. They had, also, to wheel in line. The review was followed by javelin-throwing.[3] Another review was held at the Akademeia, on a course with a hard soil (ὁ ἐπίκροτος)—good practice for cavalry intending to fight in rocky Attica. Here they had, among

[1] The mark was a suspended shield, Brit. Mus. Prize-Amphora 7, Room IV.

[2] A rough summary of Xen. *Hipparch.* i. 15-26.

[3] Xen. *Hipparch.* iii. 6.

other manœuvres, to charge at full gallop and suddenly come to a halt.[1]

One of the attractions of the cavalry service was the great Panathenaic procession, where the horsemen played a leading part : an idealised picture of them may be seen on the frieze of the Parthenon. Xenophon gives a series of directions how to make the horses prance and hold their heads up on this great occasion, and suggests devices in gait which will attract popular notice. This and kindred processions must have made recruiting for the cavalry easy.

Swimming seems to have been, as would naturally be expected, an exceedingly common accomplishment in the maritime states of Hellas ; even at inland Sparta the boys must have learnt it for their daily plunge in the Eurotas. According to tradition,[2] there was a law at Athens that every boy should be taught reading, writing, and swimming : the proverb for an utter dunce was "he knows neither his letters nor how to swim." [3] Herodotos distinctly implies that all Hellenes knew how to swim. "The Hellenic loss at Salamis," he says, "was small. For, as they knew how to swim (as opposed to the barbarians who did not), when their ships were destroyed, they swam over to the island." [4] He takes it as a matter of course that every sailor could swim. The whole crew of a captured trireme during the Peloponnesian War as often as not jumped overboard and escaped by swimming.[5] In a story in Athenaeus the boys of Lasos, on coming out of the wrestling-school, go off together for a bathe and begin to dive. A friend of Aristippos used to

---

[1] Xen. *Hipparch.* iii. 14.   [2] Petit, *Leg. Att.* ii. 4.   [3] Plato, *Laws*, 689 D.
[4] Herod. viii. 89.   [5] *e.g.* Thuc. iv. 25.

boast to him of his diving.[1] During the blockade
of Sphakteria by the Athenian fleet, numbers of
Helots swam over from the mainland to the island
under water.[2] Scanty and scrappy as they are, these
details show that swimming must have been taught
to most boys, at any rate if they were ever likely to
serve in a fleet. Plato twice[3] uses a metaphor drawn
from a man swimming on his back, showing that this
method was known. When a young disputant is being
severely handled in a discussion, Sokrates intervenes,
" wishing to give the boy a rest, since he saw that he
was getting a severe ducking and he feared that he
might lose heart."[4] The phrase suggests that the sight
of boys learning to swim was familiar. They could
learn either in the innumerable creeks and bays of the
sea, or in the lakes and rivers, or in diving-pools.[5]
There were also various " gymnastic games " which
young people played in the water together ;[6] but of
their nature nothing is known.

It cannot reasonably be doubted that in the maritime
states a large proportion of the boys, at any rate of the
lower classes, were taught to *row*, since each trireme
required a crew of 200, nearly all of whom had to use
the oar. In the good old days, according to the
Wasps, the main object was to be a good oar,[7] and
rowing-blisters were a sign of patriotism.[8] In an
emergency, the Athenians could make the whole citizen
force under a certain age embark on the fleet and could
win a victory with these rowers; this would have been
impossible if the average citizen had been ignorant of
rowing.[9] On such occasions many even of the Hippeis

---

[1] Diogenes Laert. ii. 8. 73.   [2] Thuc. iv. 26.
[3] Plato, *Rep.* 529 c ; *Phaidr.* 264 A.   [4] Plato, *Euthud.* 277 D.
[5] Plato, *Rep.* 453 D.   [6] Galen, *de loc. aff.* iv. 8. See Grasberger, i. 151.
[7] Aristoph. *Wasps*, 1095.   [8] *Ibid.* 1119.   [9] Xen. *Hellen.* i. 6. 24.

embarked : Aristophanes jestingly asserts that in an expedition to Korinth the horses tried also, shouting, "Gee-ho, put your backs into it. Do more work, Dobbin." [1] Before the close of the war,[2] Charon, the ferryman of Styx, assuming that every Hellene knows the way to row, makes the souls of the departed row themselves across. Boat-races were certainly known at this period. A client of Lusias asserts that he has won a race with a trireme off Cape Sounion.[3] Probably the trierarchoi, the rich men appointed to fit out the State navy, either voluntarily or by regular custom, made the ships race one another. Thus the races would be as much inter-tribal contests as the dithyrambs or torch-races. Two crews of the epheboi of a later date used to race in the two sacred triremes. The vessels sailing out for the Sicilian expedition raced as far as Aigina.[4] A fragment of Plato the comic poet [5] refers to similar contests :

> Thy high-heaped tomb on this fair promontory
> Shall take the greetings of our far-flung fleets,
> And watch the merchants sailing out and in,
> And be spectator when the galleons race.

EXCURSUS I

THE "gumnasiarchoi" have created some confusion among those who have discussed Attic ways. Some authorities would make them rich men performing a "leitourgia" and holding a similar position to the trierarchoi and choregoi : others make them officials appointed to superintend the gymnasia.

The gumnasiarchia is certainly reckoned among leitourgiai as a general rule. A speaker in Lusias,[6] giving a list of these duties which he had performed, says : "I supplied a chorus of

[1] Aristoph. *Knights*, 600.   [2] Aristoph. *Frogs*, 200-271, describes a rowing lesson.
      [3] *Lus.* 21. 5.   [4] Thuc. vi. 32.
      [5] Plut. *Themist.* 32.   [6] Lusias, speech 21. 1-2.

men at the Thargelia, a chorus of war-dancers at the Panathenaia, a cyclic chorus at the little Panathenaia, I was Gumnasiarchos for the Prometheia and was victorious, then choregos with a chorus of boys, then with beardless war-dancers at the little Panathenaia." In Andokides[1] a gumnasiarchos at the Hephaisteia is mentioned. The author of the treatise on the Athenian constitution says:[2] "In the case of the choregiai, gumnasiarchiai, and trierarchiai, the Athenians realise that the rich fill the offices and the populace serve under them and get the benefit. So the populace claims to be paid for singing and running and dancing and sailing in the ships." Now "singing and dancing" belong to the choregiai, and "sailing in the ships" to the trierarchiai. So "running" is left for the gumnasiarchiai. The main feature of the yearly festivals of Hephaistos and Prometheus, which the two earlier passages gave as the scene of the duties of the gumnasiarchos, was a torch-race. It may thus be inferred that the duty of the gumnasiarchos was to collect, and train, a team of his own tribe for the torch-race at these festivals.[3] In connection with this duty, they could prosecute members of their team, or any one who interfered with them, for impiety before the Archon Basileus,[4] since the race was a religious function. They were thus in the sacrosanct position which Demosthenes as choregos claims for himself in his speech against Meidias.

So far the gumnasiarchos is an ordinary performer of a leitourgia, and his duties are confined to providing a tribal team for the torch-races at the Prometheia and Hephaisteia. His team, usually at any rate, consisted of epheboi, as we learn from an inscription describing the victory of Eutuchides with his epheboi.[5]

There is also the law quoted as Solon's in Aischines' speech against Timarchos.[6] "The gumnasiarchai (note that

---

[1] Andok. 17. 20.   [2] [Xen.] *Constit. of Athen.* i. 13.
[3] So   γυμνασιαρχεῖν λαμπάδι.—Isaios, *Philoktemon*, 62. 60.
         γυμνασιαρχεῖσθαι εὖ ταῖς λαμπάσιν.—Xen. *Revenues*, 4. 52.
         λάμπάδι νικήσας γυμνασιαρχῶν.—Böckh, 257.
[4] Dem. *ag. Lakritos*, 940 ; Aristot. 'Αθ. Πολ. 57.
[5] Böckh, 243.   [6] Aesch. *Tim.* 12.

it is a different word) "are not to allow any one over age to keep company with the boys at the festival of Hermes in any way whatsoever : if he does not keep all such persons out of the gymnasia, the gumnasiarch*es* shall be liable to the law that prescribes penalties for those who corrupt free boys." But the orator himself only mentions paidotribai, and special enactments dealing with the Hermaia ; there is no mention of a gumnasiarches. The law itself is an addition made in a later period when there was a special officer to control the gymnasia. But there is no evidence for such an official in the days of the independence of Hellas.

One interesting passage remains. "I was gumnasiarchos in my deme," or country district, says a speaker in Isaios.[1] There must therefore have been local torch-races, for which rich men were called upon to pay and train teams, just as there were certainly local theatrical performances. The passage opens up a prospect of vigorous athletic life throughout the country districts and villages of Attica.

[1] Isaios, *Menekles*, § 42. See Wyse's edition on the passage.

CHAPTER V

At fourteen or soon after, it was usual for the ordinary course of letters and lyre-playing to terminate : the gymnastic lessons might be carried on till old age interrupted them. During the first three-quarters of the fifth century, the lad, on leaving school, was left to live more or less as he pleased, if he was rich enough not to have to work for his living : the sons of poorer citizens at this age, if not before, settled down to learn a trade or engaged in merchandise. Rich boys, no doubt, spent most of their time in athletic pursuits ; riding and chariot-driving were favourite amusements. But with the Periclean age arose a violent desire for a further course of intellectual study, and a system of secondary education arose, to occupy the four years which elapsed between the time when the lad finished his primary education and the time when the State summoned him to undergo his two years of military training.

Many of the primary schools of the better sort started courses of study for lads, providing, no doubt, separate class-rooms, or else the younger boys attended at different hours from those at which the elder pupils assembled. Probably some such provision had been made much earlier for those who wished to obtain a more advanced knowledge of literature and music than was offered by the primary schools. But in the time of Sokrates many masters seemed to have held classes for lads as well as for boys. On entering the schools of Dionusios,[1] the master of letters, Sokrates finds a class of lads assembled here.[2] They all belong to noble families : the poor were no doubt unable to afford education of this sort. Two of the lads were busy discussing a point of astronomy, and were quoting the authority of Oinopides[3] and Anaxagoras, for Sokrates catches these two names as he enters the room. They were drawing circles on the ground and imitating the inclination of some orbit or other with their hands. This scene shows a much more advanced sort of study than was usual at the primary school of letters. The Sophists seem to have often lectured in class-rooms.

More often secondary education was imparted, not in the regular schools by regular, established masters, but by the wandering savants, who taught every conceivable subject, and were all grouped together under the general name of Sophists.[4] From this category the mathematicians and astronomers, who in all respects occupied the same position, are often excluded. This is due to the authority of Plato, who, while detesting the other subjects taught as secondary education, had a great affection for mathematics and astronomy, the only subjects which he prescribes for lads in the *Republic* and *Laws*. But Aristophanes, taking a more logical position, includes geometry and astronomy

---

[1] Plato's own schoolmaster, Diog. Laert. iii. 5.

[2] [Plato] *Lovers*, 132.

[3] Reputed inventor of Euclid i. 12 and 23, and a great astronomer.

[4] Thus the lad Theages, who has learnt letters, lyre-playing, and wrestling, is vaguely in search of a Sophist, to make him " wise " ([Plato] *Theages*, 121 D, 122 E).

among the subjects taught by the burlesque Sophists
of the *Clouds*. In point of fact, secondary education included any subject that the lad or his parents
desired ; and the wandering professors who imparted
it, and even established teachers like Isokrates, who
kept permanent secondary schools at Athens, were all
alike, in the popular view, Sophists.

But the more important subjects do naturally fall
into two great groups, Mathematics and Rhetoric.
Mathematics, as may be seen from the *Republic*,
meant, as a part of secondary education, the Science of
Numbers, Geometry, and Astronomy, with a certain
amount of the theory of Music, which, owing partly to
Pythagorean traditions, was classed with mathematics.
We have already seen a class learning Astronomy.
Plato, in the *Theaitetos*,[1] supplies a sketch of a lesson
in more advanced arithmetic, which, by Hellenic custom,
was usually expressed in geometrical terms in order to
obtain the assistance of a diagram. The lad Theaitetos
says to Sokrates that Theodorus of Kurene, the great
contemporary mathematician, had been teaching him.
" He was giving us a lesson in Roots, with diagrams,
showing us that the root of 3 and the root of 5 did not
admit of linear measurement by the foot (that is, were
not rational). He took each root separately up to 17.
There, as it happened, he stopped. So the other pupil
and I determined, since the roots were apparently
infinite in number, to try to find a single name which
would embrace all these roots.

" We divided all number into two parts. The number
which has a square root we likened to the geometrical
square, and called ' square and equilateral ' (*e.g.* 4, 9,
16). The intermediate numbers, such as 3 and 5 and

---

[1] Plato, *Theait.* 147 D.

the rest which have no square root, but are made up of unequal factors, we likened to the rectangle with unequal sides, and called rectangular numbers." And so on. As the pupils apply the same principle to cubes and cube roots, Theodorus must have initiated them into the mysteries of solid geometry also.

Here we find a professor lecturing to a select class, in this case of only two lads, and his pupils, as in the class-room of Dionusios, discussing and elaborating among themselves afterwards the subject-matter of the lecture. Theodoros is mentioned as teaching Geometry, Astronomy, and the theory of Music, as well as the Science of Numbers. Geometry by this time included a good number of the easier propositions which were afterwards incorporated in the works of Euclid ; the school of Pythagoras, and, later, that of Plato, did much to develop it. The problem of squaring the circle was already occupying attention.[1] Compasses and the rule were the ordinary geometrical implements : diagrams were drawn on the ground, on dust or sand. In Arithmetic surds[2] were a popular subject : but arithmetical problems, being usually expressed in terms of geometry plane or solid, become as a rule a part of the latter science.

To Plato these mathematical studies are alone suitable for secondary education : the philosopher Teles,[3] carrying on the same tradition, makes arithmetic and geometry the special plagues of the lad.[4] But then the philosophers despised Rhetoric.

Rhetoric, from the time of Gorgias onwards, formed a very large part of secondary education

---

[1] Aristoph. *Birds*, 1005.
[2] Plato, *Hipp. Maj.* 303 B.   [3] Stob. 98, p. 535.
[4] And learning to ride. He is thinking of the aristocratic lad, who would afterwards enter the later exclusive ephebic college.

Isokrates was its greatest professor. He provided in his school a course of three or four years for lads, to occupy their time till they were epheboi. But the methods, the aims, and the personality of this interesting professor will be discussed later.

Besides mathematics and rhetoric, there were literary studies. The *Axiochos* gives κριτικοί among the teachers of a lad. These are the lecturers on literary subjects, who concerned themselves with interpretations, often far-fetched, of the poets ; a summary of the literary discussion in the *Protagoras* may give some idea of such a lesson.

" PROTAGORAS. I consider that it is a most important part of a man's education to be skilled in poetry ; to understand, that is, what is rightly said, and what is not, by the poets. Simonides says to Skopas, son of Kreon the Thessalian, ' To become indeed a good man is hard, a man foursquare, wrought without blame in hands and feet and mind.' You know the poem ? Do you know then that farther on in the same poem he says, ' But the saying of Pittakos, wise though he was, seems to me not said aright : he said, " 'Tis hard to be noble." ' Don't you see that the poet has contradicted himself ? "

Sokrates replies by distinguishing " being " from " becoming," and suggests that χαλεπός (hard) may mean not " difficult " but " bad." He then gives a lecture in his turn. He picks out a μέν in the first line and puts it into a most unwarrantable position in his translation, and makes " indeed " go with " hard." To become good is difficult but possible, to be and remain good quite impossible. Hence Simonides goes on to say that he is quite satisfied with those who do no positive harm. Sokrates also notes a philological point, that ἐπαίνημι in the poem is a Lesbian Aeolic form, justified because the poem is addressed to a citizen of Mitulene. It may be remarked that Hippias also possessed a lecture on the subject. A lecture on Homer by a Sophist is mentioned by Isokrates : such lectures were frequently given by the rhapsodes.

Grammar was also taught, and the right use of words. Less usual subjects were geography,[1] art, and metre. Logic was in its infancy, but the growing lad could practise himself in argument by listening to the disputes of the dialecticians. Current conversation was full of ethical and political discussions : in the fourth century there were the philosophical schools of Plato and, later, of Aristotle, and the lectures of Antisthenes the cynic in Kunosarges ; and Isokrates taught political science. Lads seem to have been expected to learn something, at any rate, of the laws of their country : no doubt they were taken up to the Akropolis to read Solon's code : occasionally they may have been present as spectators in the law-courts, in order that they might gain an idea of legal procedure. Those who intended to become speech-writers for the courts would doubtless learn more : they would also attend some well-known writer like Lusias or Isaios, and learn the art of forensic rhetoric.

It must be clearly understood that the whole of this secondary education was purely voluntary. The parent need not send his lad to hear any teaching of the sort : the poorer classes certainly would not. The richer parents could choose what subjects they or their sons

---

[1] Among the common amusements of Athenian dinner-parties was a geographical game, in which A gave, say, the name of a city in Asia beginning with K, and B had to reply with one in Europe beginning with the same letter (Athen. 457).

preferred : rhetoric or literature, geography or mathematics—it was all one to the State.   Teachers came and
went : few stayed in Athens long.   Their pupils had
either to follow them abroad, as Isokrates went to
Gorgias in Thessaly, or wait for their next visit.   It
was only the schools of Isokrates, of the great philosophers, and of a few speech-writers like Lusias and Isaios,
that had any permanence in Athens.   Isokrates himself
had taught in Chios for a time : Plato was more
than once in Sicily, and his school had to do without
him in his absence.   There is a peculiar fluidity about
secondary education in Hellas : the teachers are always
on the move.   Endowed buildings for them there were
none : they taught in their own houses and gardens, or
in those of rich hosts, or in school-rooms borrowed for
the occasion, or in public resorts like the gymnasia, or
even in the streets.   Consistent or continuous instruction
was the exception : the Sophists proper gave it only to
a few.   The average lad at this time naturally acquired
a wide and superficial knowledge of a great number of
subjects, just the amount of knowledge which is such a
dangerous thing.   The lads became Jacks-of-all-trades :
Plato, struck with the educational error of wide superficiality, wrote the *Republic* as a counterblast, preach-
ing " One man, one trade."   This protest is largely
directed against the specious superficiality of the Sophists'
teaching.

Consequently, secondary education fell into two
halves, the fluid teaching of the wandering Sophists and
the continuous teaching of the more stationary schools
of Plato and Isokrates.   It will be convenient to accept
this division, and take the fluid half first.   In subjects,
the two must overlap one another : the Sophists taught
logic as much as Plato, rhetoric as much as Isokrates,

and universal information of very much the same range as Aristotle. But the method was different, just because as a rule the Sophist was here to-day and gone to-morrow, while the stationary teachers taught the same pupils for several years together and could study their particular idiosyncrasies, and the value of education depends very largely on the teacher's understanding of, and sympathy with, the individual boys whom he teaches.

It is of interest to trace the development of the term Sophia and of the Sophists who professed it.

The earliest thoughts of the Hellenic peoples were enshrined in hexameter verse. Homer and Hesiod represent the science and philosophy, as well as the religion, of their age. The poetical tradition survived in philosophy as late as Parmenides and Empedokles : the last trace of it may perhaps be found in the myths of Plato. The religious and ritual thinkers and the composers of oracles also employed verse. Consequently "wisdom," in the earliest Hellenic literature, is mainly associated with poetry and music, and the words σοφοί and σοφισταί are applied indiscriminately to poets.[1] This sense of σοφιστής survived in later times, and Protagoras could call Homer, Hesiod, Mousaios, Orpheus, and Simonides all alike by this title. Orpheus is so styled in the *Rhesos*. Phrunichos called Lampros the musician a "hyper-sophist," and Athenaeus declares that Sophist was a general title for all students of music.

A second use of the word "wise man" had also existed from the earliest times, by which it had been applied to those who were skilful in some particular

[1] Pind. *Isthm.* 5 (4) 36.   σοφισταί; σοφός, Pind. *Ol.* i. 15 ; *Pyth.* i. 42.   σοφία, *Hymn to Hermes*, and Pind. *Ol.* i. 187.

craft, such as carpentering,[1] medicine,[2] or chariot-driving.[3]

The "Seven Sages" also received the name of Sophist,[4] and in their age the cognate words σοφός and σοφία became connected with practical and political wisdom.[5]

Then the rise of education in Hellas, in which these old poets and thinkers were largely employed, and the analogy of the other educational titles with similar endings, γραμματιστής and κιθαριστής, gave the word σοφιστής an association with the teaching profession. Scientific knowledge was beginning to accumulate. Sufficient history was known to serve as a foundation for political theory and precept. Rhetoric was becoming an essential preliminary to political life, since, with the rise of democracy, persuasion became the dominating influence in law-courts and assemblies. The desire for knowledge was never so keen as during the latter half of the fifth century in Hellas. With the demand came the men. All over the Hellenic world arose professional teachers, who carried the knowledge, which they had learnt from one another or discovered for themselves, from city to city. Everywhere their lectures attracted large and enthusiastic crowds Among the subjects which they studied and taught may be mentioned mathematics (including arithmetic, geometry, and astronomy), grammar, etymology, geography, natural history, the laws of metre and rhythm, history (under which head fell also mythology and genealogies), politics, ethics, the criticism of religion, mnemonics, logic, tactics and strategy, music, drawing and painting, scientific athletics, and, above all,

---

[1] Hom. *Il.* 15. 412.   [2] Pind. *Pyth.* 3. 96.   [3] *Ibid.* 5. 154.
[4] In Isokrates, *Antid.* 235.   [5] As in Theog. 1074.

rhetoric. To such a heterogeneous collection what name could be given but "wisdom," σοφία? The name Sophist was applied indiscriminately to all these secondary teachers.

There are several interesting accounts of these Sophists in extant literature, but the writers are always prejudiced opponents.

In the *Clouds* of Aristophanes, the Sophists and their pupils are represented as living in an underground Thinking-Shop. They are pale and squalid, engaged in all sorts of researches. Natural history is represented by the important question, "How many times the length of its own foot does a flea jump?" a problem which is solved by actual experiment. Later in the play they inquire why the sea does not overflow, since the rivers are always running into it. Scientific instead of mythological explanations of thunder and lightning are given. There is religious criticism too, such as Xenophanes had uttered long before : "If Zeus imprisoned his own father, why has he not been punished?" There is astronomy, "the paths and orbit of the sun," and a hanging basket is introduced as an observatory. Geometry and compasses are mentioned. The visitor is shown a map of the world, containing Euboia, Lakedaimon, and Attica on a large enough scale, it would seem, to mark the deme Kikunna ; perhaps, as Strepsiades expects to find dikastai on it at Athens, it had pictures of elephants and monsters in un-known districts. The students are interested in metres and rhythms. The poet laughs at grammar, forming "cockess" as the logical feminine of cock, and mak-ing the chief Sophist object to feminine nouns with masculine terminations. It is suggested that the pupils at the Thinking-Shop are dirty, half-starved vegetarians, too economical to go to the hair-cutter or the baths, abstaining from wine and the gymnasia. But the main point attacked by Aristophanes is the teaching of Argument. The whole object of learning under the Sophists is, according to him, to be able to cajole the dikastai and so win impunity to cheat, and to have an argument to justify anything. The successful scholars beat their fathers and mothers, giving logical reasons for their behaviour ; they refuse to go to school, and are too clever to believe or accept anything. But their intellectual exhilaration is spasmodic ; they have been taught, if they reach a difficult problem, to jump on to something else.

A vivid sketch of Sophist-life is given in Plato's *Protagoras*. Young Hippokrates, on returning to Athens in the evening after pursuing a runaway slave to the frontier, hears that Protagoras the great Sophist has arrived in the city. Only the lateness of the hour deters him from rushing off to find Sokrates, who will give him an introduction to the teacher. Next morning he comes round to Sokrates' house long before it is light, bangs and shouts at the door in his excitement, and announces that he is ready to spend all the money which he and all his friends possess, in fees.

They go off to the house of Kallias, where Protagoras and other Sophists are staying. The porter is so worn out by the number of visitors that he is distinctly rude. They find Protagoras walking up and down in the cloisters of the house, with three or four listeners on either side, one of whom is learning to be a Sophist himself. Behind follows a crowd, mostly composed of the foreigners whom he draws from city to city, like Orpheus, with his magic voice. Another Sophist, Hippias, is sitting on a sort of throne in the

opposite part of the cloisters ; around him on benches
are a number of inquirers, who were asking him
questions about natural science and astronomy.   A
third Sophist, Prodikos, is in a side-building, still in
bed, covered up in blankets.[1]   His audience sat on
neighbouring beds.   The whole assemblage finally
collect couches and benches together in a great circle to
hear a discussion between Sokrates and Protagoras.
Kallias, the host on this occasion, often entertained
Sophists : at another time he had Gorgias and Polos
in the house.   His cloisters must have provided a
favourite lecture-room.   The Sophists also haunted
the gymnasia.   The discussion in the *Euthudemos*
takes place in the undressing-room of the Lukeion :
the two Sophists have been walking in the cloister.
Hippias on one occasion lectures in a school-room, on
another in a public place at Olympia.

Protagoras was the first of these teachers to take
pay.   His system was very fair.   On the close of their
course of instruction his pupils, if they chose, paid the
fee for which he asked ; otherwise, they went into a
temple, and, after taking an oath, paid as much as they
said his instruction was worth.[2]   Hippias made about
£600 in a very short time in Sicily, receiving some £80
from the tiny town of Inukos, although Protagoras
was also lecturing in the island at the time.   Prodikos
charged £2 for a particular lecture on correct speech,[3]
but there was also a less complete form of it which cost
only 10d. ;   he seems to have been noted for the grada-
tions in his charges, for there were also lectures at 5d.,
1s. 8d., and 3s. 4d.[4]   The sum which Euenos of Paros
asked for teaching the whole duties of a man and a

---

[1] He was an invalid.
[2] Plato, *Protag.* 328 c.
[3] Plato, *Krat.* 384 B.
[4] [Plato] *Axioch.* 366 c.

citizen was £20.[1] Probably, however, the charges of
these Sophists, and the money which they made, were
much exaggerated by their contemporaries. Isokrates,
the pupil of Gorgias, gives a much lower estimate.
"None of the so-called Sophists," he says, "will be
found to have collected much money. On the contrary,
some passed their lives in poverty and the rest in quite
ordinary circumstances. The richest Sophist within
my memory was Gorgias. He spent most of his time
in Thessaly, the most prosperous part of Hellas. He
lived to a great age and followed his profession for a
great many years. He did not take upon himself any
public burdens by settling in any one city. He did not
marry or have children to bring up. Yet with all these
opportunities of growing wealthy, he only left about
£800 at his death."[2] It must be remembered that the
Sophists received money only from those who definitely
enrolled themselves as pupils or came to a few advertised
lectures. Hippias lectured at Sparta frequently, and
never received a penny. Any one might go and ask a
Sophist a question, and would almost always receive a
voluminous answer. The eloquence and practical
skill of these men were also always at the disposal of
their own city. Like the greater Renaissance scholars,
Hippias, Gorgias, and Prodikos were much occupied
in going on embassies. For the larger part of their
life-work they received no payment whatever ; what
they actually received was possibly less than what their
philosophic opponents obtained in donations from
friendly tyrants.

At any rate, their fees were not heavy enough to
damp the ardour of their pupils. Young men left
their relations and friends to follow Sophists from

---

[1] Plato, *Apol.* iv. 20 B.   [2] Isok. *Antid.* 156.

city to city. These enthusiastic disciples were almost ready to carry their teachers about on their shoulders, so great was their affection for them. Why this enthusiasm? Partly because the Sophists were men of great personal charm. Partly because in that age the thirst for knowledge was unbounded. Partly from a desire to learn the way of virtue, which the Sophists claimed to teach. But the most potent reason was ambition. The young wished to shine in conversation, the great occupation of the age, and to be able to discuss every conceivable topic with intelligence. But education was also the road to political success. The Sophists taught systematic rhetoric, and logic of a sort. They also supplied the subject-matter for orations, in their practical handling of political science, of history, of ethical commonplaces; for a public oration was expected to be a storehouse of erudition. Rhetoric was needful not only for power, but also for security; for in the courts it had more influence than mere argument and facts.

About the individual Sophists little is known. They appear for us only in the pages of those who traduced them. Plato is mainly occupied with various conclusions which he draws from their philosophic theories, which were not a part of their teaching. *Protagoras*, the eldest of them, a most dignified personage, set himself to train good citizens: he claimed that he enabled his pupils to manage their households and govern their states. He imparted to them all the worldly wisdom which he had gained by long years of personal experience. He made a special study of political science, no doubt for this purpose, and left a treatise upon the subject, which was sufficiently excellent for a certain

Aristoxenos to be able to say that Plato had plagiarised most of the *Republic* from it.[1] Being businesslike, he favoured clearness of thought, and studied grammar : he was the first to separate nouns into the three genders.[2]

Prodikos belonged to the same practical school. He began by teaching his pupils the right use of words.[3] Thus he told Sokrates not to use δεινός when he meant "clever" ; for its proper meaning was "terrible," applicable to war, disease, or the like.[4] There is an amusing skit on his pet subject in Plato.[5] "The audience in a philosophical debate should give an impartial but not an equal attention to both speakers ; for it is not the same thing. For it is right to give an impartial hearing, but you ought to incline, not equally towards both, but rather towards the wiser speaker. I also ask you to agree, and to discuss, not to dispute. For friends discuss with friends for friendship's sake, but enemies dispute. In this way our meeting will be best conducted. For you, the speakers, would thus win from the audience most repute, not praise (for repute is without deception in the minds of the hearers, but praise is an outward expression of what is often not felt) ; and we, the audience, would thus receive most happiness, not pleasure ; for happiness is produced by the mental reception of knowledge and wisdom, pleasure by eating or by some other pleasant physical state." It was easy to laugh, but, as Plato himself shows, these distinctions of meaning were extremely useful in meeting logical quibbles, and were much needed in contemporary logic. Besides this, Prodikos was a moral teacher, and composed the famous *Choice of Herakles*,

---

[1] Diog. Laert. iii. 25.

[2] Aristot. *Rhet.* iii. 3. 5.   [3] Plato, *Euthud.* 277 E.

[4] Plato, *Protag.* 341 A.   [5] *Ibid.* 337 A-C.

in which he inculcated the duty of hard work as opposed to a life of laziness and pleasure. He was an invalid, but worked on in spite of ill-health ; the result was, perhaps, a certain amount of pessimism.

Hippias was a marvellously all-round genius. He once came to the Olympian festival with everything that he wore or carried made by himself, ring, oil bottle, shoes, clothes, a wonderful Persian girdle ; he also brought epic poems, tragedies, dithyrambs, and all sorts of prose-works.[1] He knew astronomy, geometry, arithmetic, grammar. At Sparta he taught history and archæology. He had a wonderful system of mnemonics, by which, if he once heard a string of fifty names, he could remember them all.[2] He lectured on Homer and other poets. He also composed a moral discourse, which won great applause at Sparta, where quibbles or bad morality would have been sternly repressed ; it was afterwards delivered in an Athenian school-room. Hippias was always ready to answer any question which was put to him, and was rarely at a loss.

A less prominent Sophist was *Antiphon*, who must be carefully distinguished from his namesake the Attic orator. He published works on physics, on concord (ὁμόνοια), and on political science. The fragments are interesting, and show some popular handling of ethical teaching. The following extracts[3] will give some idea of the man :—

" First among things human I reckon education. For if you begin anything whatever in the right way, the end will probably be right also. The nature of the harvest depends upon the seed you sow. If you plant

---

[1] Plato, *Hipp. Min.* 368.   [2] Plato, *Hipp. Maj.* and *Protag.* 318.

[3] Quoted in the Teubner Antiphon from Stobaeus. *Flor.* 98. 533. *Flor.* Appendix, 16. 36. This Antiphon comes in Xen. *Mem.* i. 6. 1.

good education in a young body, it bears leaves and fruit the whole life long, and no rain or drought can destroy it."

" Life is like a day's sentry-duty, and the length of life is comparable to a single day. While our day lasts, we look up to the sunlight, then we pass on our duty to our successors."

" A miser stored up money in a hiding-place, and did not lend or use it. Then it was stolen. A man to whom he had refused to lend it told him to put a stone in the hiding-place instead, and imagine that it was money ; it would be just as useful."

Among the Sophists were some apparently who were merely jesters, and used their brains solely in arousing laughter. It may well be doubted whether the account which Plato gives of *Euthudemos* and *Dionusodoros* is true to life ; but they probably represent a type. As teachers, no sane man could take them seriously. They had been gladiators, and had taught forensic rhetoric ; afterwards they discovered a genius for quibbles. They were ready to make out any statement to be true or false. The respondent may only answer " Yes " or " No," and no previous statement could be quoted against them, since they did not claim to teach anything consistent. A sample [1] of their arguments will make their methods clearer. " *A*. Your father is a dog. *B*. So is yours. *A*. If you answer my questions, you will admit it. Have you a dog ? *B*. Yes, a very bad one. *A*. Has it puppies? *B*. Mongrels like itself. *A*. Then the dog is a father ? *B*. Yes. *A*. Isn't the dog yours ? *B*. Certainly. *A*. Then being yours and a father, it is your father, and you are the brother of puppies." Absurd as it is, such discussions are a good

[1] Plato, *Euthud.* 298 D.

means of teaching logic, since they make the search for
rules intellectually compulsory.

No doubt there were black sheep among the lesser
Sophists, to whom Plato's bitter definitions in the
Sophist were quite applicable, who were " hunters
after young men of wealth and position, with sham
education as their bait, and a fee for their object, making
money by a scientific use of quibbles in private conversation, while quite aware that what they were teaching
was wrong." But they do not appear in extant literature, which has only recorded a very few, and those the
very pick, of the hundreds of Sophists that there must
have been in the Socratic age.[1]

The Sophists who have been mentioned so far have
been but little concerned with Rhetoric : they form
rather a school of Logic, opposed to the rhetorical school
of *Gorgias* and his followers.

Of the rise of Rhetoric in Hellas I need say little :
the whole subject has been admirably treated elsewhere.[2]
For educational purposes, Hellenic rhetoric started with
several fatal drawbacks and some counterbalancing
advantages. The southern nature of the Hellenes preferred sensuous charm of sound to logical accuracy of
fact ; their rhetoric, arising as it did out of poetry, and
modelling itself upon its literary parent, pandered only
too readily to their taste. With truth it had no more
to do than Homer had ; its object was to please the ear
by curious rhythms, balanced clauses, parisosis, and all
other possible devices. As long as the form was excellent, no matter how trivial the subject :[3] mice or salt

---

[1] It is not fair to condemn Polos and Thrasumachos on the score of the opinions
which Plato puts into their mouths.

[2] Jebb, *Attic Orators.*   [3] Compare Renaissance poetry in Italy.

PLATE VIII.

IN THE PALAISTRA: FLUTE-PLAYERS (WITH φορβεια), JAVELIN-THROWER, DISK-THROWER, AND BOXER

Gerhard's *Auerlesene Vasenbilder*, cclxxii. Fig. 1.

From a Kulix, now at Berlin, signed by Epiktetos (No. 2262).

were good enough for a theme. The oration must, of course, be full of passion, but that could be simulated : rhetoric had inherited the legacy of acting from its parent, Lyric Poetry. So rhetoric became simply a question of style, not of argument ; and since arguments were not required, the strength or weakness of a case did not matter : rhetoric could make any cause attractive to a sensuous Hellenic ear by its tricks of style, and thus make " the weaker cause the stronger." The method by which its professors taught their pupils brought out this attitude clearly. They were accustomed to take an imaginary case, and then to teach their pupils how to write a speech on either side of it : the extant " Tetralogies " of Antiphon are examples of the method, which was excellent educationally ; for it is good to see the arguments on both sides of a case. It was the carelessness about fact and indifference to truth, and the element of acting, that were so dangerous to the pupils. These elements certainly wrecked the justice of the Athenian courts ; their effect on Hellenic character was probably equally unsatisfactory.

Rhetoric also inherited the " gnome " or commonplace, a general statement about ethics or politics or what not, which could be developed into a sententious little essay. Budding orators learned to compose a little store of these and keep them ready for use, to be inserted in a speech whenever an opportunity occurred. For writing these essays, a certain amount of independent thought about politics and ethics was necessary ; and both the thought and the essay-writing were no doubt good for the lads.

The flowery and poetic style, which was the main characteristic of early Hellenic rhetoric, was the creation of Gorgias. A fragment of a funeral oration, in which no doubt he put forth all his powers, may be given as a sample of the sort of thing which his pupils learned to write :—

"As witness to their deeds these dead set up trophies over the foe, offerings to Zeus, offered by themselves. They were not unskilled in natural Ares nor lawful loves nor armèd strife nor beauty-loving Peace ; revering the Gods by Justice, honouring their parents by Service, just to their countrymen by Equality, faithful to their friends by Loyalty. Therefore, when they died, love for them died not with them, but deathless in bodies no longer bodies it lives when they live no longer." In the *Encomium on Helen* we have "fright exceeding fearful, and pity exceeding tearful, and yearning exceeding painful," and "productive of pleasure, destructive of pain." In the *Palamedes* Gorgias even uses puns.

His poetical compounds and those of his pupil *Alkidamas* were famous. In short, at this time there was no boundary whatever between poetry and prose : prose, if anything, was the more poetical of the two.

This strange hothouse Euphuistic style of Gorgias took Hellas by storm, and his influence was enormous : it even half-mastered the austere mind of Thucydides. As reformed by the greater critical faculties of his pupil Isokrates, it became the parent of Ciceronian Latin and so of the prose literature of centuries.

The other rhetorical Sophists of the time are less interesting. *Likumnios* and *Polos*, teacher and pupil, seem to have devoted themselves to questions of rhythm : they employed quaint conceits and affectations, like Gorgias. *Theodoros* and *Euenos* divided and subdivided the parts of an oration into " confirmation " and " additional confirmation," and " by-blames " and " by-

panegyrics " :   in which work Polos joined them.
Thrasumachos of Chalcedon, who seems to have been a
bigger man altogether, began to attack the psychological
side of rhetoric by studying the questions of pathos and
indignation ; these studies he embodied in pamphlets,
and no doubt his results were imparted to his pupils.

One of the beauties of old Hellenic education had
been that it did not make the rich a class apart from
the poor by giving a widely different form of culture.
The rise of the Sophists changed all this : their fees
excluded the poor.   The odium of resultant class-
separation fell upon the teachers.   Their pupils, rich,
aristocratic, and cultured, inclined towards oligarchy.
Hellenic sentiment held the teacher responsible for the
whole career of his pupils.   So for this reason again the
democracies regarded the Sophists with suspicion, as
the trainers of oligarchs and tyrants.   It was chiefly
because he had been the teacher of Kritias and Alkibiades
that Sokrates was put to death by the restored democracy.   The persuasive powers which the rhetoricians
gave to their pupils might be, and often were, mis-
used ;   the pupils might mislead the Ekklesia into
bad policy or the law-courts into injustice by their
eloquence.   However much the Sophists might protest
that they taught only rhetoric, not ethics, they were
held responsible for the dishonesty as well as for the
eloquence of such pupils.   Besides, rhetoric gave the
rich man, who alone could buy it, a most undemocratic
influence in the State.   The odium against the Sophists
was increased by their religious and political views.
They were free thinkers in all things.   Protagoras was
a frank agnostic ; Gorgias believed that nothing whatever existed.   Their political theories were equally
revolutionary, full of the idea of Social Contracts and

the right of the one strong man. All this was extremely distasteful to the majority, who were democratic
and orthodox. But it must be remembered that no
such views appeared in lectures : they were confined to
an occasional book or to private conversation. Out-
wardly the Sophists were law-abiding and respectable
servants of the constitution, and their lectures were, if
anything, rather commonplace.

Thus the prejudice against them was excited partly
by their freethinking and partly by their fees. The
first of these two reasons applied still more to Sokrates
and the philosophic schools. But Sokrates neither
asked nor received fees : Plato and Aristotle only
accepted presents. Consequently when the philosophic
party tried to dissociate themselves in the popular mind
from the Sophists with whom they were confounded,
they attempted to revive the old Hellenic prejudice
against taking fees for " wisdom," which had given
trouble to the lyric poets, and to emphasise the money-
making aspects of the Sophists' profession. This rather
absurd appeal to the gallery has influenced posterity;
but it did not win universal acceptation in Hellas.
Aischines still calls Sokrates a Sophist. Under the
Roman Empire " Sophist " became a title of distinction
applied to artistic stylists and teachers like Libanius.

CHAPTER VI

ATHENS was the place in which the fluid educational system of the Sophists would naturally begin to crystallise. Not only were the Athenians the keenest and most intellectual of the Hellenes: owing to the vast trade of their city, merchants, astronomers, inventors, poets, thinkers of all sorts, poured into it, and men of all trades and all tongues collected there. Many stayed there for a few days only, in passing; for Athens was a sort of Clapham Junction in those days. All these brought a perpetual supply of new ideas into the city, which the inhabitants were quick to assimilate.

But, possessing all the advantages of a commercial centre, Athens was free from the disadvantages. The clamour and vulgarity of trade were confined to the Peiraieus : in the gymnasia or the streets or the colonnades of Athens the philosopher and the thinker could teach and meditate in peace, in an atmosphere ennobled by her treasures of architecture and art and sculpture, which subdued the most blatant visitor, amid the literary circles which her dramatic contests attracted and encouraged. Here was an ideal spot for the meeting-place of the best minds in Hellas and the growth of a great educational system. The city was an education in itself. Perikles had called Athens the school of

Hellas ; the name was now to be justified in its most literal sense.

Early in the fourth century there arose established secondary schools in Athens. Plato began to teach Logic and Philosophy, Isokrates Rhetoric, not for a few weeks at a time, but permanently : their courses lasted three or four years. Characteristically, there was no State organisation or interference ; Isokrates taught in his own house, near the Lukeion, Plato in his garden near Kolonos and in the Akademeia. Their pupils came from all parts of the civilised world, staying in Athens during their course of study. Plato imposed a preliminary examination in mathematics upon his pupils ; Isokrates only commended a knowledge of such subjects. The students of these two schools became recognised features of Athenian life.

Plato led his pupils towards intellectual research and a life of retirement ; the tendency of the school was markedly aristocratic, and several of the lads became tyrants in after life. Isokrates inculcated the practical life : his teaching was meant as a preparation for success in society and politics. But as his school naturally was only for the comparatively wealthy and leisured classes, it also tended to be aristocratic ; however, it produced some of the leading democratic statesmen of the day.

Besides these two great schools others grew up. It is hard to distinguish exactly between the boys who went to Isokrates in order to learn political speaking and those who went to a " logographos " like Lusias or Demosthenes to learn forensic oratory. The " logographoi " do not seem to have claimed to impart culture, but only technical instruction : they are thus on the boundary line of education. But Demosthenes went to the " logographos " Isaios to get precisely the instruction which Isokrates had refused him : so it is hard to make a clear distinction. I shall therefore give a short sketch of the " logographoi " also.[1]

By the time that these schools began to establish themselves the Sophists were beginning to die out. Times were harder in the fourth century, and fewer people had money to spend on these expensive teachers. The intellectual movement of the Periclean age had spent itself, and the desire for universal knowledge was no longer so keen. Moreover, it is quite probable that settled schools, like that of Isokrates at Athens, were forming in many of the great centres : it is known that Isokrates himself taught for a while in Chios. The great demerit of the Sophists' teaching, namely, that it was too much in a hurry and gave no time for personal endeavour on the part of the pupil, had been recognised: and the result was that the Sophists settled down in a single place and gave continuous courses of instruction.

But a good many Sophists of the old type remained, to vex Isokrates by their criticisms and rivalries. They still came to Athens at the great festivals, and gave hurried lectures.[2] But they had not the originality of their predecessors, and people preferred to read the works of Protagoras or Gorgias for themselves to hearing them repeated as original by a lecturer. Books were already a serious rival to lecturing, and were a cause of much searching of heart to Plato : Isokrates, however, preferred to write himself and so advertise his school.

Besides the wandering Sophists there were probably a good many teachers, both of Philosophy and of

---

[1] Isokrates clearly felt them to be his educational rivals. See *Antid.* 310 A, and the end of the *Paneg.*

[2] There is a sketch of them in Isok. *Panath.* 236 c ; to a lecture on Homer three or four of them had appended an attack upon Isokrates.

Rhetoric, established permanently at Athens. Isokrates mentions casually that all the schools[1] produce only two or three first-class speakers. In his educational prospectus, *Against the Sophists*, he criticises these rivals freely. " They merely try to attract pupils by low fees and big promises. The speeches which they write themselves are worse than the improvisations of the wholly untrained, yet they promise to make a complete orator out of any one who comes to them ; for they make no allowance for natural talent or for experience, but regard eloquence as an exact science, just like the A B C and equally communicable ; whereas it is really a progressive art, where the same thing must never be said twice, and its rules must be relative to the occasion and the circumstances." [2] It is clear that these rivals committed the serious crime of underselling Isokrates and also of issuing more attractive prospectuses ; perhaps, too, they are the captious critics to whom he is always referring.

Isokrates is still more severe on various philosophical teachers ; he cannot mean Plato alone, for he mentions their fees, and Plato made no charge. There must have been a large number of philosophical professors, of whom Plato was only the most brilliant. But in many points Isokrates no doubt meant his denunciations to apply to Plato also. The summary of his attack is as follows :—" They make impossible offers, promising to impart to their pupils an exact science of conduct, by means of which they will always know what to do. Yet for this science they charge only 3 or 4 μναῖ ($£12$ or $£16$), a ridiculously small sum. They try to attract pupils by the specious titles of the subjects which they claim to teach, such as Justice and Prudence. But the

---

[1] Isok. *Antid.* 99.   [2] Isok. *Soph.* 10. 293 A.

Justice and the Prudence which they teach are of a very
peculiar sort, and they give a meaning to the words
quite different from that which ordinary people give ;
in fact, they cannot be sure about the meaning themselves, but can only dispute about it. Although they
profess to teach Justice, they refuse to trust their pupils,
but make them deposit the fees with a third party
before the course begins." [1] Here we have a picture of
a distinct group of ethical teachers all trying to work
at that Socratic paradox that virtue is knowledge, and
imparting their results to pupils for low fees.

All these Professors of Ethics seem to have made
Mathematics and Astronomy a part of their course,
just as Plato did. " To the old Athenian education, of
Letters and Music and Gymnastics, they have added a
more advanced course, consisting of Geometry and
Astronomy and such subjects, together with eristic
dialogues," that is, Dialectic. [2] This course seems to have
been much criticised as being a mere waste of time, since
it was of no practical use and the knowledge so obtained
was soon forgotten in after life. But Isokrates, although
these subjects played no part in his own school, was
sufficiently good an educationalist to see their merits :
the study of subtle and difficult matters like Astronomy
and Geometry " trains a boy to keep his attention
closely fixed upon the point at issue and not to allow his
mind to wander ; so, being practised in this way and
having his wits sharpened, he will be made capable of
learning more important matters with greater ease and
speed." [3] But all these unpractical, if improving,
studies should be abandoned before the nineteenth
year : for they dry up the human nature and make men

[1] Isok. *Soph.* 4. 291 D. Cp. the modern " caution-money."
[2] Isok. *Pan.* 26. 238 A.   [3] Isok. *Antid.* 118. 265.

unbusinesslike. "Some of those who have become so
adept in these subjects that they teach them to others,
show themselves in the practical conduct of life less
wise than their pupils, not to say than their servants."[1]
Consequently, those who care to study mathematics and
eristic should confine them to the years between fourteen and eighteen : and then pass on to learn rhetoric
with Isokrates ; the rest can come to his school as lads,
as many did.

But, although he differentiated himself so carefully
from what moderns would call the philosophical schools,
Isokrates styled himself a teacher of philosophy quite as
much as they did. To him, as to the Romans, philosophy was the art of living a practical life. "That
which is of no immediate use either for speech or for
action does not deserve the name of Philosophy."[2] The
true philosopher is not the dreamer who neglects what
is practical and essential, but the man of the world who
learns and studies subjects which will make him able to
manage his household and govern his state well ; for
this is the object of all labour and all philosophy.[2]
With this practical end in view he ridicules the metaphysical researches of "the old Sophists, of whom
Demokritos said that the number of realities was infinite,
and Empedokles declared for four, and Ion for not
more than three, and Alkmaion for only two, and
Parmenides and Melissos for one, while Gorgias asserted
that nothing existed at all."[3]

In the promises which he makes of imparting to his
pupils this practical wisdom which he calls philosophy,
Isokrates is characteristically cautious. An exact
science, which will embrace all possible questions and
circumstances which may arise in domestic and political

[1] Isok. *Panath.* 238 D.   [2] Isok. *Antid.* 118. 266.   [3] *Ibid.* 118. 268.

matters, is an impossibility ; men must be content with
a general capacity of forming a right judgment in view
of each particular case when it arises.   Consequently he
defines as " wise men," σοφοί, " those whose judgment
usually hits upon the right course of action," and as
" seekers after wisdom " or philosophers, φιλόσοφοι,
" those who occupy themselves with those studies and
pursuits from which they will most quickly obtain this
practical wisdom,"[1] or capacity of forming correct
judgments.   But a judgment can only be formed
properly after a proper deliberation : so the work of
Philosophy is to practise her pupils in this deliberation.[2]
This practice is, of course, provided in the school
of Isokrates ; for his school was, in fact, a debating
or deliberating society, in which the pupils wrote and
recited carefully composed speeches on given themes,
or listened to the harangues of their master.   Sometimes
they discussed events of the day and matters of general
interest[3] at the moment ; at another time their topic
was some constitutional or historical question, or the
comparative merits of different nations and governments.[4]
At another time, as may be seen from the example of
Isokrates' own orations, they dealt with those mythical
characters who were historical realities as well as sacred
personages to the average Hellene, Theseus and Helen
and Bousiris : this in their eyes was almost equivalent
to religious instruction and they were virtually writing
theological essays.   No doubt also the pupils wrote
and recited those " commonplaces " or short essays on
general topics, composed in a most elaborate style,
which ancient orators kept in stock, ready to be inserted

---

[1] Isok. *Antid.* 118. 268.   [2] *Ibid.* 91.   [3] Isok. letter to Alexander.
[4] Isok. *Panath.* 275.   It is noticeable how many of his pupils became historians—
Ephoros, Theopompos, Androtion, Asklepiades.

in a speech when a suitable opening presented itself
Isokrates' own works are particularly full of these
highly finished little essays:[1] so it is at least extremely
probable that he insisted upon their composition in his
school. Before his pupils, too, Isokrates would recite
those fine sermons of his, like the *Demonikos*; and
effective pieces of moral exhortation they must have
been.

Thus the Isocratean school claimed to be, and was,
a school of morals : it was also a school of good style
and composition. The boys' essays had to be written
in a particular style, grandiloquent and ornate, to suit
their themes. "For it is absurd to suppose that the
matter and manner of ordinary conversation or of
forensic oratory are suitable to Pan-Hellenic themes ;
on the contrary, in this kind of speech the thoughts
must be more original and more lofty, the style more
striking, and the diction more poetical and elaborate."[2]
Style, diction, and matter must, in fact, be that which
Isokrates worked out in his own speeches. That style[3]
I do not mean to discuss here. The fact that he wrote
in a study and never spoke in public, has made him
exaggerate the merits of the artistic prose-style of which
he was the first really great exponent ; but of its
popularity with an Hellenic audience there can be no
question. The pupils of Isokrates became the most
eminent politicians and the most eminent prose-writers
of the time ; his house, as Cicero puts it, was the school
of Hellas and the manufactory of eloquence.

To acquire this kind of oratory, there was need both
of natural ability and of diligent study. Isokrates

---

[1] See, for example, "On Slander " (*Antid.* 313 E), "On Speech " (115. 255).

[2] Isok. *Antid.* 48.

[3] For a complete analysis of it, see Jebb's *Attic Orators*.

professes to supply, first an exact science of all the
rhetorical devices and the various forms which speech
can take, and then practice in the right employment
and arrangement of these several parts. To learn the
technique of rhetoric is comparatively easy, if the
aspirant applies to the right man ; but the right use of
the technique can never be brought under any set of
rules, or taught by one man to another : it can only be
learnt by experience. The future orator must try the
effect of each arrangement and combination of technique
on the audience, and so draw up his own system.[1] The
requisite audience for these experiments will be provided by the other pupils of the school, with the master
as chief critic. A good master is essential. By his
personal influence he will be able to communicate those
finer elements of style which cannot be communicated
in formal teaching. If he is worth his salt, all his
pupils will bear the stamp of his own manner, and will
easily be distinguished from every one else by the
similarity of their style to his and to one another's.[2]
Education in rhetoric at Isokrates' school seems to have
begun with the study of his own works. In the
Panathenaikos he describes himself as reading the
speech over with two or three of his regular pupils ;
they revise and criticise it as they go along. This
would give Isokrates the opportunity of expounding
his own views of technique, with his own works before
him as illustrations. It may be inferred from the
beginning of the *Bousiris* that the written speeches
of other Sophists were also studied, and their faults, or
aberrations from Isocratean canons, pointed out, in
order that they might be avoided in future. At any
rate, Isokrates complains that other professors of the

[1] Isok. *ag. Soph.* 294 c ; *Antid.* 91-93, etc.   [2] *Ibid.* 294 E.

same sort of Rhetoric at Athens made use of his writings for teaching their own pupils, though, of course, according to him, they did so in order to show the boys what to admire, not what to avoid. When this technique had been fully mastered Isokrates set his pupils to write speeches on their own account, choosing for them some great and improving theme : in these speeches they had to apply the rules which they had learnt, and the subtler influences which they had imbibed, from their teacher. But they had also to think out the subject-matter, and in this lies much of the merit of the whole system. For, as Isokrates observes, the essayist who writes upon such themes will have to think noble thoughts, and select noble deeds as his instances and illustrations. This contemplation of what is noble will be a greater incentive to virtue than any so-called science of ethics : [1] for there is no science which can create goodness in wicked natures, but exhortation and persuasion can work wonders. Moreover, since the orator's best argument is, after all, a good reputation, the young orator will see that his conduct and character are as excellent as possible.[1] And the practice of weighing just what thoughts and actions are suitable to the speech involves that faculty of sound deliberation which is necessary for the formation of right judgments. In fact, Isocratean " Philosophy " does more to form character than it does to produce eloquence.[2]

The pupils practised themselves, as we have seen, by delivering their harangues before Isokrates and their fellow-pupils. The school formed a select clique of trained critics of Rhetoric ; the encouragement of criticism by this means must have been valuable. To

---

[1] Isok. *Antid.* 121.   [2] Isok. *ag. Soph.* 295 D.

this council Isokrates submitted his own orations before publication ; former pupils were also invited to attend on these occasions. There is an interesting account of such an assembly at the end of the *Panathenaikos*. " I was revising the speech as it stands down to this point," Isokrates says, " with three or four of the lads who are accustomed to study with me. On reading it through, we were satisfied with it and thought it only needed a peroration. I determined, however, to send for one of those among my pupils who had been brought up in an oligarchy and had set themselves to praise Lakedaimon, so that he might notice any false charge which we had unwittingly brought against the Spartans." The pupil comes, and, while praising the speech enthusiastically, makes an unguarded criticism of its matter which led to a long discussion, in the course of which he and Isokrates deliver lengthy harangues. Finally, the pupil is crushed. The boys who had been present throughout the discussion were completely convinced by Isokrates and applauded him warmly. But the master himself was not satisfied. So three or four days later he called together all his old pupils who were in Athens, and the speech was submitted to their judgment, and received with enthusiastic applause. The former critic then delivered a brilliant harangue, trying to elucidate a hidden meaning in the speech. " The crowd of pupils, which is usually ready to applaud, shouted, flocked round him, and congratulated him, thoroughly agreeing with his eulogy of me," says Isokrates. " I praised him too, but did not reveal whether he had hit off my secret meaning or not."

The whole tone of the passage suggests that such an appeal to the pupils for criticism and advice was common, the only extraordinary feature being the

presence of the "old boys." This view is supported
by other passages. In the *Areiopagitikos*[1] Isokrates
tells his imaginary audience that "Some who heard me
on a former occasion describe this constitution which
Athens once enjoyed, while praising it enthusiastically
and calling our ancestors happy, . . . told me that I
was not likely to persuade you to adopt it." On
another occasion his speech made such an impression
upon this preliminary audience that "No one praised
the beauty of the style, as they usually do, but all
admired the truth of the argument." When he first
told his pupils that he meant to send an advisory
speech to Philip, "they all thought he was mad, and
had the impudence to rebuke him, a thing which they
had never done before. . . . But when they had heard
the speech, they changed their minds completely and
thought that Philip, Athens, and all Hellas would alike
be grateful to him."[2]

Isokrates' great political pamphlets, with their
wonderfully polished style and their striking themes,
naturally served him as an excellent advertisement, as
he naïvely admits in the *Antidosis*. Those who
required further information about his educational
methods and aims would turn to the prospectus
Against the Sophists, which he published at the
beginning of his career. Owing to these attractions,
pupils came to him from all parts of the Hellenic
world, from Pontos, Sicily, and Cyprus ;[3] he had
"more than all the other teachers of philosophy put
together."[4] They were not merely private citizens,
but statesmen, generals, kings, and tyrants.[5] Probably
the age at which they came varied greatly, but most

---

[1] Isok. *Areiop.* 151 B.   [2] Isok. *Philip*, 85, 86.
[3] Isok. *Antid.* 106.   [4] *Ibid.* 318 c.   [5] *Ibid.* 316 c.

of his actual pupils would probably be between fifteen
and twenty-one. He often speaks of μειράκια as among
them. Moreover, he speaks of parents bringing their
sons to him,[1] which they certainly would not do if the
boys were over eighteen. Public life in the average
Hellenic state began at twenty ; so boys would wish
to be ready for it by that age. The course at Isokrates'
school lasted for three or four years.[2] The Athenian
lad was more or less busy with his military duties from
eighteen to twenty, so he would probably take the
course between fourteen and eighteen ; natives of other
states would fit it in according to their local customs.
The fee for the whole course was 10 mnai, or £40.[3]
The story[4] goes that Demosthenes, having only £8,
offered to pay that sum for one-fifth of the course.
But Isokrates replied that he could not sell his philosophy in slices ; the customer must take the whole fish
or none at all. Probably, however, the tale is a fiction :
Isokrates himself claims not to have made any money
out of his countrymen, and only to have charged his
foreign pupils.

Since, soon after the opening of his school, he had
a hundred pupils, the accounts of his great wealth,
which he repudiated so indignantly, cannot have been
far wrong, especially as he received 20 talents
(nearly £5000) for his panegyric on Euagoras. His
own comparison of his wealth with that of Gorgias,
who left only £800 at his death, is curious, if the above
statements are true.

But his pupils, drawn from a class that had sufficient
substance to live at leisure,[5] seem to have been well
satisfied with what they got for their money. "At

[1] Isok. *Antid.* 110.   [2] *Ibid.* 62.   [3] [Demos.] *Lakritos*, 15 and 42.
[4] [Plutarch] *Ten Orators*, 837.   [5] Isok. *Antid.* 129.

the end of their time, when they were on the point
of sailing home to their friends, they so loved their
life in Athens that they parted from it with tears and
sighs." Isokrates kept on friendly terms with them
afterwards. Thus he writes to Timotheos, tyrant of
Herakleia and an old pupil, to congratulate him on
his accession and commend to him another old pupil,
Autokrator. Then there is the charming letter in
which he introduces Diodotos, another of his pupils, to
the Macedonian Antipater, at some personal risk, for
there was war between Athens and Macedon at the
time. " I have had many pupils," the letter runs,
" some of whom have become great orators, some men
of action, some great thinkers, some, with no particular
talents, have at any rate become upright and cultured
gentlemen: Diodotos combines all these qualities."

The chief boast of the school of Isokrates was
that it produced gentlemen. Isokrates defines education not as a knowledge of metaphysics and a contemplation of the Good, nor yet as technical ability
in some particular profession, art, or trade, but as a
sort of culture and polish. " This is my definition of
the educated man," he says. " First, he is capable of
dealing with the ordinary events of life, by possessing a
happy sense of fitness and a faculty of usually hitting
upon the right course of action.

" Secondly, his behaviour in any society is always
correct and proper. If he is thrown with offensive or
disagreeable company, he can meet it with easy good-
temper ; and he treats every one with the utmost
fairness and gentleness.

" Thirdly, he always has the mastery over his
pleasures, and does not give way unduly under misfortune and pain, but behaves in such cases with

manliness and worthily of the nature which has been given to us.

" Fourthly (the most important point) he is not spoilt or puffed up nor is his head turned by success, but he continues throughout to behave like a wise man, taking less pleasure in the good things which chance has given him at birth than in the products of his own talents and intelligence.

" Those whose soul is well tuned to play its part in all these ways, those I call wise and perfect men, and declare to possess all the virtues ; those I regard as truly educated." [1]

Thus the object of Isokrates was rather to impart culture and polish to his pupils than to teach them rhetoric ; it is in this point that he differs from the other professors who taught the same sort of rhetoric as he did at Athens and have now been forgotten, and from the logographoi, who taught the kind of speaking which suited the Athenian law-courts, without professing to supply anything but a technical knowledge of their particular subject.

In an Athenian trial the prosecutor and defendant had each to deliver a speech for themselves ; afterwards, regular advocates might address the jury in some cases, but this was rare.   So the duty of an Athenian lawyer was simply to write speeches for his clients to deliver, not to speak himself.   Thus the metic Lusias, who had no right to speak in a court himself, was a famous lawyer, or logographos, speech-writer, as the Hellenes called him.

Mantitheos, say, finds himself involved in a lawsuit. He comes to Lusias and explains the circumstances. Lusias masters the details, looks up the laws on the

[1] Isok. *Panath.* 239.

question, and studies his client's age, character, and so
forth.   He then writes a speech sufficiently dramatised
to come naturally from Mantitheos' mouth.   In composing it he will simulate the indignation which he
supposes his client to feel, he will adopt the nonchalant
air of injured innocence which Mantitheos showed in
telling the story, and so on, till the speech is a real
bit of dramatisation like the speeches in a tragedy.
When composed, the speech would be carried off by
Mantitheos, learnt by heart, and duly recited.   It is
all a bit of acting on Lusias' part.   The habit of
simulating feelings when writing speeches was dangerous,
when the logographos came forward to speak in his
own person on some question.   Demosthenes never
quite escapes the suspicion of acting and posing, even
in his most impressive moments.

Besides these clients, the Athenian lawyers had
permanent pupils, who either intended to be lawyers
themselves or thought the study would help them in
a political life.   Their methods of teaching, as may
be seen from Plato's *Phaidros*, resembled those of
Isokrates.   In the dialogue called by his name, Phaidros
is going out to walk off the effects of sitting indoors
too long.[1]   He had been listening to Lusias, "the
cleverest speech-writer of the age," reciting one of his
speeches, on which he had spent much labour.   Phaidros
had made him repeat it several times, and has now
borrowed the book in order to learn it by heart during
his walk.   Sokrates persuades him to read it aloud, in
doing which he is quite carried away by its eloquence.[2]
Sokrates then proceeds to criticise the style and
matter of the speech,[3] and to compose one of his

[1] Plato, *Phaidr.* 227-228.   [2] *Ibid.* 234 D.
[3] The criticisms do not suit Lusias ; they fit Isokrates much better.

own on the same subject to show how it ought to be treated.

This reveals the method of teaching. The teacher, as here and in Isokrates' case, recites a speech of his own, explaining how it was done and asking for criticism from the pupils. Then the pupil would learn it by heart and declaim it in some solitary place. On other occasions, as Sokrates does here, the master would take the speech of some rival professor and criticise it severely, composing a better speech himself. The *Bousiris* and *Helen* of Isokrates show this method. Or else the pupil replied to the teacher, or the teacher wrote two speeches on opposite sides of the question. The extant work of Antiphon and the lost work of Gorgias [1] are of this type.

Most of the Attic orators seem to have taken pupils. Isaios taught Demosthenes. Demosthenes in his turn seems to have had great popularity as a teacher. He " promises to teach young men the art of speaking " ; [2] " he filled Aristarchos with empty hopes of becoming the prince of orators all in a moment " ; [3] " he invited some of his pupils to come and listen to the speech *On the False Embassy*, promising to show them how to cheat and mislead the audience " ; [4] " later on he will brag before his boys of his tricks." These passages give an interesting picture of Demosthenes and his pupils, as seen through his opponent's green spectacles.

In opposition to the schools of Rhetoric stood the schools of Philosophy, leading their pupils towards the life of retirement and contemplation and away from the

[1] Cicero, *Brutus*, xii. 46-47.　　[2] Aischines, *Timarch.* 171, 173.
[3] *Ibid.* 171.　　[4] *Ibid.* 175.

strenuous life of political and social activity.[1]　We
have seen that there were many professors of Philosophy
at Athens in Isokrates' time, charging fees of three or four
mnai for their course.　But only one of them is known
to posterity, and he gave lessons gratis.　Otherwise,
Plato must be taken as a member of a class, albeit the
most brilliant member.　The teaching of Plato centred,
as is well known, round the Akademeia.　Plato possessed
a house and garden, which he bequeathed to his school,
between that gymnasium and Kolonos.　When he and
his pupils wished to be private they could withdraw into
his gardens ; otherwise they frequented the Akademeia,
from which their school took its name.　It was not
every one who could obtain admission to the school,
for, as Plato taught gratuitously, he could pick and
choose his pupils.　He expected would-be students to
be well grounded in Geometry : there must have been
some sort of entrance-examination.　His successor,
Xenokrates, finding that an applicant was ignorant of
Music, Geometry, and Astronomy, told him to go away :
" for you give philosophy no chance of getting a grip
upon you." [2]　The inner circle of the school had their
meals in common : the banquets were extremely plain.
Timotheos, the Athenian general, who was accustomed
to rich living, after having been a guest at one of these
meals, remarked, on meeting Plato next day, " Your
suppers are more pleasant on the following day than
they are at the time." [3]　After the meal, a larger
number of friends probably came in ; this, at any rate,
was a custom at the similar meetings held by the
philosopher Menedemos a generation later.[4]　The discourse often went on all night.　There was a fixed code

---

[1] Plato, *Gorg.* 484-486 ; end of *Euthud.* ; *Theait.* 172-177 ; *Rep.* 496.
[2] Diog. Laert. iv. 2. 6.　　[3] Athen. 419 d.　　[4] *Ibid.* 419 e and 55 d.

of rules to regulate these meals,[1] which is suggestive of
Plato's pleasantries in the *Laws* about the educational
value of strictly regulated bouts of intoxication.   But
drunkenness was, of course, not allowed : Plato had a
particular objection to it, and used to tell drunkards to
look in the looking-glass and they would never err in
that way again.[2]   It offended his strict canons of
physical beauty and propriety.   It is interesting to note
that the author of the *Republic* admitted women on
terms of equality to this inner circle of the Akademeia,
in defiance of Athenian prejudice.   Lastheneia of
Mantineia and Axiothea of Phlious, who dressed in
male attire, are the first champions of women's rights
to a University education who appear in history.[3]   The
discussions of this clique were probably conducted after
the model of the Platonic dialogue, and doubtless were
in Plato's mind when in the *Laws* he constructed
his curious ethical and political debating-society for the
older and wiser members of his state.

But admission to these mysteries must have been
reserved for comparatively few, personal friends and
mature thinkers : the members formed rather a private
club than an educational system.   The young Athenian
who wished, when his primary education was finished,
to study philosophy under Plato, had two means open
to him : there were lectures in various public places ;
there was also a school for lads in the Akademeia.

The only lecture,[4] of which any very definite trace
is left, was not a great success from the educational
point of view.   Plato announced beforehand that
his subject would be " The Good."   A great crowd

---

[1] Athen. 186 b.   [2] Diog. Laert. iii. 26.   [3] *Ibid*. iii. 31.

[4] See for this lecture Simplikios (on Aristot. *Physics*, p. 202 B, 36), and Aristoxenos, *Harmon*. beg. of Bk. ii.   On one occasion, at least, it was delivered in the
Peiraieus (Themist. *Orat*. 21. 245).

collected, expecting to hear a neat Isocratean discussion of such things as Health, Wealth, Friendship, which were popularly considered to be rival claimants for the title of the Good. But Plato began to talk about arithmetic and geometry and astronomy, and discussed the One as the Good. The whole lecture was couched in enigmatical language. The majority of the audience went away in despair.[1] Only practised Platonists like Aristotle and Herakleides and Hestiaios did their best to understand the lecture, and took notes. The whole idea of a " popular lecture " must have been repugnant to Plato. In his view, knowledge was only for the few, who, starting with great natural abilities, could devote themselves for years at a time to continual study and research. The pupil must be talented to start with : he must undergo a long course of preparatory studies in Logic and Mathematics : only when middle-aged might he approach the inner mysteries of Philosophy. Holding such educational ideas as these, Plato naturally made his lectures unintelligible to all but a few : his main subject for public exposition seems to have been that curious mathematical metaphysic which Aristotle combats as Platonic, although it is nowhere found in the extant dialogues. By reading the *Metaphysics* of Aristotle the modern inquirer can perhaps realise how difficult Plato's lectures must have been.[2]

At the school in the Akademeia, Plato seems to have instructed his lads chiefly in Logic and Mathematics. Logic consisted chiefly of definitions, such as those for which Sokrates was always hunting, and that curious

[1] The popular attitude may be seen in Amphis' *Amphrikates* (Diog. Laert. iii. 25) : " I no more know what good you'll get than I know what Plato's Good is."

[2] Plato seems also to have recited his dialogues in public. Favonius asserted that Aristotle alone of the audience stayed to the end when Plato thus delivered the *Phaidon* (Diog. Laert. iii. 25).

process of "division" which is exemplified at such length in the *Sophist* and *Politikos*. Diogenes Laertius [1] gives a long catalogue of such divisions, of which only a few can be found in extant works : the rest must have figured in the school, and survived as traditions in the commentaries. A comic poet has left a picture of the logic school at work [2] :—

"*A.* What of Plato and Speusippos and Menedemos ? Upon what are they now engaged ? What is their thought ? What argument is investigated among them ? Tell me, I pray, if you know.

"*B.* I can tell you clearly. For at the Panathenaia I saw a herd (ἀγέλη : note the Spartan word) of lads in the gymnasium of the Akademeia, and listened to strange, portentous arguments. They were drawing up definitions about natural history. They separated the life of animals and the nature of trees and the tribes of vegetables : then, among these last, they inquired to what tribe the cucumber belonged. . . . First of all they stood speechless, and, putting their heads down, thought for a long time. Then suddenly, while the lads still had their heads down, and were thinking, one of them said it was a circular vegetable, another declared that it was a herb, another suggested a tree. A Sicilian Doctor who was present ridiculed them most rudely. But the lads took no notice ; and Plato, very gently and without losing his temper at all, told them to try again to define the species to which it belonged. So they began their divisions again."

In the *Sophist* the mysterious stranger divides Art into (1) creative or productive, (2) acquisitive. Then acquisitive art into (1) acquisition by exchange, (2) acquisition by capture. Then the art which acquires

---

[1] Diog. Laert. iii. 45, etc.   [2] Epikrates (in Athen. 59 d, e).

its object by capture is divided into public or competitive
and secret or hunting. Then, when hunting has been
duly divided and subdivided, a definition of angling is
obtained. In the parody by Epikrates, the same process
is employed in order to define "cucumber," although
the stages are, of course, confused. A cucumber is a
form of life. Life is divided into animals and vegetation : vegetation into trees and vegetables. Then the
doubt arises, to which half does the cucumber belong.
Some of the pupils say it is a vegetable, some a tree.
So the lesson begins again.

Plato's pupils seem to have been expected to take
great care of their personal appearance : their neatness
is a common butt of contemporary comedians [1] : —

> Then rose a smart young man from the Akademeia
> Of Plato. . . .
> His hair was neatly smoothed, his foot was neatly
> Laced in the sandal, bound with even lengths
> Of shoe-lace curved about his ankle-bones :
> And neat the corselet of his weighty cloak.

And again :

> A. Who's that old fellow yonder, do you know ?
> B. He looks a Hellene, wears a mantle white,
>   A fair grey tunic, little soft felt hat,
>   A well-tuned [2] staff, in fact, to put it short,
>   'Tis like a glimpse of the "Academy." [3]

Of Plato himself, as he walked up and down among
his pupils, wrestling with intellectual difficulties, several
pictures survive in literature. A character in Alexis [4]
remarks to a friend who has come to visit him :

---

[1] Ephippos, *Shipwrecked Man* (Athen. 509).

[2] εὔρυθμος, probably a hit at Plato's demand for "rhythm."

[3] Antiphanes, *Antaros* (Athen. 545 a).

[4] Alexis, *Meropis* (Diog. Laert. iii. 22).

You've come in the nick of time. I'm in a fix.
Though walking up and down, like Plato, I've
Found nothing clever : but my legs are tired.[1]

Amphis, in his *Dexidemides*, said :

Plato, all you can do is to frown, drawing up your eyebrows
severely, like a shellfish.[2]

The psychological yearning of the *Phaidon*, per-
petually interrupted by cold currents of scepticism,
must have found an echo in Plato's school-teaching, as
the following dialogues from Comedy show [2] :—

A.   My mortal frame grew dry :
     My deathless part rushed forth into the air.
B.   Why, bless us, are we in the school of Plato ?

And

A.   You're a man, clearly, and have got a soul.
B.   Like Plato, I don't know but I suspect it.[2]

Of discipline in the Akademeia under Plato nothing
is known : the following story [3] belongs to the school
a little after his death. A certain Polemon agreed with
some young friends of his, who attended the school,
that he would rush into the room during the lesson,
drunk and garlanded. This he carried out. But the
teacher, Xenokrates, went calmly on with his lecture,
which happened to deal with Sobriety. This conduct
quite overcame Polemon, and he became a most diligent
pupil, and finally succeeded Xenokrates as teacher.

Of Plato's affection for his pupils, his own poems
afford sufficient proof. One of them was named Aster,
or Star. One day, as the lad was studying the heavens,
his master wrote the following epigram about him :—

---

[1] This walking up and down was characteristic of Hellenic teaching. Compare
the *Peripatetics*, and Archutas in the temple-gardens at Tarentum (Athen. 545 b).

[2] Diog. Laert. iii. 22.   [3] *Ibid.* iv. 3. 1.

> Star of my soul, thou gazest
> Upon the starry skies ;
> I envy Heaven, that watches
> Thy face with countless eyes.

And when he died, Plato wrote his epitaph :

> Thou wert the morning Star among the living,
> Ere thy fair light had fled :
> Now, being dead, thou art as Hesperus, giving
> New splendour to the dead.[1]

Additional evidence is given by his efforts on behalf of Dionusios and Dion, which led him into so many perils in Sicily.

Plato was teaching in Athens almost continually from 388 till 347. His pupils included, no doubt, many of the chief men of the day : Chabrias, Iphikrates, Hupereides, Phokion, Lukourgos, and Demosthenes are mentioned, besides the philosophers Speusippos, Xenokrates, Herakleides of Pontos, and Aristotle. But posterity ascribed pupils recklessly to all the great teachers of antiquity, so the catalogue carries little weight. It is interesting to observe that the school as a whole was attacked for producing tyrants : the bitter description of the miseries of tyranny in the *Republic* are at once a sad reflection upon former pupils and a warning to those whom he was instructing at the time. But the Philosopher-king, who embodied Plato's ideal form of Government, may well have had a corrupting influence upon the pupils. Dion, the philosopher and patriot who became a tyrant, is an interesting commentary upon the *Republic*.

Teaching in the Akademeia was given gratuitously ; but those who were so disposed might give presents to

---

[1] The first translation is my own, the second Shelley's.

their teacher. Dionusios presented Plato with over 80 talents.[1]

The school of Aristotle in the Lukeion differed little in its methods from the school of Plato in the Akademeia. He had been a pupil of Plato for twenty years before he began to teach on his own account. He used to give instruction walking up and down in the walks of the Lukeion. In his earlier period, at any rate, he seems to have taught rhetoric, and taught it in Isocratean fashion : we hear of him setting a theme, on which he and the pupils delivered harangues "in rhetorical fashion." Later the school became a home of universal knowledge and research ; in this respect Aristotle is the heir of the much-abused Sophists. He adopted Xenokrates' custom of appointing one of the pupils to be Archon of the school for ten days, and then another : this system must have relieved him of much petty business.[2] He delivered two courses of lectures daily : one in the morning on abstruse subjects to picked pupils ; and the other in the afternoon, open to all comers and more intelligible in matter and manner.[3] His fame as a teacher was sufficient to win him the honour of being chosen to be Alexander's tutor, and he seems to have retained his pupil's respect, if not perhaps his affection. Aristotle, dreaming of a tiny city-state, and Alexander, dreaming of a world-empire and carrying out his dream, are an ill-assorted pair. What would Plato have given for the chance of educating such a Philosopher-king ?

That there were bitter feuds between the various educational leaders in Athens, goes without saying. A

---

[1] Saturos and Onetor in Diog. Laert. iii. 11.

[2] The above details are mainly from Diog. Laert. v.

[3] Aul. Gell. xx. 5. 4.

Hellene could no more brook a rival than could an
Italian of the Renaissance. Isokrates attacks Plato,[1]
Plato Isokrates, and then their pupils take the quarrel
on into the next generation. Both attack with equal
animus the wandering Sophists and the Eristics, who
retaliated with vigour. A would-be pupil must have
found it hard to choose a professor under whom to
study, when so much evil had been spoken of them all.[2]

The schools of Rhetoric and of Philosophy were
only for the rich and the leisured classes : the poor had
neither the time nor the money requisite for attending
them. But they were not wholly debarred from the
higher knowledge. There were still Sophists lecturing
for advertisement in public places. Still more, there
were books, which were beginning to be both numerous
and cheap : every Athenian could read. How important a part books were beginning to take in national
education may be seen from the works of Isokrates and
Plato, who are both excessively indignant at the intrusion
of such a rival.

" I know that what is read has less power of persuasion than what is heard. It is universally believed that
a speech, if actually delivered, deals with serious and
important subjects ; but if only written and never
spoken, it is supposed to aim merely at effect and the
fulfilment of a contract. This opinion is quite reasonable. For the written speech is deprived of the prestige
of the author's presence and of his voice and of the
proper rhetorical delivery : it is read when the occasion
which called it forth is past, and the points which it

[1] Plato had also his feuds with Antisthenes, who wrote a dialogue against him,
calling him Satho, with Aristippos, and with Aischines the Sokratic (Diog. Laert.
iii. 24).
[2] Kriton feels this difficulty in *Euthud.* 306 D, E.

discusses are consequently less interesting.   The slave
who reads it aloud puts no character into it, but drones
it out as though he were reckoning up the items of a
bill." -Such is Isokrates' view, somewhat freely translated, of " the written word," which his shyness
compelled him to use instead of the spoken, and he
beseeches Philip of Macedon, whom he is addressing,
to put aside the usual prejudice against writings.

Plato regarded the written word with even greater
contempt.   To him it is the cause of forgetfulness ;
those who employ writing learn to rely on their notes,
not on their memory, and are accustomed to register
their impressions on tables of wax, not of the mind.[1]
Again, it is impossible for an author to control the
circulation of his works ; they may reach those for
whom they are not intended.[2]   For Plato expects
speaker and writer alike to express only what is suitable
to their audience ; the teacher must, by a study of
psychology, know what arguments will do good and
what will do harm to each particular pupil.   But a
book cannot impart knowledge, in the Platonic sense
of the word, at all ; for it is unable to answer questions
or to explain its author's meaning when the reader fails
to follow.[3]   Comprehension of a fact or of a statement
made on a writer's authority, without comprehension
of the meaning and the explanation, is not knowledge.[4]
Consequently, not even a lecture [5] or a sermon, far less
a book whose author is absent or dead, can impart
knowledge ; to gain this, long study and a severe course
of dialectic are essential.   The possessor of true know-

---

[1] Plato, *Phaidr.* 275 A.   [2] *Ibid.* 275 E.

[3] Plato, *Phaidr.* 275 D ; *Theait.* 164 ; *Protag.* 329 A, and 347 E.

[4] So book-knowledge is a hothouse plant which has sprung up unnaturally all in a
moment, and very delicate when exposed to the open air of criticism (*Phaidr.* 276-7).

[5] Plato, *Sophist,* 230 A.

ledge must be able to defend his view against any
opposing arguments and to support it by discussion
himself : [1] neither book nor lecture can give this intimate
acquaintance with every point of view. Moreover,
teaching is like agriculture. There are different soils
and different minds. The seed of knowledge will bear
different fruit in different soils, and there are types of
minds in which some particular seeds must not be sown
at all. Thus the same teacher will produce quite
different philosophical results in different minds : just
as Sokrates did with his various pupils. It is the
development of the individual intellect and aptitudes
of each pupil, not the inculcation of his own theories,
that is the teacher's true object.[2] Consequently, even
a consistent scheme of dogmas is wrong for educational
purposes ; for it may suit the intellect of the teacher
himself, but it cannot suit all his pupils.

Hence, in order to be consistent with his own
educational ideals, Plato makes his works inconsistent :
they are not a body of rigid dogmas. Also, he provides
in them just that discussion which he notes as lacking
in most books ; it is possible to ask his books a certain
number of questions, for he anticipates and answers
them himself in the dialogue. In this way he makes
his words pass through the alembic [3] of each pupil's
brain, and come out according to the type of mind
through which they have passed. There is no enforce-
ment of authority in true Platonism.

Plato refused to publish any philosophy in his own
name. By speaking through the mouth of others, he
could vary his attitudes just as he wished. The written
word, he declares, must necessarily contain much trifling.

---

[1] Plato, *Menon*, 97 ; *Rep.* 534 B, C.   [2] Plato, *Rep.* 518.
[3] Plato, *Phaidr.* 277 A.

Its composition is a good amusement for leisure hours.[1] Its one use is that it serves to remind the writer of what he knows already, when the forgetfulness of old age comes upon him. But the writer is quite worthless if he possesses nothing better in his mind than what he has written on paper,[2] "twisting words up and down, glueing them together and pulling them apart."[3]

Books, however, were already serious rivals to personal intercourse, as a means of education. The libraries founded by Peisistratos at Athens and by Polukrates at Samos were, it is true, almost certainly fabulous ; for Euripides was satirised for possessing a collection of books, so it must have been a novelty in his time. Books were probably very rare before the Periclean age, but then they multiplied with great rapidity. The children used them in the schools. Schoolmasters were expected to possess them : Alkibiades beat one for not having a copy of Homer. The comic poet Alexis makes Herakles' master, Linos, possess copies of Orpheus, Hesiod, the tragedians, Choirilos, Homer, Epicharmos, and all sorts of prose works, including a cookery-book. A cargo of books was wrecked at Salmudessos,[4] a fact which points to a large book-trade in Hellenic waters. Euthudemos, the companion of Sokrates, possessed a fine collection of the best-known poets and Sophists, including the works of Homer.[5] Sokrates suggests that he may be collecting his books in order to learn Medicine, on which subject there were many treatises, or Architecture or Geometry or

[1] Plato, *Phaidr.* 276 D, E.

[2] Plato apparently regarded his dialogues as mere trifles compared with what he taught to his inner circle.

[3] Plato, *Phaidr.* 278 D.

[4] Xen. *Anab.* vii. 5. 14.

[5] Xen. *Mem.* iv. 2.

Astronomy. This shows how handbooks dealing with all manner of subjects were multiplying.

Xenophon's treatise on *The Horse* had been preceded by a similar work by Simon ;[1] he himself also wrote on *Hunting*, on *The Duties of a Cavalry Officer*, on *The Management of a Farm*, and *The Constitution of Sparta*, besides his more definitely historical and philosophical works. His *Education of Kuros* conceals a treatise on the duties of a general. The subjects are significant of the new movement ; for earlier Hellenes had supposed that Homer and Hesiod taught the whole art of agriculture and generalship. Other agricultural treatises, containing much theory but very little practical knowledge, were also in circulation.[2] Later in the fourth century Aineias the Tactician contributed a manual for generals. Medical treatises emanated in great numbers from the school of Hippokrates, and probably from elsewhere. Chares and Apollodoros published works on Husbandry,[3] Mithaikos a *Sicilian Cookery - Book*,[4] Metrodoros a book of Homeric allegories. Books of travels and geography are also mentioned by Aristotle.[5] Handbooks on " Rhetoric " were first compiled by Korax and Tisias : they dealt with the subject of " arguments from probability." Show pieces were written by Antiphon and Gorgias. A treatise by Polos upon the systematic arrangement of a speech was read by Sokrates. Thrasumachos published a work upon *Appeals to Compassion*.

The prices were probably not high, for the labour of copying could be cheaply performed by means of slaves. Sokrates, in the Platonic Apology,[6] mentions that a

[1] Xen. *Horsemanship*, i.
[2] Xen. *Econ.* xvi.
[3] Aristot. *Pol.* i. 11. 7.
[4] Plato, *Gorg.* 518 B.
[5] Aristot. *Pol.* ii. 3. 9.
[6] Plato, *Apol.* 26 D.

copy of Anaxagoras could sometimes be picked up for a drachma ; and there is no reason to suppose that Anaxagoras was particularly cheap. If this was an average price, books must have been within the reach of most Athenians.

CHAPTER VII

TERTIARY EDUCATION

WHEN he reached eighteen years, the young Athenian partly came of age. His property passed into his possession, if he had been a ward, and he could now prosecute his guardians if they had defrauded him. But he could not appear in any other sort of lawsuit, or take part in the National Assembly, nor could he be taxed, till he was twenty.

First of all, his deme or parish had to examine him to see if he was of proper parentage and of the requisite age.[1] If they rejected him, the case came before the regular Court of Athens. In the event of being again rejected, if it was on the score of age, he returned to the ranks of the boys to wait a further trial, but if on the score of parentage, he might be sold as a slave and his price put into the Treasury. If his deme accepted him he was again examined by the Boule of 500 at Athens, who might rescind their decision.[2]

When he had passed all these preliminary examinations, the boy was inscribed upon the roll of his deme, the ληξιαρχικὸν γραμματεῖον, and became in the eyes of the law an ephebos. It was then incumbent upon him to take a solemn oath in the temple of Aglauros, in the following terms[3] :—

[1] Aristot. 'Aθ. Πολ. 42 for these examinations.
[2] Luk. ag. Leok. 18. 76.   [3] Pollux, viii. 105-106, etc.

"I will not disgrace my sacred weapons nor desert the comrade who is placed by my side. I will fight for things holy and things profane, whether I am alone or with others. I will hand on my fatherland greater and better than I found it. I will hearken to the magistrates, and obey the existing laws and those hereafter established[1] by the people. I will not consent unto any that destroys or disobeys the constitution, but will prevent him, whether I am alone or with others. I will honour the temples and the religion which my forefathers established. So help me Aglauros, Enualios, Ares, Zeus, Thallo, Auxo, Hegemone."

This oath and ceremony must be ancient. The orator Lukourgos[2] includes them among "the ancient laws and customs of the original founders," and claims that the oath of the Hellenic army at Plataea in 479 was imitated from the oath of the Athenian epheboi. By this solemn act the ephebos accepted the duties and responsibilities of an Athenian citizen. So in Plato's dialogue, the *Kriton*,[3] where the Laws of Athens are introduced as pleading their cause, they say, "When any one has passed his examination, and has seen the constitution of the city and us, the Laws of Athens, we bid him, if he is dissatisfied with us, to take what is his and go whither he pleases. But if he stays, we consider that he has promised to obey us." For there is good evidence, besides that which is afforded by the above passage, to show that Athenian boys were taught what the laws of their city were, before they promised to obey them. Thus Aischines says : "When any one is inscribed upon the muster roll of his deme and knows the laws of the city."[4] Plato puts it even more

---

[1] κραίνοντες. Note the archaic word.
[3] Plato, *Krit.* 51 D, E.
[2] Luk. *ag. Leok.* 18. 75.
[4] Aischin. *ag. Timarch.* 18.

definitely : " When the children leave school,[1] the city compels them to learn the laws." [2] So the ephebos knew what he was doing when he swore to obey the law of the land.

Meanwhile the tribes had met and each chosen three men of over forty years of age, from whom the assembled people elected one, to look after the epheboi of each tribe.[3] These supervisors were called Sophronistai or Moderators. That these Moderators probably dated back to Solonic times, and possessed a general, but rarely exercised, supervision over all education, I have endeavoured to show in Chapter II. Their province was the morality and discipline of the epheboi, whose military training was naturally controlled by the military officers, the Generals and Taxiarchoi ; later, however, when the epheboi ceased to be a military body, these latter functionaries ceased to have any connection with them. Towards the close of the fourth century the people elected a single Kosmetes or Chancellor for the epheboi ; he is first mentioned, if a probably spurious passage in the *Axiochos* is rejected, in an inscription, in which he is associated with the epheboi and Moderators of the year in awarding a crown to Theophanes in the Archonship of Nikostratos (333-332 B.C.).[4] But in 280 B.C., in the list of the officers and masters of the epheboi, the Kosmetes is mentioned, but no Sophronistai : [5] at that time the epheboi were too few to need an officer to each tribe.

---

[1] I have already suggested that metrical versions may have been taught at the music-schools.

[2] Plato, *Protag.* 326 D. Boys used to listen to cases in the law-courts. This would give them some idea of legal procedure. (Compare the custom at some English public schools of letting the boys go to hear the local assizes.) Demosthenes thus went with his paidagogos to hear the trial of Kallistratos.

[3] Aristot. ʼΑθ. Πολ. 42. 2.   [4] *C.I.A.* iv. ii. 1571 B.

[5] *C.I.A.* ii. 316.

These newly appointed magistrates took the epheboi of their year in charge at once. The young recruits were first taken round the temples, and then put into garrison in Mounuchia and Peiraieus. They had masters and under-masters appointed for them by the Sophronistai to teach them the use of heavy arms, and also of the bow, javelin, and catapult. There were also two Paido-tribai, for gymnastics. These masters, together with later introductions such as literary teachers, chaplains, doctors, and so forth, appear regularly in the inscriptions after 300 B.C.[1] The Sophronistai were paid a drachma a day for their services. They also received four obols for every ephebos in their tribe, out of which they had to provide the rations, etc. ; the ephebos did not handle the money himself. Each tribe messed together.[2]

Besides the Sophronistai and Kosmetes, the Council of the Areiopagos also kept a watch over the epheboi. Discipline seems to have been fairly strict : the *Axiochos*[3] talks of "rods and immensities of evils." But there were plenty of amusements, and, apparently, plenty of vacations. There were a very large number of special festivals, in which the epheboi took part. There were also the torch-races at the feasts of Hephaistos and Prometheus, for teams of epheboi from each tribe, trained at the expense of a gumnasiarchos. The epheboi had also a special part of the theatre reserved for them.[4]

No doubt a large part of the time of these epheboi was spent in severe physical exercise in the gymnasia. The analogy of the epheboi in Plato's *Republic* and *Laws* would suggest this. The *Axiochos* mentions, as consequent upon enrolment in the epheboi, "the Lukeion and Akademeia," *i.e.* practices in these

---

[1] e.g. *C.I.A.* ii. 316. 338.
[2] Aristot. 'Αθ. Πολ. 42. 3.
[3] [Plato] *Axiochos*, 367 A.
[4] Schol. on Aristoph. *Birds*, 794.

gymnasia. Xenophon,[1] just before mentioning the
" peripoloi " or epheboi in their second year, talks of
" those who are ordered to practise gymnastic exercises," clearly referring to this period. He suggests
that their duties would be better and more cheerfully
performed if they received a larger supply of rations
than those who were training for torch-races ; to these
latter no doubt a liberal gumnasiarchos might serve
out meals costing much more than four obols a day.
Probably those who were physically inferior alone were
told off for these compulsory gymnastics : Xenophon's
phrase seems to distinguish them from the epheboi
selected for the torch-race, who would naturally be the
physically fittest in the tribal contingent.

At the end of their first year of training, the epheboi
appeared in the theatre at the great Dionusia to show
off their military evolutions and the drill which they
had learned. After the review they received a spear
and shield from the State.[2] The sons of those who
had fallen in battle, being the wards of the State,[3]
received a complete outfit of armour. These arms,
which the epheboi received from the State, were
considered to be sacred : consequently to throw away
the shield in flight was regarded as a serious offence,
almost an act of sacrilege.[4]

After receiving their arms from the State, the
epheboi were marched out of Athens, and spent most
of the next year patrolling the country and frontiers,
and garrisoning the forts.[5] Attica was studded with

---

[1] Xen. *Revenues*, iv. 52.   [2] Aristot. 'Aθ. Πολ. 42. 4.   [3] Thuc. ii. 46.

[4] Lucias, x. 1, and Aristophanes anent Kleonumos, *passim*.

[5] Properly speaking, it was only during his second year that the ephebos was a
peripolos or patrol. Aischines, however, claims to have served two years as a
peripolos. The term may have been used loosely, or else in times of crisis the
epheboi may have been hurried off to the frontier as soon as they were enrolled.

PLATE IX.

A RIDING LESSON—MOUNTING

Archæologische Zeitung, 1885, Plate 11.

From a Kulix at Munich, attributed to Euphronios.

these περιπόλια or patrol-stations, from Oinoé and Phulé on the north-western frontier to Anaphlustos and Thorikos in the south. The epheboi, like the κρυπτοί in Plato's *Laws* and at Sparta, were shifted about from district to district, in order that they might acquire a thorough knowledge of their country's geographical peculiarities. The tribal companies, into which they were divided, relieved one another in various stations. Thus in the course of 334-333 we know that both the Hippothontid and the Kekropid tribes were successively stationed at Eleusis, for the people of that district pass two separate votes of thanks to them for the excellent discipline which they had preserved.[1]   There may also have been open-air camps : the Eleusinian inscriptions talk of ὑπαίθριοι.

The epheboi seem to have been assisted in their patrol-duties by a mercenary force of foreigners. Thucydides[2] declares that Phrunichos was assassinated by a peripolos : the Athenian people, according to Lusias, rewarded Thrasuboulos of Kaludon as the slayer and recorded his name on a pillar.[3]   If the historian had meant to dispute this award, he must have referred to it, for it was clearly the accepted version. He also states that the plot was arranged at the house of the captain of the peripoloi, and mentions an Argive as one of the accomplices : Lusias mentions a Megarian. Both these foreigners were probably peripoloi. But foreign youths cannot at this period have been permitted to serve with the tribal companies of epheboi. A legend, it is true, asserts that this privilege was granted to the young men of Kos, in honour of the great doctor Hippokrates ; but even

[1] *C.I.A.* iv. ii. 574 D, and 563 B.
[2] Thuc. viii. 92.   [3] Lusias, xiii. 71.

this only shows that all other states were excluded. Indeed, foreigners were not enrolled among the Athenian epheboi until a much later epoch, when the system was no longer military.

What, then, was this " Foreign Legion " ?   M. Girard identifies it with the Mounted Archers, on the strength of a passage in Aristophanes' *Birds*.   An unknown deity has invaded the territory of Cloud-Cuckoo town.   Peisthetairos exclaims, " Why didn't you despatch peripoloi after him at once ? "   To which the messenger replies, " We did send 30,000 Mounted Archers."   The inscriptions at Eleusis also make a force of non-citizen troops serve under the captain of the peripoloi.   These mercenary troops, having no civil duties, would naturally be used as a patrol.   More-over, to an Athenian, " archer " meant " policeman." Athens was policed by foreign " Archers ": it would be natural for Attica to be policed in like manner, only by a mounted force, as a greater distance had to be covered.[1]   But it is also possible that the non-Athenian peripoloi were the sons of μέτοικοι ἰσοτελεῖς, who, being forced to serve as hoplites when grown up, would require some preliminary training ; these alien hoplites are coupled by Thucydides[2] with the recruits and veterans, who garrisoned the Athenian walls and forts : they seem to have served as a perpetual patrol.

The first three classes of Athenian citizens in wealth must all have passed through this training ; for, although the two first were liable to cavalry service, they might also be called upon to serve as hoplites.[3] Rich young epheboi, who had plenty of time on their

[1] The force may also have included citizens, for the younger Alkibiades once served in it (Lus. xv. 6).   But that was a special occasion, when the ordinary cavalry had refused to receive him.

[2] Thuc. ii. 13. 6-7.   [3] Lus. xvi. 13, xiv. 10.

hands, would naturally learn both cavalry and infantry drill. The poorer Zeugitai would only have to learn their duties as heavy infantry, and were probably allowed to spend a good proportion of their time on their farms in Athens. But what about the fourth class, the Thetes? They were not liable to be called out as hoplites, but had to serve on land as light-armed troops or at sea as rowers. Did they also have a recruit course? Now the garrisons of the Athenian forts and walls were hoplites :[1] there is no trace of the Thetes here. But the patrol duties in the mountains can hardly have been performed by heavy troops : it is noticeable that in Xenophon light troops are suggested for this purpose, when Sokrates is developing an elaborate scheme for holding the frontiers of Attica against all invaders.[2] In the next century, at any rate, light troops were used for this purpose. In a later work Xenophon talks of "those who are ordered to occupy the forts and those who have to serve as peltasts and patrol the country,"[3] in a passage where he is clearly referring to the epheboi. Thus there are two classes, the garrisons, who would naturally be hoplites, and the patrols, who are peltasts, suitably equipped for mountaineering. But the peltasts only began to appear towards the close of the Peloponnesian War : the first mention of them is in Thucydides' account of the army of Brasidas. Before this time, the light troops were archers and some slingers ; thus, in the monument to those of the Erechtheid tribe who fell in the year 459, after the hoplites four archers are mentioned.[4] But they were a small force : there

---

[1] Thuc. ii. 13. 6-7.   [2] Xen. *Mem.* iii. 5. 27.
[3] Xen. *Revenues*, iv. 52.
[4] *C.I.A.* i. 143. Cp. *C.I.A.* i. 79 for citizen-archers.

were only 1600 of them in 431 B.C. The majority of the Thetes served in the ships. In the *Birds* of Aristophanes, which appeared in 414, when it was a question of repelling a sudden raid, just after the peripoloi have been mentioned, Peisthetairos bids his immediate attendants arm themselves with slings and bows: these are clearly the weapons for a flying column despatched in pursuit of raiders.[1]

The passage of Xenophon makes it clear that there were peltasts in the ephebic force in the fourth century ; that of Aristophanes suggests the probability of archers and slingers among them in the fifth. But whether these light - armed troops consisted of enterprising Zeugitai who added this training to their hoplite drill, or were a small detachment of Thetes, cannot be fixed. Thetes must, at any rate, not have been numerous in the ephebic force, for they could not have spared the time necessary for such lengthy training.[2]

As a rule, the epheboi were not expected to do more than guard the frontier and repel an occasional foray : even this, however, must have given them plenty of employment in war-time. But they shared in Muronides' great victory in the Megarid in 458, when Athens had to use her reserves.[3] Either they or the " foreign legion " joined in a later invasion of Megara.[4] But as a rule they served for home defence only. Their recruit-course ended with their twentieth year : henceforth they were ordinary Athenian citizens and soldiers.

In about 332 B.C., when Lukourgos delivered his speech against Leokrates, the old ephebic system seems

---

[1] It is noticeable that in Aristotle's time the epheboi were taught by a " Teacher of Archery." He may be a survival.

[2] In Boiotia and the Megarid the epheboi served as cavalry, hoplites, or peltasts (*C.I.G.* Boiot. and Meg. 2715, 2717-21, 1747-48, etc.).

[3] Thuc. i. 105.   [4] *Ibid.* iv. 67.

still to have been in force. The suggestion that
Leokrates might have evaded the ephebic oath is only
rhetorical, for the orator immediately goes on to assume
that he took it.[1] In 328, the probable date of Aristotle's
Athenian Constitution, it seems still to have been in
existence, for the philosopher records it as part of the
contemporary regime. The inscriptions support these
authorities. A list of epheboi of the Kekropid tribe
enrolled in 334 is given under the vote of thanks :
the upper part of the list is gone, but the numbers were
apparently large.[2] Some forty-four names can be inferred from the fragments, belonging to six or seven
demes out of the twelve which composed the tribe ; but
apparently the smallest contingents are at the bottom,
so there may well have been a hundred names in the
tribe, and 1000 epheboi altogether. Considering the
impoverishment of Attica and the consequent decrease
in the hoplite classes, this is probably a fair proportion
of epheboi.[3] A tribal contingent is still large enough
to serve as a garrison for Eleusis, and to act by itself.

But in the next century the numbers drop down to
twenty-nine and twenty-three. The service must have
been voluntary. Moreover, brothers are found serving
together, from which it may be inferred that the exact
age qualification was no longer regarded.[4] Philosophy
and literature become subjects of study ; and a
library, swollen by gifts from old epheboi, is collected.
Foreigners begin to be enrolled in the second century,

---

[1] Luk. *ag. Leok.* 76.   [2] *C.I.A.* iv. ii. 563 b.

[3] In 431 B.C. Athens had 13,000 hoplites of between twenty and forty years of
age. On this average there would be perhaps about 1000 epheboi per year, or 2000
altogether—the same number as here. The 16,000 of the reserve in 431 includes
veterans and metics as well as epheboi.

[4] The changes seem to have happened shortly before 305, for in an inscription
of that year the numbers have dropped greatly and brothers serve together.

and in course of time outnumber the native Athenians. Although the old military service is preserved, no doubt in a mummified condition, the system of the epheboi develops into the Athenian university, where young Romans like Cicero's son came to learn philosophy, though they had little to learn from Athens in military matters. The Sophronistai and Kosmetes become the Proctors and Chancellor, the special festivals the compulsory services, of the new University. The torch-races, the military duties, and the naval races [1] become its athletics. It is the old conscription system of Athens, not the schools of Plato or Isokrates, that gives birth to the first University.

The system of epheboi was represented at Sparta by the κρυπτοί. We hear of an archephebos at Argos, and a gumnasiarchos who manages the epheboi at Troizen.[2] In the Megarid and in Boiotia the epheboi were trained as cavalry, hoplites, or peltasts.[3] An ephebarchos can be traced in Teos. There were patrol-houses, and so possibly epheboi patrols in the territory of Syracuse.[4] This period of special training for military duties seems to have been general all over Hellas. Plato adopts it without demur in the *Republic* and *Laws*.

[1] *C.I.A.* ii. 466. 470.
[3] See note 2 on p. 218.
[2] *C.I.G.* Pelop. 589, 749, 753.
[4] Thuc. vi. 45, vii. 48.

THE EPHEBIC INSCRIPTIONS OF THE
FOURTH CENTURY

(Dealing with Attica only)

I. *C.I.A.* IV. ii. 574 d.

" The epheboi of the Hippothontid tribe, who were enrolled
when Ktesikles was Archon (334-333 B.C.), having been
crowned by the Boule and Demos, offered this offering."

Then follows a mutilated vote of thanks from the people
of Eleusis to the epheboi for the discipline which they had
preserved while garrisoning the town, and to their Sophronistes,
who is to receive a crown, and to have a front seat at local
festivals.

II. *C.I.A.* IV. ii. 563 b.

Decrees in honour of the epheboi of the Kekropid tribe.

(*a*) By the Kekropid tribe.

" Kallikrates of Aixoné proposed. Whereas the epheboi
of the Kekropid tribe, who were enrolled when Ktesikles was
Archon (334-333 B.C.), are orderly and do everything that the
laws enjoin upon them, and are obedient to the Sophronistes
appointed by the people, we pass a vote of thanks to them and
crown them with a golden crown of 500 drachmas for their
excellent discipline and behaviour. We also pass a vote of
thanks to the Sophronistes, Adeistos, son of Antimachos, and
award him a golden crown of the aforesaid weight, for that he
hath well and diligently directed the epheboi of the Kekropid
tribe. This vote to be recorded on a stone pillar and set
up in the shrine of Kekrops."

(b) Vote of the Athenian people.

" Hegemachos, son of Chairemon, proposed. Whereas the epheboi of the Kekropid tribe stationed at Eleusis do well and diligently pay heed to the orders of the Boule and Demos, and do behave themselves orderly, we pass a vote of thanks to them for their good discipline and behaviour, and enact that each of them be crowned with an olive crown. We also pass a vote of thanks to their Sophronistes, Adeistos, son or Antimachos, and decree to him a crown of olive, when he has passed his scrutiny. This vote to be recorded on the offering which the epheboi of the Kekropid tribe offer."

(c) Vote of Eleusinians.

" Protias proposed. Whereas the epheboi of the Kekropid tribe and their Sophronistes, Adeistos, son of Antimachos, do well and diligently garrison Eleusis, the people of the deme pass a vote of thanks to them and crown each of them with a crown of olive."

The vote to be recorded as before.

(d) Similar vote of the Athmonian deme in honour of their fellow-demesman, Adeistos.

With this is a list of the epheboi in question, much mutilated.

III. *C.I.A.* IV. ii. 1571 b.

" Theophanes, son of Hierophon, offered this to Hermes, having been crowned by the epheboi and Sophronistai and Kosmetai."

This is signed by the epheboi for the years 333-332, 332-331, and 331-330.

IV. *C.I.A.* IV. ii. 251 b.

A vote of thanks from the Boule and Demos to the epheboi as a whole for their exemplary behaviour, and to their Kosmetes and Sophronistai and teachers. A mutilated list of epheboi follows. This belongs to the year 305-304 B.C.

V. *C.I.A.* iv. ii. 565 b.

A vote of thanks of the Pandionid tribe to Philonides, who had been elected by the people Sophronistes of their epheboi, and had performed his duty well.

VI. Böckh, 214 (belonging to 320 B.C.).

(Dug up at Aixoné.)

An extract :—" We pass a vote of thanks to the Sophronistai and crown each of them with a crown of olive, namely, Kimon, son of Megakles, and Puthodoros, son of Putheas . . . for the zeal they showed in regard to the all-night revel."

The epheboi took part in a sacrifice and revel in honour of Hebe. Apparently, as a rule, they were noisy and gave trouble to the inhabitants of the neighbourhood. But this year they were kept in order by the Sophronistai. Hence the vote.

PART II

THE THEORY OF EDUCATION

CHAPTER VIII

THE greater part of the religious instruction in Hellas was given outside the schools, in the home and in public life. The child learnt the current ritual observances proper to each particular deity or occasion by participating in them himself. His religious devotion was practised and stimulated by the festivals and sacred songs and dances which made up so large a part of Hellenic life. In a religion like the Hellenic, which was so largely a matter of forms and ceremonies, there was little dogma to be learnt by children ; no catechism, no sectarian teaching was necessary. Such dogma as there was consisted in the myths which were current about the various deities and heroes ; and of these myths there were so many varieties that heterodoxy about them became almost impossible.

Such as it was, this dogma, consisting of manifold and often contradictory myths, was enshrined in the poetry of the race, so that most of the poems became sacred books, regarded by the orthodox as inspired. This sacred literature, as we have seen, was the chief object of study in the primary schools at Athens, where it was read, written, and learnt by heart. At Sparta almost the whole of literary and intellectual education consisted of sacred songs in honour of gods and heroes.

The myths were the very essence of primary education in Hellas.

In order to understand the attitude of the educational theorists towards these myths which run through most of the Hellenic poetry, it is necessary to realise the extraordinary authority which was given to the poets, and especially to Homer and Hesiod.   Every word of them was regarded as inspired and strictly true : their authority was indisputable.   At the beginning of the sixth century an interpolated line in the *Iliad* was made the main support of the Athenian claim to the Island of Salamis.   Gelon, the tyrant of Syracuse, according to the current legend, was refused the command of the Hellenic forces against Persia because, as the Spartan envoy put it, Agamemnon would groan if he heard of such a thing, and because Homer had said that an Athenian was the best man at drawing up and marshalling a host, for which cause the Athenians now claimed the command.[1]   That such arguments could be employed shows in what veneration Homer was held.   He was considered to be especially inspired.[2]   His admirers asserted that he had educated Hellas, and that his works provided fit instruction for the whole conduct of life.[3]   More specifically, it was said that " The divine Homer won his glory and renown from this, that he taught good things, drill, valour and the arming of troops." [4]   He was misquoted to support peculiar views, as in Plato.[5]   People had their favourite texts : Sokrates' was " In due proportion to thy means pay honour to the gods."   It was a not unheard-of accomplishment to know the whole *Iliad* and *Odyssey* by heart.

---

[1] Herod. vii. 159-161.   [2] Plato, *Ion*, 24 c.

[3] *Rep.* 606 ᴇ.   So in Isokrates, *To Nikokles*, 530 ʙ.

[4] Aristoph. *Frogs*, 1034-1036.   [5] Plato, *Rep.* 391 ʙ.

Moral lessons were drawn from them. Thus the story of Kirké was a warning against self-indulgence. Kirké made the companions of Odusseus swine through their over-indulgence in the pleasures of the table ; Odusseus himself, by Hermes' advice and his own self-restraint in such matters, escaped this fate.[1]

In time, however, the higher morality of the leading Hellenic thinkers revolted against the low morality, to say nothing more, of much of the mythology embodied in the poets. Xenophanes began the attack. "Homer and Hesiod," he cries, "ascribed to the gods all that is considered disgraceful among men." Herakleitos declared that Homer deserved a thrashing. Even the pious Pindar tried to alter some of the myths to suit his own morality, and Aeschylus fights hard for an underlying monotheism. In the next generation the storm broke : awakening intelligence, fostered by the Sophists and the philosophers, shrank away from the horrors of the *Theogony*. Tragedy, by bringing mythology before the eyes, had made its impossibility more apparent. The researches of the earlier historians in comparative mythology had undermined the bases of belief. Herodotos had found that a god named Herakles had been recognised in Egypt 17,000 years before his time ; consequently the Hellenic Herakles, only six centuries before the historian's age, must be only a man of the same name.[2] Rationalism began to master the mythology : Thucydides tried to apply scientific methods to the Trojan War, making, for

[1] Sokrates in Xenophon, *Mem.* i. 3, 7. The moralisation is quite un-Homeric.
[2] Herod. ii. 43-46. This tendency culminated in Euhemeros, at the end of the fourth century, who claimed to have found inscriptions in Crete giving the careers of mortal kings named Ouranos, Kronos, and Zeus. He argued that the gods were distinguished men, deified by admiring posterity. His theory passed to Rome in Ennius' translation and supported the imperial cult.

example, its duration due to the difficulty of obtaining
supplies for so large a force. The rationalism of
Euripides is well known. Metrodoros, a pupil of
Anaxagoras, made the gods natural forces and varieties
of matter—a device already employed by Empedokles
for poetical convenience. In this way Sokrates
rationalises the Boreas-myth in the *Phaidros*,[1] where
Plato states that the wise disbelieve such tales ; but
Sokrates was too busy studying his own personality
to raise all these numerous questions, so he accepts
the customary belief. The defenders of Homer, led
by Metrodoros and Stesimbrotos,[2] tried to allegorise
him, declaring that the worst myths had a moral
meaning in the background. The allegories were
often ludicrous : Plato rejects them wholly for educational purposes, as children always take the literal
interpretation.

But public opinion was still fiercely attached to the
old deities, as the incident of the Hermai and the
condemnation of Anaxagoras, Protagoras, and Sokrates
showed. The deities could not be sacrificed : consequently it was the myths that had to go. The myths
said that Zeus dethroned his own father and committed
adultery : if the myth is true, since Zeus is Supreme
God, these crimes are justifiable.[3] Therefore the myth
must be untrue. Homer and Hesiod lied : their works
are mainly a blasphemous fiction.[4] Isokrates[5] sums
up this new attitude. "The poets," he declares,
"blasphemously represented the sons of the Immortals
as having done and suffered worse deeds than the most
impious of men: they spoke such things about the

[1] Plato, *Phaidr.* 229 c.

[2] Plato, *Ion*, 530. Cp. Xen. *Banquet*, iii. 6, where Anaximandros is mentioned.

[3] Cp. Aristoph. *Clouds*, 905, 1080, representing "Sophist" arguments.

[4] Plato, *Rep.* 377 D.   [5] Isok. *Bous.* 228 D.

gods as no one would venture to allege of his worst enemy ; not only do they make them steal, commit adultery, and fall into slavery to mortals, but even represent them as eating their children, mutilating their fathers, and binding their mothers in chains. . . . For this the poets did not go unpunished, but some of them were wanderers and begged their bread, some became blind, another was an exile all his life long, and Orpheus, who devoted himself especially to such stories, was torn in pieces." [1]

The greatest objection to these immoral legends was that they were taught in the nursery and the elementary school, at the most impressionable age.[2] Hence Plato wishes to lay down strict canons for the myths, legends, and fables which are to be taught to children. " For the beginning of everything is half the battle, especially in the case of what is young and tender. Young children are like soft wax, ready to take a clear and deep impression of any seal which is laid upon them. Hence the immense importance of the earliest stages of education, the myths and stories taught in the nursery and at school. . . . The compositions of Homer and Hesiod are fiction, and unlovely fiction at that ; even if true, they had better not be told to the young and undiscerning. . . . The myths must be improving on the surface, not by allegory." [3]

Plato is not prepared to rewrite the Hellenic Bible : he will only draw up the canons which the poets must follow. It is to be noticed that these canons are peculiar, and would exclude not merely most of Homer and Hesiod, but a large part of the Old and some of

---

[1] Cp. the statement of Herodotos (ii. 53) that Homer and Hesiod created the details of Hellenic mythology, even the names and functions of the deities.

[2] Plato, *Rep.* 377 B.   [3] *Ibid.* 378.

the New Testament.   The first canon is that God, being good, cannot be the cause or originator of any harm or evil to mankind ; for these things some other cause must be discovered.   The greater part of the human lot is evil : so God is not the cause of the majority of human events.

This excludes Homer's lines :

Two butts of human fortunes by the gates of Heaven stood,
One full of all things evil, and one of all things good.
To whom God gives a mixture, his life is weal and woe,
But to whom He gives of the evil alone, he lives as a beggar below.

And

Zeus is the world's housekeeper, who serves out weal and woe.

And Aeschylus'

God plants the seed of sin among mankind,
Whene'er He wills to bring a race to naught.

If God is represented as the cause of misfortunes, the poet must say that the misfortunes were good for the sufferers, making them better and happier.[1]

The second canon is that God is not a wizard, appearing now in one form, now in another.   Why should He change ?   External forces are not likely to change Him : He would not change Himself, since it would necessarily be a transition to the less good and less beautiful, since He is perfect.   So the lines—

Disguised as human strangers, in many a changing guise,
Gods roam about the cities, to spy iniquities,

and the tales of Proteus and other metamorphoses, are false.   Consequently mothers should not tell their children that a god may always be present in disguise, for it is a lie and is also likely to make the children

[1] Plato, *Rep.* 380.

cowardly. Lying is only useful in dealing with enemies, for managing lunatics, and for making a satisfactory explanation where certainty is impossible. God has no such reason for lying or deception.

· The character of the Deity having been thus purged of mythological accretions, Plato passes on to the treatment of the future state. This must not be described as in any way terrible, or the children will learn to prefer dishonourable life to honourable death. So reject—

> O better be a poor man's serf, and share his scanty bread,
> Than be the crownèd king of all the nations of the dead.

And

> From him his soul bewailing her hapless fortunes fled,
> Her youth and beauty leaving, to the kingdoms of the dead !

All such passages must be expurgated from school editions ; nor is it right to admit the fearful scenery of Hell, the rivers of Hate (Styx) and Wailing (Kokutos), ghosts, banshees, and other terrible words, for fear of making the children nervous.

Then comes the discussion of the ideal man, in which Achilles falls from the pedestal which he had previously occupied as the ideal of Hellenic manhood. Great men must not indulge in immoderate lamentations for their dead friends. The lament of Achilles for Patroklos and of Priam for Hektor, when he rolled in the dust and the dungheap, must be rejected. " For if the young should take such stories seriously and not laugh them to scorn as contemptibly improbable, they would be most unlikely to consider such lamentations degrading, or to check themselves when they felt any impulse to act in such a way, but, without shame or restraint, they would whine out many dirges over tiny misfortunes." [1]

Nor must the heroes be made too fond of laughing. For immoderate laughter leads by reaction to immoderate grief. So reject—

> Then rose among the blessed gods a laugh unquenchable.

The myths must instil self-control, obedience to rulers and elders and to the better instincts. This leads Plato to expurgate—

> Thou drunkard, shameless as a dog, and fearful as a deer :

but commend—

> Good father, sit in silence, and hearken to what I say.

Then Homer teaches gluttony, by making Odusseus, the wisest of men, say—

> Best thing in life I count it, a heavy-laden board,
> While in the goblets ceaselessly the good strong wine is poured.

Still worse are the tales of the lusts of Zeus or of Ares and Aphrodite, and of the covetousness of the gods.

> Gifts win the heart of gods : gifts win the heart of kings.

Nor must the heroes be allowed to blaspheme. "My respect for Homer makes me shrink from saying it, but it is impious to state or to believe that Achilles was ready to fight against the river, a god, or that he dragged Hektor's body round Patroklos' tomb or slaughtered captives upon it, or that he gave to the dead Patroklos the hair which he had dedicated to the river god Spercheios." [2] Nor must poets say that

[1] Plato, *Rep.* 388 D.

[2] *Ibid.* 391 B. Plato maligns Achilles. He only promised the hair to Spercheios on condition that he returned home alive, which he knew he would not do if he slew Hektor.

wicked men are enviable, if they are not found out, or
that justice does good to others but is a loss to oneself.
On the contrary, they must invent myths to establish
the opposite, whether it be true or not, because it is
profitable.

Plato cares very little for literal truth in mythology ; he is only desirous that the fiction should be
improving and in accordance with sound ethics.   It
is impossible to know the truth, he thinks, about things
primeval and the gods, so it is necessary to invent stories
as near the truth as possible and such that they will be
improving.   The majority of men, as Isokrates also
noticed, prefer myths to anything else ; for their intelligence can only grasp ethical and metaphysical truths
when they are embodied in stories and parables and
fables.[1] These fictions, however, are like powerful drugs :
their concoction must only be entrusted to competent
hands, or the result will be deadly.   The rulers of the
State, the philosophers, must construct the national
mythology, not unskilled and irresponsible persons like
poets.[2]   Plato himself gives a good many instances
of such profitable myths ; he enshrines in them, as in
a popular form, many of his deepest beliefs, his
psychology,[3] his views of the immortality of the soul,[4]
his political theory that all men are not equal.[5]   In his
opinion mythology was the proper food for the un-
enlightened many who were incapable of philosophic
certainty ; the philosopher, by the light of his exact

---

[1] Compare Tennyson, *In Memoriam*, xxxvi. :

> For Wisdom dealt with mortal powers,
>   Where truth in closest words shall fail,
>   When truth embodied in a tale
> Shall enter in at lowly doors.

[2] Plato, *Rep.* 389 c.   [3] In the *Phaidros*.

[4] In the *Republic*, and elsewhere.

[5] *Rep.* 414-417, etc.   For the use which Plato made of myths as popular exposi-
tions of his views, cp. *Laws*, 663, 664, 713, 714, 716.

knowledge of ethics and metaphysics, was to concoct this food.

In pursuance of this theory an ideal character, in history or fiction, was required to personify and make real to the multitude the disembodied ideals of Ethics.[1] Achilles had been tumbled from his pedestal by philosophy. Who was to replace him? Plato tries to put an idealised Sokrates in this position, but he could not square the historical personality with the ideal man postulated in the *Republic*. Xenophon, also thinking that a pattern man is "an excellent invention for the study of morality," proposes Agesilaos.[2] Prodikos tried to make Herakles the model of the young. Aristotle formulated the μεγαλόψυχος, but never personified him. Stoicism sought for its Wise Man or Perfect Saint, but never found him; Epicureanism was satisfied with its founder. But the search for the personification of the ethical ideal becomes the central feature of Hellenic philosophy and religion from the time of Plato onwards.

---

[1] Isokrates recognised this too, *Antid.* 105 c.   [2] Xen. *Ag.* x. 2.

CHAPTER IX

SINCE poetry, music, singing, and dancing were the chief components of a Hellenic boy's education, the æsthetic canons by which these were regulated came to be of great importance in the moral history of Hellas, and were the objects of much thought and inquiry on the part of the educational theorists. It is hard for a modern reader to understand the attitude which Plato and Aristotle adopt towards poetry, art, and music, partly owing to the way in which these subjects are neglected in many modern schools, and still more owing to the immense changes which have taken place both in the subjects themselves and in their relations to the State as a whole.

In ancient Hellas art, literature, and music were addressed to the whole citizen-body, not to a cultured upper class. The epics were recited to crowds that might number thousands. The choral lyrics were danced and sung by large choruses in the presence of a whole city. Tragedy and Comedy were acted before the whole Athenian populace, swollen by crowds from every part of Hellas. The great orations were spoken either to the national assembly, where every grown man might be present, or to a jury of several hundred citizens. So with Hellenic art. The statues and pictures were not created for private drawing-rooms, but for public temples, colonnades, or gymnasia.

Thus it was national, not individual taste which was the standard of Hellenic art and literature : they had to follow the taste of the city, not of a clique. But every city in Hellas, as in the Italy of the Renaissance, had an intense individuality of its own, which dominated its poets, artists, and musicians. The art-schools of the islands, of Argos, of Athens were as distinct from one another as those of Venice, Florence, Perugia. The greater centres had types of music so far distinct that they required different instruments. Language, character, and politics in like manner presented a different aspect in each community. But underneath this ubiquitous local individuality lay the fundamental distinction between the Dorian, on the one hand, and the Ionian, with whom for æsthetic purposes may be classed the Aeolian, on the other. For Hellenism began to run its course in two distinct channels, the Doric and the Ionic.[1]

The Doric characteristics were the sacrifice of the detail and the individual to the whole and the community, a love of terseness and simplicity, a strong sense of harmony, order, and proportion, a hatred of complexity, mystery, vagueness, and luxury, and a preference for the perfect body over the developed intellect. The Dorians were essentially one-sided, and lacking in imagination, intellect, and invention ; they were strong conservatives, and any innovation was repugnant to them.

The Ionians were a very different people. Indi-

---

[1] The characteristics are sketched in Thuc. i. 70. Cp. the difference between Florence and Venice in Renaissance Italy.

vidualism was strong in them from the first. They had a tendency to floridity, to exaggeration of detail, and to luxury. A quick-witted and imaginative race, they were fond of perpetual innovation. Versatility was characteristic of them. They preferred intellectual to physical success. Their imagination outran their powers of execution. They had none of the solidity of the less brilliant Dorian, none of his discipline, self-restraint, directness, or perseverance. They were his inferiors in most physical and ethical qualities, his superiors in all intellectual pursuits.

Till the fifth century the two conflicting types exercise little influence upon one another. The Ionians produce a sensuous, dreamy, refined, and imaginative sculpture ; the Dorians a series of physically excellent but wholly unintellectual athlete-statues. The Aeolians produce the personal lyrics of love and wine ; the Dorians the choral poetry of athletic triumphs and gymnastic dances. The Dorians can claim the ethical and collectivist philosophy of Pythagoras ; the Ionians the intellectual and individualist philosophy of the so-called Ionian schools.

Athens during this period was purely Ionic, as her statues, the remains of which are now being recovered from the rubbish heaps where Xerxes threw them, abundantly testify. Further evidence comes from the style of dress shown in these statues and in other works of art of the period : it is almost oriental.[1] The statues reveal an excess of detail and over-refinement : the most common type was a draped woman. The Dorians, on the other hand, were most successful in the nude male type ; and the great Aeginetan school quite failed to represent the goddess Athena.

[1] See also Thuc. i. 6 ; Athen. 512 B.C.

The same principle of differentiation applied to music as well as to art, in Hellas: the Dorian, the Ionian, the Aeolian, as well as the neighbouring Phrygian and Lydian, each produced a type of their own, or " harmony," as it was called. Each " harmony " bore the mark of the " ethos," or moral character, of the tribe or race which produced it, plainly and unmistakably. Music in early Hellas must have been of a primitive type, and an acute musical ear had not yet been developed by long training. Consequently, the average Hellenic audience was in the position of the utterly unmusical man of modern times : the complicated music of modern masters would have been wholly unintelligible to them, and the only meanings which they could extract from music were certain broad ethical impressions. The unmusical man is stirred by a good marching tune, moved to a certain depression by a dirge or dead march, enlivened and excited by a rollicking bacchanalian song, and reduced to a solemn and half-religious frame of mind by the tones of a great organ. So with the average Hellene : he extracted this amount of impressions from his music, and no more. Any idea of music as the voice of the unutterable was quite foreign to his mind ; in fact, he disliked any music that was unaccompanied by singing : tunes without words were unknown in earlier Hellas.

How these different harmonies were produced, by what combination of notes and scales each was regulated, may be left to the specialists : it is one of those questions which will probably never be settled con-clusively. The fact remains that they existed, each with an unmistakable moral characteristic of its own. But what exactly the moral characteristic of each was, is rendered doubtful by the conflicting evidence of different writers ; probably, as musical taste changed and developed, the same "harmony" came to cause a different impression.   Plato's ear, accustomed to the prevalent Dorian, found the Lydian doleful and depressing ; Aristotle and his contemporaries, more used to softer music, praised it as valuable for educational purposes.[1]   Herakleides of Pontos,[2] who made a special study of music, gives, in a fragment, a sketch of the old Hellenic "harmonies."   The Dorian, according to him, was manly, dignified, stern, and robust, not effeminate nor merry nor variegated nor versatile.[3]   The Aeolic, afterwards called "Hypo-Dorian," was haughty and pretentious, rather conceited, not, however, base in any way, but inflated and confident.   It was the right music for "woman, wine, and song."   The Ionic, representing the old Ionic character before the race degenerated, was passionate, headstrong, contentious, showing no signs of benevolence or merriment, but revealing a certain hardness of heart and temperament.   It was not florid nor cheerful, but austere and harsh, with a not ignoble dignity which fitted it to accompany Tragedy.   Later, the race and the "harmony" seem to have degenerated, and are charged with being luxurious and effeminate.   There used also to be a Locrian "harmony," which was used by Pindar and Simonides, but afterwards it fell into contempt and died out.

Besides these purely Hellenic types, there were two which came from barbarian races, the Lydian and the Phrygian.   Of the Lydian there were several varieties. The Mixed-Lydian was doleful and suitable to dirges :

[1] No doubt all the theorists had a fatal temptation to judge the harmony by the opinion which they held of the race which produced it.   The Lydian may have recovered prestige during the fourth century, for it included Karian, and Karia became a great power under Mausolos.   [2] Athen. 624 c.

[3] It is the only true Hellenic harmony (Plato, *Lach.* 188 D).

it made the audience feel mournful and grave. The
Syntono-Lydian was very similar. The pure Lydian is
rejected as effeminate by Plato;[1] but Aristotle, resting
on the musical experts, declares that it involves order
and arrangement (κόσμος) and is well adapted for
education. About the Phrygian opinion is still more
divided. Plato commends it. According to him it
suitably represents the notes and accents of a self-
controlled man " in peaceful and unconstrained circumstances, trying to persuade some one or making a
request, praying to a god or advising a man, or giving
his attention to the request or advice or arguments of
some one else ; and if he attains his object, not puffed
up, but in all things acting, and accepting the conse-
quences of his actions, with moderation and self-
control." The philosopher then goes on to reject
the flute, as suitable only to hysterical enthusiasm.
But this, as Aristotle pointed out, was inconsistent.
For the Phrygian harmony and the flute went hand in
hand : the wild orgies of Dionusos and other worships
of an enthusiastic nature were usually accompanied by
the flute and could only be set to the Phrygian
harmony. The dithyramb, for instance, could only be
set in this way ; when Philoxenos definitely tried to
write one to the Dorian, he slid back without being able
to prevent it into the Phrygian. Aristotle therefore,
accounting it an enthusiastic harmony, reserves it as a
" purge " (κάθαρσις), which, by providing under well-
regulated conditions an occasional outlet for hysteria, will
work such affections out of the system for a long period :
at the end of which another dose will be required.[2]

---

[1] Plato's opinion of the harmonies is in *Rep.* 398-399. Aristotle, who professes
only to summarise the views of experts, discusses them in *Pol.* viii. 7.

[2] Plato apparently accepts this principle with regard to the Korubantic dances
(*Laws*, 790 D).

In Hellas music was held to be an efficacious medicine for the ills alike of body, soul, and mind. Even the grave and learned philosopher Theophrastos, the pupil of Aristotle, asserted that the Phrygian " harmony " on the flute was the proper means of curing lumbago.[1] Pindar states that Apollo " gives to men and women cures for grievous sickness, and invented the harp, and gives the Muse to whom he will, bringing warless peace into the heart " :[2] the god of medicine is the son of the god of the harp. The Pythagorean philosopher Kleinias, when he was in a bad temper, used to take up his harp, saying, " I am calming myself." [3] He and his school regarded the harp as the true means of attaining that peace and solemn orderliness of soul which as true Dorian musicians they desired. Lukourgos produced at Sparta the state of mind necessary to enable his reforms to be carried, by sending from Crete a lyric poet named Thales, whose songs, by their calm and orderly tune and rhythm, were an incentive to discipline and con-cord : by this means the Spartans were imperceptibly calmed in character.[4] The Arcadians, according to their compatriot Polubios, from ancient times onwards " made music their foster-brother " from their cradles till they were thirty years of age, in order to counteract the brutalising tendencies of their rough life and harsh climate ; and the inhabitants of one district, Kunaitha, which neglected this preventive, were notorious for their wickedness.[5]

Thus music came to be regarded as the best means of forming character. It was only necessary to apply the right sort of " harmony " to the young and sus-ceptible personality, and the right " ethos " would be

[1] Athen. 624 b.   [2] Pind. *P.* 5. 60-63.   Cp. the story of Saul and David.
[3] Athen. 624 a.   [4] Plut. *Luk.* 4.   [5] *Pol.* iv. 20. 2.

produced. The Dorian was most in request for educational purposes: its merits were universally recognised. For it " suitably represented the notes and accents of a brave man in the presence of war or of any other violent action, going to meet wounds or death or fallen into any other misfortune, facing his fate with unflinching resolution." [1] Of the others, as has been said, Plato preferred the Phrygian and Aristotle the Lydian.

Not only beautiful music, but beautiful art also, was believed to produce, by an unconscious but irresistible influence, beautiful characters in those who came into contact with it ; while, on the other hand, bad art, as well as bad music, was the cause of vice and low moral ideals.[2] This, they naturally thought, was particularly true in the case of children, who are so sensitive to all external influences ; moreover, it is the early impressions that make most difference in a man's life. To serve this educational end, the Hellenes expected every statue and painting, as well as every poem and tune, to have ἦθος, that is, according to Aristotle's definition,[3] to be such that its moral purpose was manifest to the average man. For this purpose Hellenic art had to become impersonal : the great statues represent a single trait of character. The smaller individualising traits are omitted : the single trait chosen is then idealised and carried to its utmost possible development. This produced a single and easily intelligible effect. The frieze on the Parthenon represented the perfect knight in various attitudes, not So-and-so and Somebody-else.

---

[1] Plato, *Rep.* 399 A.

[2] Londoners must devoutly hope that the Hellenic theory is false.

[3] Aristot. *Rhet.* ii. 21. 16.

The same idealised abstractions can be traced in the
" Theseus " of the Pediment, and in most of the dramas
of Sophocles.

The realisation of this artistic ideal was made possible
by the fusion of the two currents, Doric and Ionic.   At
the end of the sixth century a wave of Doricism passes
over Athens, and the first competent athlete-sculptors
arise there.   A second wave came in the middle of the
next century, in the period of Perikles.   The Dorian
characteristics now dominate Attic artists alike in poetry,
sculpture, and vase-painting.   Aeschylus had possessed
the best traits of the Ionic temperament, chastened by
the great crisis of the Persian wars : his imagination is
half oriental, and he has often been compared to a
Hebrew prophet.   But the canons of Sophocles are
purely Doric, as are those of Pheidias.   The mixture
of Doric ethics with Ionic imagination produces the
great age of Hellenic art and literature.   With art in
such an educative condition, the effect of the great
public buildings and temples, which adorned even quite
humble villages, and of the glorious statues of which
every temple, agora, and gymnasium formed a perfect
treasure-house, must have been very great upon the
Hellenes, who were probably the most susceptible of all
peoples to artistic influences.   Moderns vaguely realise
that a great Gothic Cathedral does direct the emotions
quite perceptibly.   The more susceptible Athenians
must have been much more strongly influenced by
the Parthenon and the Propulaia.   In fact, it is related
that Epaminondas declared that his countrymen could
never become great unless they removed these buildings
bodily to Thebes.   Strangers visiting Athens were so
overcome by her architectural glories that they thought
her the natural capital of the world—an effect which

Perikles may well have intended. Great works of art produce great effects : it is not unnatural to suppose that smaller works produce a not inconsiderable, if smaller, effect. Modern theorists often declare that the pictures and wall-paper of the nursery ought to be in the best taste. Plato and Aristotle ruled that everything, however humble, which surrounds the growing child should be in accordance with the best canons of art, since art influenced morality so strongly. " Ought we not to keep an eye," says Plato,[1] " on the craftsmen also, and prevent them from representing moral evil or disorderliness or bad taste or lack of grace or lack of harmony either in their imitations of animals or in their buildings or in any other object of their craft ? If they are unable to carry out our directions in this matter, ought we not to expel them from the community, lest boys who are brought up in the bad pasture of these bad representations may pluck poison daily from everything around them, and little by little insensibly accumulate a large amount of evil in their souls ? Must we not rather search for such craftsmen as are able, by their native genius, to discover what is beautiful and graceful ? For in this way our children, dwelling in a region of health, will be influenced for good by every sound and every sight of these works of beauty, inhaling as it were a healthy breeze that blows to them from a goodly land." Every article of furniture, every detail of architecture, is to take its part in educating the citizens. But if art and music are so potent a factor in education, they require to be carefully regulated : a depravation of popular taste, which will cause a depravation of the dependent artists, will by its educating influence increase the national

[1] Plato, *Rep.* 401 B.

decadence both of taste and of morals, in an ever-widening degree.

Poetry had at least an equally potent influence upon contemporary ethics. The works of the great poets were the chief medium of education, and large quantities of them were learned by heart in all the elementary schools.[1] What the boys learned, they then recited, with as much dramatic action as they were capable of : the rhapsodes provided them with models. Thus the boys really *acted* the poets as far as they could. Acting was a new thing in Hellas in Solon's time, and it was received with apprehension. When Thespis first acted one of his plays, Solon asked him if he was not ashamed to tell such lies in public, making himself out to be what he was not. Thespis replied that it was only in fun. Then Solon struck the ground with his stick and said, "We shall soon find this fun of yours invading our commercial transactions." Later, when Peisistratos obtained the bodyguard, to which he owed his tyranny, by pretending to have been wounded by his enemies, Solon said the stratagem was a case of acting.[2] This objection was echoed by Plato, and is not wholly unjustified by the course of history. For the great vice of Hellenic life was its insincerity : it is impossible to tell how far a Hellene is in earnest. It is this vice which ruins their oratory ; it is this which, in later times, made the "hungry little Greek" the type of a fawning liar in Roman opinion. It was not only in recitations that acting played a great part. The

[1] A poetical education probably develops the imagination at the expense of the logical mind. Plato is a good instance of this : his imagination, against his will, outweighs his reason. It may be this personal experience which gives so much bitterness to his attack on poetry.

[2] Plut. *Solon*, 29. 30.

dances were essentially dramatic : it was this quality
which enabled them to give birth to the drama. In
the war-dance all the gestures and attitudes of attack
and defence in actual battle were represented. The
Dionysiac dances were originally the acts of devotees
trying to assimilate themselves to the god in his
sufferings and triumphs.

How vividly a Hellene entered into the dramatisation may be seen from the case of the rhapsode Ion.
When he recited Homer, his eyes filled with water and
his hair stood on end ; and his audience were in much
the same condition. The effect in the " Mimetic "
dances, where music, gestures, rhythm, and poetry all
combined to produce a single impression, must have
been greater still ; the audience, as well as the performers, must often have been quite carried away.
Such performances were very frequent. Is it unnatural
to suppose that such frequent assimilation had an
important effect on the Hellenes, with their artistic
temperament and great susceptibility ? At any rate,
Plato, Aristotle, and Aristophanes, not to mention lesser
names, believed that it had.

Among these potent poetic influences, the drama
must certainly not be forgotten. Sokrates regarded the
Clouds of Aristophanes as a far more deadly attack
upon his career than anything that Anutos and Meletos
could say. To Plato, the theatre plays the part of the
" Great Sophist," the educating influence which forms
the opinion and the character of the young.

It must be remembered that Hellenic poetry enshrined the religion of the race : this fact gave it an
enormous influence. The characters in Aeschylus and
Sophocles are divine or semi-divine ; many of the audience in the theatre were wont to revere Agamemnon

or Theseus ; all paid worship to Athena and Apollo. The Athenian drama was sacred to a Hellene as is the play at Oberammergau to a Christian. Had Shakespeare dramatised the Bible, modern children might have recited his speeches and acted his plays with somewhat similar feelings to those with which Hellenic boys recited Homer or Aeschylus. Suppose Shakespeare had thus dramatised the story of Esau and Jacob, and an imaginative child was set to learn Jacob's speeches and repeat them ; suppose he was also in the habit of hearing them recited by a first-class actor who knew how to bring out the minuter traits of character.[1] Is it not, at any rate, quite rational to argue that the child would gradually absorb some of these traits of character, just as children often pick up the peculiarities of nurses and others with whom they have no hereditary connection ? Might not underhand habits be reasonably attributed to frequent acting of the part of Jacob ? Yet in ancient Hellas the influence was much stronger, for the people were more susceptible and the characters were believed to be half-divine.

Thus in ancient Hellas music, art, and poetry had an immense effect on the characters and morals of the race. This influence may well have been exaggerated by Hellenic thinkers. Damon the musician declared that every change in artistic standards produced a change in the tone and constitution of a State ; and Plato agreed with him.[2] The danger of such innovations is a large part of the theme of the *Laws*, and, in a less degree, of the *Republic*. Sparta accepted

---

[1] Children have a natural tendency to act, and need little inducement or instruction.

[2] Plato, *Rep.* 424 c.

this attitude and forbade all change. The opinion was certainly widely held, and must have rested on experience.

Just as the thinkers were beginning to realise this principle, it happened that a very great change in the artistic canons did take place. Sophocles is succeeded by Euripides, Pheidias by Praxiteles : music suffers a similar transformation. Idealism gives way to realism : Sophocles and Pheidias had represented men as they ought to be, Euripides and Praxiteles represent them as they are. Poets and sculptors still pretend to be delineating deities, but in reality they are delineating contemporary life.[1] Their creations not only cease to be idealised, they cease to have only a single trait. The " Hermes " of Praxiteles is a dreamy but vigorous young Athenian who might have been met in the Akademeia or Lukeion ; the " Herakles " of Euripides is now a homicidal maniac, now a reckless mercenary.[2] The characters become human by losing their divineness. In the next generation the divine names are dropped, and Menander can depict contemporary life without using legendary names. Music also ceased to be so severely separated off into types. All manner of musical innovations arise, which it is very hard for a modern to grasp. But the result is clear enough. It became no longer possible to detect the ethical meaning of a tune : music was becoming complex, just as characters in drama and sculpture were becoming complex. It was also more homely in subject. It became daringly " mimetic " also, imitating all the sounds of nature. This was an age of daring experiments, and musicians shared the general movement.

---

[1] So in the later Renaissance the " Madonna " is the artist's wife.
[2] According to Dr. Verrall.

To the Conservative party in Hellas and to the educational theorists these changes naturally appeared ruinous. In their opinion, Euripides was practically parodying the Bible and making divine characters share all the follies and weaknesses, and use the homely language, of mere men. Boys, learning such poetry by heart, would cease to have ideals : everything would be commonplace to them. They would recite the most homely language, and act the most homely parts, under the idea that they were half-divine. Moreover, with the attack of the new school upon the old religion, the more immoral parts of Hellenic mythology were brought into undue prominence. Euripides seems to have chosen some questionable subjects ; the dithyrambic poets were worse, and chose themes quite unsuitable for children to act or hear. And music ceased to have any ethical value ; it was all trills and onomatopœia. Such changes meant a revolution in the results of education.

The poet Aristophanes is the first to raise his voice against the change. A few months before the utter ruin of Athens, he produces the *Frogs*, which really repeats the attack of the *Clouds*, with Euripides instead of Sokrates for the defendant. The poet is attacked as at once the prophet of the new culture of the Sophists and of the new artistic standards. The following are some of the chief faults which Aristophanes finds with the new school represented by Euripides :[1] (1) an undignified style of music, worthy only of the bones as an accompaniment ; (2) its habit of mixing all sorts of incongruous musical rubbish together, " lewd love-songs, drinking catches of Meletos, Karian flute-music, dirges, and dances " ; (3) its trills or shakes, as in εἱειειειειλίσσετε ; (4) its mixture of incongruous

---

[1] Aristoph. *Frogs*, 1301, 1340.

pictures, "dolphins, spiders, halcyons, prophet-chambers, and race-courses," pathos and bathos, commonplace and solemnity ; (5) bad metre, licenses of every sort, and frequent " resolved " feet. As a parody of its habitual incongruity Aristophanes gives :

" O God of the sea, that's what it is. O ye neighbours, behold yon monstrous deed : Gluke's gone off with my cock. Nymphs, ye daughters of the hills ! Mary Ann, lend a hand."

Aristophanes' voice comes with a certain pathos, for the play is the last utterance of Periclean Athens, just at the point of falling and trying to find a scapegoat on whom to lay the responsibility of its ruin : and the scapegoat chosen is the new artistic and musical standard. The Ionic temperament had, in fact, broken away from all restraint. The Doric canons of order, symmetry, regularity, and solidity were thrown aside. Everything antique was treated with disdain ; all authority was rejected with scorn. No standards, ethical or artistic, were tolerated. Perpetual change, daily novelty, became the one desire of Athens. The foundations of belief, the bases of the moral code, were broken down. The whole world seemed to be crumbling away, and nothing was arising to take its place. Spectators became dizzy with the eternal fluctuations. What wonder if they turned longing eyes towards the one centre of gravity in Hellas, towards the one place where politics, art, and ethics retained their old stability, towards Sparta ? So Sparta becomes the philosopher's ideal, and it is the Spartan canon that Plato tries to reimpose on Ionicism running riot.[1] The fault which he finds with contemporary art and music

---

[1] Ionicism = Herakleiteanism, πάντα ῥεῖ. Doricism = Parmenideanism, τὸ πᾶν μένει.

is that they simply try to please and amuse the audience, not to educate and improve it.[1] They are like parents who try to soothe a fractious child with sweetmeats when his health requires castor oil. But the poets and artists are the slaves of the mob which pays them. They must be freed from this control, and made the servants of the government. Strict canons must be drawn up, which they must follow on pain of being expelled from the State. The canons must be drawn up by a select body of experts ; the mob is incapable of judging in such matters ; the critic must guide their taste, not follow it.[2] Good music and art must bear the stamp of a good "ethos," and, since men appreciate the character most which most resembles their own, it will be the good man who will most appreciate good music :[3] so the good man becomes the standard. In order to point his moral, Plato sketches the history of the Athenian drama, showing how its dependence on popular opinion ruined it[4] :—

"At the time of the Persian wars Athens was a limited democracy, with the magistracies arranged according to a property qualification. The spirit of obedience and discipline prevailed in those days, and was strengthened by the dread of Persia. The populace willingly obeyed the laws that fixed the artistic and musical standards. By these regulations the different types of song and accompaniment, hymns or prayers to the gods, lamentations, pæans, dithyrambs, and so forth were kept quite distinct, no one being allowed to mix them together ; the standard, too, was not fixed, as now, by the shouts and stampings and confused applause of the mob, but every one listened in silence until the end

---

[1] Plato, *Gorg.* 501-502 ; *Polit.* 288 c.   [2] Plato, *Laws,* 657-659.
[3] *Ibid.* 656.   [4] *Ibid.* 698-701 c.

of the play, the educated classes from preference, and boys and their paidagogoi, and the mob generally, under the direction of the rod. Thus the mass of the citizens were ready to obey in an orderly manner, not venturing to make noisy criticisms. In course of time some poets, who ought to have known better, led the way in breaking down these laws. Frenzied and distracted by their desire for pleasure, they mixed lamentations with hymns and pæans with dithyrambs, they imitated the flute on the lyre, they confused everything with everything else. Blinded by ignorance, they lied and said that there was no question of accuracy of representation in music : the only standard was the pleasure of the hearer, whatever sort of man he might be. With such style of poetry, and arguments to match, they inspired the many with contempt for the laws of Art, and gave them the idea that they were capable of criticising it. So the audience was no longer silent but noisy, since it supposed that it knew what was good and what was bad. Art was no longer governed by good taste, but by the bad taste of the mob. Nor was this the worst of it. From Art the infection spread to other spheres, and every one began to think that he knew everything, and consequently to break the laws. For, thinking themselves wiser than the laws, they no longer feared them. . . . Next comes a refusal to obey the Archons, then contempt for the orders of parents and elders, then a desire to be free from the restraints of a constitution. The end is utter contempt for oaths and covenants and the gods."

It is the lack of order and system in contemporary music which Plato dislikes.[1] In modern dances, he

---

[1] The essence of dancing is that it is *orderly* movement ; of singing that it is *orderly* sound (*Laws*, 654).

complains, manly words are set to effeminate tunes or gestures, and the voices of men and beasts and instruments are mixed together into a confused and unintelligible hodgepodge.[1]   Music without words is equally detestable.   Music that runs on without the proper pauses and loves mere speed and meaningless clamour, using flutes and harps without words, is in the worst taste.   The meaning must be quite plain.

Music must also be good.   Poets say much that is good, much that is bad : they are irresponsible beings.[2] The State ought to appoint censors who will reject all unsuitable poems and tunes and dances.   Those which are already in existence must be selected and expurgated. If this ruins the poetry, never mind : moral tone is far more important than poetical skill.   In fact, poetry ought to be written by moral citizens without any regard being paid to their poetical talents : it would also be well if they did not compose till they were fifty ![3] A sketch of a Platonic Censor re-editing Homer is given in Books ii. and iii. of the *Republic* : his methods are drastic.

But Plato's chief denunciation is reserved for the " mimetic " or imitative aspect of poetry.   The poet teaches " posing."   Homer, when he described the siege of Troy, is posing as a skilled tactician (as his admirers often claimed that he was), when really the silence of history proves that he was nothing of the sort.   So too the painter who represents a plough is posing as an authority upon agriculture : question him, and he will prove to be completely ignorant of the subject.   Both poetry and painting are a fraud and a deception ; by their pretence of knowledge, they encourage the mind in the habit, to which it is so prone, of accepting vague

---

[1] Plato, *Laws*, 669-70.   [2] *Ibid*. 800-802.   [3] *Ibid*. 829 c.

opinions as certainties without testing their truth.[1] They foster that belief in the sense-perceptions which it is the object of Platonic education to destroy.

But the poet not only poses himself : he makes his audience, his reader, his performer pose. The boy who recites the dying speech of Aias in Sophocles' play is posing as Aias, pretending to be Aias, and adopting the tone and the traits of Aias. The boy who dances in the dithyramb *Semelé* is trying to enter into Semelé's feelings and moods, being helped by the music and the gestures and the words.[2] Such posing, if begun in early years, will invade the character and change it : the boy will become like the personages whom he is accustomed to act. Hence Plato lays down strict laws dealing with the recitations and dances of the young.[3] " If they speak in character, it must only be in the character of those who are, what they themselves must be when they are grown up, brave, temperate, pious gentlemen. They must have no skill in taking unsuitable characters, lest from their dramatic representation of what is vulgar and base they become infected with the reality of vulgarity and baseness. For imitation, if begun in early years and carried far, sinks into a boy's habits and nature, and influences his voice, his gestures, and his ideas. . . . So boys must not be allowed to take the character of a woman, young or old, abusing her husband or blaspheming against the gods or uttering lamentations,—certainly not of a woman in sickness or in love or in pangs; nor the

---

[1] Consequently the painter and the poet are, in Plato's opinion, allies of the Sophist.

[2] This is true, in a less degree, of the audience. Cp. Plutarch's account of the Spartans (*Lac. Inst.* 239 A) : " They did not listen to tragedies or comedies, in order that neither in earnest nor in jest they might hear men gainsaying the laws."

[3] Plato, *Rep.* 395 ff.

character of slaves performing slavish duties ; nor of bad men, cowards, insulting or mocking one another, using foul language, drunk or sober ; nor yet of madmen." [1] It will be seen that this will exclude much of Hellenic drama, especially of the plays of Euripides and Aristophanes. Comedy, according to Plato, should only be acted by foreigners, and should serve as an awful warning of everything that a gentleman ought not to do. The new music is subjected to similar rules. " Boys must not imitate blacksmiths at the forge, or craftsmen occupied in any trade, or sailors rowing, or boatswains giving them orders, or anything of the sort ; nor yet horses neighing, or bulls roaring, or the noise of rivers or the sea or thunder or wind or hail or chariot-wheels or pulleys or trumpets or flutes or pipes . . . ; nor the sounds made by dogs and sheep and birds." So the proper style of poetry for educational purposes will be mostly narrative, with occasional dramatisation of virtuous men. To accompany this simplified and purified poetry only the Dorian and Phrygian " harmonies " will be required : all the others may be rejected. Simple instruments alone will be wanted : many-stringed lyres and the flute can be banished. The seven-stringed lyre and the shepherd's pipe will be left.

Plato finds it too difficult to carry these principles into rhythm, since he is not an expert in the subject. But he thinks that the metres could be regulated in accordance with his canons ; the expert Damon declared that some had a demoralising tendency.

As a whole, Plato's aim is to restore Doric standards, to combat amateurism and dabbling, by which boys

---

[1] Plato holds that no one likes to imitate his inferiors ; so the good man will not care to imitate any but the good. He ascribes this attitude to the Deity.

were made Jacks-of-all-trades, and above all to insist
that the refined few ought to set the standard of taste in
matters musical, literary, and artistic, not the unrefined
many.   With his view may be contrasted Perikles'
boast to the Athenian people, "We can all criticise
adequately, if we cannot all invent," and Aristotle's
belief that a crowd judges better than an individual
because its judgment is compounded of many judgments.

But when we come to Aristotle the creative instinct
of the Hellenic nation, apart from a few gifted
individuals, is dead.   To him and his contemporaries
music and painting are no longer rendered necessary
parts of education owing to the irresistible craving
of an artistic temperament for expression.   Listen
to his theory.   Painting gives boys an eye for
beauty, and prevents them from being cheated in
art-dealing : there is no inward compulsion to paint.
Boys had better learn to sing and play, since children
must needs make a noise.   All they really need is the
power of criticising professional music.   This power,
unluckily, cannot be acquired without personal study.
But let them drop their music as soon as they can,
or they might be mistaken for vulgar professionals.
Such words could hardly have been addressed to a
nation that was still musical and artistic.   So Aristotle's
æsthetic criticism is really a study of the past, the
discussion of a dead age.   He has no natural affinity
for such things himself : he prefers to sum up the
opinions of experts.   Consequently his remarks on the
subject are scientific but no more ; for a real appreciation of the Hellenic artistic and musical spirit it is
necessary to go to Plato, who combated it so fiercely
just because he was more in sympathy with it than
suited his philosophic desires.

PLATE X. A.

IN A RIDING-SCHOOL

From a Kulix by Euphronios, now in the Louvre. Hartwig's *Meisterschalen*, Plate 53.

PLATE X. B.

IN A RIDING-SCHOOL

From a Kulix by Euphronios, now in the Louvre. Hartwig's *Meisterschalen*, Plate 53.

CHAPTER X

THE central figure in many parishes in England is a retired Major-General or Colonel. He constitutes the chief pillar of the neighbouring church, reads the Lessons on Sundays, teaches in the Sunday School, gives away the prizes at School-treats held in his own grounds, and heads every subscription list; while his leisure is given to the compilation of a military memoir or two, and perhaps, if he is very literary, of a few short stories. Just such a man was Xenophon. On retiring from active service, he withdrew to the little village of Skïllous in Elis, where he owned a house and a park. The whole country swarmed with fish and game, so that he and his sons could have as much hunting as they pleased. Guests were numerous, for past his gates ran the great high-road from Lakedaimon to Olympia. In his grounds he built a chapel to Artemis, the expenses being defrayed from a tithe of the spoils he had taken in the heart of the Persian Empire. The tenth of the produce of his land was paid to the goddess, and once a year he gave a great sacrificial feast in her honour, to which all the neighbours were invited. In this way the retired General lived for twenty years, devoted to his religion, his hunting, and the composition of his books. Having two sons of his own, he naturally gave some attention to the problems of education. His treatise on the constitution of Lakedaimon is simply a sketch of the Spartan school system, no doubt intended for his boys, who were brought up at Sparta. A curious passage in his *Economics*[1] shows that he considered the most effective mode of teaching to be a series of appeals, by means of question and answer, to personal observation and common-sense. Ischomachos asks Sokrates whether he knows how to plant trees. Sokrates at first replies "No," but when he is questioned point by point, whether on his excursions to Lukabettos, he has noticed the depth of the trenches in the orchards, and some similar details, and when his common-sense has shown him that plants grow quicker through soft than through hard soil, he finds that he is an expert nurseryman, and decides that questioning must be the way to teach.

But the most important of Xenophon's educational works is the *Education of Kuros*. In this he becomes the classical Miss Edgeworth and Henty combined. The book is really an historical novel, mostly fiction, embodying a moral story for the young, an ideal system of education, and a practical treatise on the whole duty of a general. The ideal system comes first, as a sort of preface, and presents a curious parallel to the rival schemes of his contemporary Plato. Xenophon makes the reader suppose that his system was practised in Persia in the time of Kuros' boyhood, but there is no authority for his statement. Persia is in this case a convenient title for Utopia.

The ordinary State, according to Xenophon, leaves its citizens to form their own characters; but the

Xen. *Econ.* 19.

Persian system definitely aims at producing virtue.   In
every Persian city there is what is called the " Free
Agora." [1]   This is an open square, like the ordinary
market-place, but unlike it in being without shops or
booths, for the vulgar bustle and clamour of buying and
selling is forbidden here, as likely to disturb the peace
and calm of the educated.   Round it lie the royal palace
and the State buildings, so that it would be a place of
some architectural pretensions and not unlike the quad-
rangle of a College at an English University.   The
square is divided into four parts—one for the children,
one for the epheboi, one for full-grown men, and one
for the old ; for men of all ages have their place in
this College.   Any Persian is at liberty to send his son
to school here, but only the rich can afford to support
their sons while they attend the classes : the poor man's
children, in Utopian Persia as in modern England, must
needs work for their living at an early age.   The schools
are apparently only for boys : Xenophon has nothing to
say here about feminine education, although he approves
of the Spartan system.

All boys under sixteen are ranged together in twelve
companies, according to the number of Persian tribes ;
of arrangement in classes by age or intelligence nothing
is said.   They have to be in their quarter of the Free
Agora at daybreak.   Their education is under the control
of twelve masters chosen from the elder men.   What
they learn in school is *Justice*, as boys elsewhere learn
letters.   The system is as curious as the subject.   A sort
of miniature law-court is constituted, where the masters
act as judges and the boys accuse one another before
them.   The accusations must not be concocted for the

---

[1] Aristotle (*Pol.* vii. 12) says that " Free Agoras " were customary in Thessaly.
He adopts the system for his ideal state—a clear compliment to Xenophon.

occasion, for any one found guilty of bringing a false charge against a schoolfellow is severely punished. Smith Major has stolen Brown's bow and arrows, or Jones has called Robinson various opprobrious names ; the offenders are hauled up before the tribunal, duly tried, and, if convicted, flogged.[1] Ingratitude is regarded as a particularly heinous crime. It appears that promising pupils were allowed to act as judges sometimes. The boy Kuros tells his mother how he received this honour and once gave a wrong verdict, to his own discomfiture. " The case was like this, mother," he is made to say. " A big boy wearing a small coat met a small boy wearing a big coat, and compelled him to exchange. I was told to decide the case, and said that it was best that each should have the coat which fitted him. Then the master flogged me. For the point was, To whom did the big coat belong ? not, Whom did it fit best ? It belonged to the boy who bought or made it, not to the boy who took it by force, breaking the law."

Besides " Justice," the children were taught the properties of plants, in order that they might avoid those that were harmful and use those which were good.[2] This seems a curious anticipation of " Nature-study," with a strictly utilitarian object, and Xenophon deserves credit for an original suggestion.

The boys are assisted in the formation of good habits by the sight of their elders in the adjacent quarter of the Free Agora, setting them an example in temperance and obedience and self-restraint. They also learn not to be greedy, by taking their meals, when ordered, in the school, under supervision, off the very simple fare of

---

[1] Floggings were apparently to be frequent. " Tears are a master's instruments of instruction " (ii. 2. 14).   [2] viii. 8. 14.

bread, water, and a sort of seed resembling the modern mustard, which is all that they are allowed to bring with them from home for the purpose. What is more, this probably constituted the only meal which the children had on such days. It must have been a pretty stiff lesson in abstinence! How they would have hated a master who ordered it too often! For games and exercise they had shooting with the bow and hurling the javelin—that is, military training.

The other three ages are also organised each under twelve masters in its own quarter of the Agora of Education. The epheboi, who in Utopia include all from sixteen to twenty-six, even sleep there, acting as a standing army and a police force to guard the palace and the State buildings. Xenophon thinks it well that the men of this age, who need more attention, in his opinion, than even the boys, should be always under the eye of the authorities. They are organised into twelve companies, one from each of the Persian tribes. Their time is largely occupied in police-work, such as catching brigands, and in hunting. Xenophon attaches great importance to hunting of all sorts, as being the best training for war.[1] For it involves exposure to heat and cold and other hardships, training in marching and running, and skill with bow and javelin;[2] it also requires courage, to meet the sudden charge of a panther; and long and patient strategy, to catch birds and hares.[3] So, several times a month, the king goes out hunting and takes six companies of the epheboi with him, armed with bows and arrows, a dagger, a light shield, and two spears—one for throwing and one for stabbing. When not engaged in hunting or in police-work, the epheboi revise what they learned as boys, and practise shooting, competing with

---

[1] Hence his treatise on hunting.   [2] i. 2. 10.   [3] i. 6. 39-40.

one another ; there are also public contests, with prizes. Prizes are also given to the officer in charge of the company which shows itself the most intelligent, courageous, and trustworthy ; the master who taught this company in its school-days is also commended.

The men from twenty-six to fifty occupy the third, and the elders the fourth, quarter of the Agora. The former act as a standing army of heavy infantry ; the latter as a reserve force for home defence, as Judges, as the electors to the offices of State, and as the teachers of the children. The other offices are filled by the third age. Any freeborn Persian can climb this four-runged Ladder of Education to the very top ; but no one may enter a higher class without having served his full time in those below it. To Xenophon, it appears, belongs the credit of being the first theorist to recognise the merits of this Thessalian custom of the " Free Agora," the State-provided centre of culture, after-wards adopted so extensively in Alexandria, where the educated classes of all ages might meet in an intellectual atmosphere and amid beautiful surroundings, and provide that exchange and mart of ideas by personal intercourse which Newman considered to be the essence of a University. In the Free Agora of Utopian Persia all the educated spend their days, influencing one another by talk and example, exchanging and criticising ideas, competing in warlike exercises—and all in an atmosphere untainted by the vulgarity of money-making. On the other hand, culture there does not mean idleness ; to Xenophon, as to Plato, education seemed to entail great responsibilities, and the educated classes provide the sole standing army of the State and have to give their countrymen the benefit of their intelligence by serving as Rulers and Judges.

But Xenophon's University provides only legal and military instruction ; intellectual culture is not recognised in his "Persia." The boys learn the principles of their national law ; for, as Xenophon is careful to proclaim, the Justice which they are taught is no Platonic elaboration, but simple conformity to the law of the land.[1] Their other lessons aim solely at the soldier's life : this is the object of their severe diet, their botany, and their training in arms. General morality is to be imbibed from contact in the Agora with their exemplary seniors, not by ethical contemplation. The system has the merit of being extremely practical, as would be expected from a man of Xenophon's stamp. The boys are to be soldiers all their lives, and Rulers and Judges in their old age. Consequently they are to be taught only what is essential to this calling. The soldier must be well versed in the use of arms and capable of enduring hardships ; so the boys are taught to use the bow and javelin and lead a sternly simple life. The chief essential to the Ruler and Judge is a sound knowledge of the national law : the boys are taught law from the first, in a highly practical way, and even learn to administer it, acting as judges to their schoolfellows. No better means could be devised for teaching boys the legal procedure of their native land than this of constituting them into a miniature Court.[2] It is a scheme, however, which would be repugnant to the whole idea of an English public school, where the boys are expected to fight their own battles and set their own tone without calling in the master's assistance except in grave cases. But the Hellenic boy was never

[1] i. 3. 17.

[2] Cp. the experiment which was, I believe, tried in an American school, where the boys learned the national constitution by themselves electing in due form a President, Congress, etc.

left without supervision : the paidagogos, or some elder, was always in attendance.[1]   Probably the chief criticism which it would have occurred to an Athenian of that age to urge against Xenophon's system would be, not that it encouraged tale-bearing, nor that it failed to teach self-reliance, but that his countrymen were quite sufficiently litigious already without any teaching. The absence of literature and music would also have seemed a fatal objection.

The " Persian " schools are apparently open, free of charge, to any boy whose father chooses to send him. For the only expense which the parents are mentioned as incurring is the loss of any wages which their son might have been earning if set to a trade instead of being sent to school.   Xenophon thus institutes free education without compulsion.   Pupils may be withdrawn at any age ; if they or their families have enough private means to enable them to live in leisure all their lives they can rise through the various stages to the highest offices of the State, provided that they are not rejected as unfit during their upward passage.   Theoretically the educational ladder is open to all ; practically it is closed to all but those who are well-to-do and fairly capable to boot.   But the education provided is not a general culture, intellectually and morally good for all children, nor yet utilitarian knowledge, such as arithmetic or writing, which will serve as a useful, or even neces- sary, basis for a trade or profession : it is a strictly technical education in the work of War and Govern- ment.   Few parents, therefore, would send their boys to Xenophon's schools, at any rate for a longer period than would be required for learning just the rudiments

[1] " The perpetual presence of masters," according to Xenophon, " best inculcates proper modesty and discipline."

of national law and morality, unless they designed them
for a public career.

Thus Xenophon, like his beloved Spartans, has made
war the main object of education, and, like the Romans,
uses law as the chief instrument of instruction.   But he
has seen the demerits of the Spartan " Mess-clubs," and
his boys take their meals and sleep, as a rule, at home ;
only the epheboi, as in Crete, dine and sleep always in
the agora.   His chief merit is that he recognised that
an educational atmosphere, εὐκοσμία τῶν πεπαιδευμένων,
free from the associations of money-making, is essential
to an educational establishment.

After this deeply interesting sketch of Xenophon's
educational ideals, the *Education of Kuros* becomes a
historical novel with a purpose, an idealised Kuros
acting as example throughout.   In Book i. there is the
description of him as the model boy, courteous to his
elders, quick and eager to learn, brave, impetuous,
loved by all, but rather a prig.   The description is full
of improving anecdotes and little sermons.   The book
concludes with a lecture on the duties of a general,
dealing with tactics and the best means of training
the army and providing supplies.   Xenophon puts
all his personal experience into this, and there is plenty
of adventure to make the book palatable to his young
readers.

A few extracts will make the characteristics of this
curious work plain.

When quite young, Kuros went with his mother
Mandané to stay with his grandfather Astuages, King of
Media.   The old man, thinking that the boy would be
homesick and wishing to comfort him, sent for him at
dinner the first evening and set all sorts of rich meats
and sauces before him.   Then Kuros said, " Grandfather,

you must find it a great nuisance, if you have to help yourself to so many courses and taste so many kinds of food." His grandfather replied, "Why, don't you think this a much finer dinner than what you get at home?" "No, grandfather," replied Kuros; "at home we satisfy our appetites by a short-cut, just bread and meat, but here, although your object is the same, you wind in and out so much on the way that it takes you ever so much longer to reach it." "But, my boy, the delay is only so much pleasure, as you will see if you try." Kuros, however, persisted in refusing the unwholesome dainties, so his grandfather compensated him by giving him an enormous help of meat. "Is all this meant for me," asked Kuros, "to do what I like with?" "Yes, my boy." Then Kuros took the meat and distributed it to the servants who were waiting at table, saying to one, "This is because you taught me to ride"; to another, "This is because you gave me a javelin"; to a third, "This is for waiting on my grandfather so nicely." From this example the young reader doubtless learned not to desire too many courses or too rich sweets at table, and perhaps also to be grateful to every one, even servants. After this Kuros remained in Media, while his mother returned home. "He soon won the love of his schoolfellows, and quite charmed their parents when invited to their houses by the affection which he showed for their sons." A good moral, this, for little boys who go out to parties.

This model boy does not die young, but grows up. He had been rather a chatterbox when small (a warning to the young readers), but only owing to his desire for knowledge and his readiness to answer questions; besides, he chattered in such a nice way that it was a pleasure to hear him. But as he grew older, he grew more bashful. " He always blushed when he met his elders, and he talked in a quieter tone. When he played with his schoolfellows, he chose the games where he expected to be beaten, not those in which he expected to win ; and he was always ready to lead the laugh against himself when beaten." Model youth ! Of course, he soon became the champion at every form of sport, just as in a modern book of the kind he would have won at least five " Blues."

Kuros next appears as a mighty hunter, and then at the age of fifteen takes a leading part in a battle against the Assyrians ; in fact, it is his strategy and prowess that decide the day. What more could be wanted in a book for boys ? The modern author would give him a grizzly bear, a lion, and a V.C. : Xenophon gives him the Persian equivalents.

After this, little more is said of Kuros' boyhood. He is next introduced as a man of twenty-six, just put into command of a Persian expedition to help Media against the Assyrians.[1] Henceforth Xenophon's object is no longer to point a moral, but to instruct budding generals and princes in strategy and government. The remaining books are a " Handbook of Tactics, with hints on the proper treatment of inferiors " ; so they fitly begin with a long lecture by Kuros' father on the whole duty of a general.[2] There is, however, a good deal of moral advice and occasional allegory interspersed amid the tactics. For instance, a certain Gobruas came to dine with the Persian army. " Seeing how plain the food was, he regarded the Persians as rather *bourgeois*. But then he observed what good manners the guests had. No educated Persian would allow himself to be seen staring at a dish, or helping himself hurriedly,

[1] i. 5. 5.   [2] i. 6. 1-46.

or acting at table without proper deliberation. For they think it piggish to be excited by the presence of food or drink. He noticed, too, that they never asked one another questions which might cause pain, that their jests were never malicious nor their wit rude, that everything that they did was in the best taste, and that they never lost their tempers with one another." And so on. " Manners for men," we might call it, by Xenophon.

A curiously interesting case of allegory, which well shows how imaginary most of the history is, may be found in the third book.[1] The son of the king of Armenia had had for a companion and tutor a certain Sophist, of whose wisdom he was very proud. But his father condemned the Sophist for corrupting[2] the boy. When he was being led to execution, the man showed what a saint and hero he was by calling the boy and saying, " Do not be angry with your father for putting me to death. For it is no wicked purpose which makes him do it, but only ignorance. All sins which men commit in ignorance I rank as involuntary errors." Later, the father confesses that he put the Sophist to death for stealing away his son's affections, " for I feared that my boy might love him more than he loved me." Kuros admits that such jealousy is an explanation and regards it as pardonable.

The analogy to Sokrates is obvious to any one. The half-apology for the Athenian people is very interesting in the mouth of the old Socratic companion Xenophon.

But the object of the *Education of Kuros* is, after all, to teach generalship. A couple of examples of the way in which this is done will suffice. On one

---

[1] iii. 1. 38.   [2] διαφθείρειν, the word used in Sokrates' accusation.

occasion[1] Kuros orders the foot-cuirassiers to lead the way in a forced march, and kindly explains the object of such a manoeuvre. "This command I give," he says, "because they are the heaviest part of the army. When the heaviest part is in the van, obviously it is quite easy for the other arms, being lighter, to keep up. But if the quickest detachment is in front on a night march, it is not surprising if the army straggles, for the vanguard goes faster than the rest." Again, Kuros could call all his officers by name, to their great surprise.[2] "For he thought it very absurd that tradesmen should know the names of all their tools, and yet a general should be so stupid as not to know the names of his officers whom he must use as his tools in the most serious emergencies. Soldiers who thought that their general knew their names would, he considered, be more eager to do heroic deeds in his presence, and less eager to play the coward. It seemed also to be foolish to be obliged to give orders, when he wanted something done, in the way some masters do in their households, 'Fetch me some water, Somebody'; or 'Cut some firewood, Someone.' For when the order is addressed to no one in particular, each stands looking at his neighbour and expecting him to carry it out."

The military part is exceedingly well done. Xenophon was one of the few good strategists whom Hellas produced, and his remarks on tactics, the hygiene of an army, and discipline are sound and useful. What is more, his novel is interesting and occasionally witty : it is distinctly good reading. He has disguised his powder in the most appetising jam, and so has achieved with success the difficult task of writing a novel with

[1] v. 3. 37.   [2] v. 3. 46.   Notice the Socratic comparison.

a purpose. Had books been common then, his work would have been both popular and useful in Boys' Libraries, and have done good service as a school prize. But from Plato it only provoked the malicious and not very deep criticism that it was unhistorical and unsound.[1] "Of Kuros," he says, "I conjecture that, though he was a good general and a patriot, he had not come across the merest scrap of sound education, and never applied his mind to the art of managing a household.[2] For, being absent on campaigns all his life, he allowed the women to bring up his children. The women spoilt the boys, letting no one gainsay them, and made them effeminate, not teaching them the Persian habits or their father's profession, but Median luxury. Hence the collapse of Persia under Kambuses."

[1] Plato, *Laws*, 694 c-d.   [2] A hit at Xenophon's *Economics*.

PART III

CHAPTER XI

THE preceding chapters have sufficiently established, as it seems to me, that Hellenic education alike at Sparta and at Athens, in theory and in practice, aimed at producing the best possible citizen, not the best possible money-maker ; it sought the good of the community, not the good of the individual. The methods and materials of education naturally differed with the conception of good citizenship held in each locality, but the ideal object was always the same.

The Spartan, with his schoolboy conception of life, believed that the whole duty of man was to be brave, to be indifferent to hardships and pain, to be a good soldier, and to be always in perfect physical condition ; when his Hellenic instincts needed æsthetic satisfaction, he made his military drill into a musical dance and sang songs in honour of valour. Long speaking and lengthy meditation he regarded with contempt, for he preferred deeds to words or thoughts, and the essence of a situation could always be expressed in a single sentence. This Spartan conception of citizenship fixed the aim of Spartan education. Daily hardships, endless physical training, perpetual tests of pluck and endurance, were the lot of the Spartan boy. He did not learn to read or write or count ; he was trained to speak only in single words or in the shortest of sentences, for what need had a Spartan of letters or of chattering ? His imagination had also to be subordinated to the national ideal : his dances, his songs, his very deities, were all military.

The Athenian's conception of the perfect citizen was much wider and much more difficult of attainment. Pluck and harmony of physical development did not satisfy him : there must be equal training of mind and imagination, without any sacrifice of bodily health. He demanded of the ideal citizen perfection of body, extensive mental activity and culture, and irreproachable taste. " We love and pursue wisdom, yet avoid bodily sloth ; we love and pursue beauty, yet avoid bad taste and extravagance," proclaims Perikles in his summary of Athenian ideals. Consequently Athenian education was triple in its aims ; its activities were divided between body, mind, and taste. The body of the young Athenian was symmetrically developed by the scientifically designed exercises of the palaistra. At eighteen the State imposed upon him two years of physical training at public cost. In after life he could exercise himself in the public gymnasia without any payment ; there was no actual compulsion, except the perpetual imminence of military service, which, however, almost amounted to compulsion.

As to mental instruction, every boy had to learn reading, writing, arithmetic, and gain such acquaintance with the national literature as these studies involved. The other branch of primary education, playing and singing, intended to develop the musical ear and taste, was optional, but rarely neglected. The secondary education given by the Sophists, rhetors, and philosophers was only intended for the comparatively few who had wealth and leisure.

Taste and imagination were cultivated in the music- and art-schools, but the influences of the theatre, the Akropolis, the temples and public monuments, and the dances which accompanied every festival and religious occasion, were still more potent, and were exercised upon all alike. This æsthetic aspect of education was regarded as particularly important in Hellas owing to the prevalent idea that art and music had a strong influence over character.

For the training of character was before all things the object of Hellenic education; it was this which Hellenic parents particularly demanded of the school-master. So strongly did they believe that virtue could be taught, that they held the teacher responsible for any subsequent misdemeanour of his pupils. Alkibiades and Kritias had ruined Athens : they were Sokrates' pupils : therefore execute Sokrates ; this seemed per-fectly logical to an Athenian. If a Sophist sued a defaulting pupil for an unpaid bill, he was regarded as ridiculous, for it was his business to teach justice, and if those who had learned under him behaved unjustly, it was clearly because his teaching had been worthless.

Since the main object of the schools of Hellas was to train and mould the character of the young, it would be natural to suppose that the schoolmasters and every one else who was to come into contact with the boys were chosen with immense care, special attention being given to their reputation for virtue and conduct. At Sparta this principle was certainly observed. Education was controlled by a paidonomos, selected from the citizens of the highest position and reputation, and the teaching was given, not by hired foreigners or slaves, but by the citizens themselves under his supervision. But then the teaching at Sparta dealt mostly with the manners and customs of the State, or with bodily and military exercises, known to every grown man, and the citizens had plenty of leisure. The Athenians were in a more difficult position. There were more subjects for the boy to learn, and some of them the parents might have neither the capacity nor the time to teach. Owing also to the day-school system at Athens and the peculiarities of Hellenic manners, the boys needed some one always at hand to take them to and from school and palaistra. Thus both paid teachers and attendants were needed. But it was also necessary not to let education become too expensive, lest the poor should be unable to afford it. Consequently the paidagogoi came often to be the cheapest and most worthless slaves, and the schoolmasters as a class to be regarded with supreme contempt. No doubt careful parents chose excellent paidagogoi, schoolmasters, and paidotribai for their sons, and made the choice a matter of much deliberation : the teachers at the best schools and palaistrai were often men of position and repute. But that the class as a whole was regarded with contempt there can be little doubt. The children went into a school as they would have gone into any other shop, with a sense of superiority, bringing with them their pets, leopards and cats and dogs, and playing with them during lesson-times. Idlers and loungers came into the schools and palaistrai, as they came into the market-booths, to chatter and look on, seriously interrupting the work. The schoolmasters and paido-tribai at Athens were, in fact, too dependent upon their public for subsistence to take a strong line, and, in spite of their power, often exercised, of inflicting corporal punishment, they seem to have been distinctly at the mercy of the pupils and their friends. The paidagogoi too, though they seem to have kept their pupils in order, were often not the right people to control a boy's conduct; they were apt to have a villainous accent, and still more villainous habits. It must be confessed that the Athenians, in their desire to make education cheap, ran a very great risk of spoiling what in their opinion was its chief object, the training of character.

Otherwise, they sought this end whole-heartedly. The games, physical exercises, and hardships of a boy's life were meant to develop his pluck, fortitude, and endurance. For, according to the Hellenic view, now too much neglected in many quarters, the condition and treatment of the body had a very important effect both upon mental activities and upon character. It was for this reason that physical training formed at least half of every system of education practised in Hellenic states or recommended by Hellenic philosophers. A National School which trained the minds only, and neglected the bodies of the pupils, would have been inconceivable to a Hellene. It was not merely that physical infirmities interrupted the free exercise of thought, or led to peevishness and lack of decision. Man was a whole to the Hellenes, and one part of him could not be sound if the other parts were not. So strongly did they hold this opinion, that they more than half believed that physical beauty was a sign of moral beauty; it was this latent idea which added an additional significance to the exercises of the palaistra with their symmetrical development of the body, and to the competitions for manly beauty which were prevalent throughout the country; it lent, moreover, a nobler aspect to that passion for the outward loveliness of youth which the vases, sculpture, and literature of ancient Hellas reveal so surprisingly. But, besides this vaguer and more doubtful connection with character, bodily exercise and development were supposed to have a special and indubitable effect in strengthening the resolution and will-power. The object of physical training was only in a minor degree to keep the body in good condition ; its main aim was to develop strength of character, determination, fortitude, endurance, pluck, and energy. But, in accordance with that Hellenic canon of " moderation in all things," which was worked out so thoroughly by Aristotle, there might be too much, as well as too little, of all these ethical qualities. Consequently physical exercise must be taken only in due moderation, and carefully balanced by artistic and musical training, which militated in an opposite direction, leading, if pursued in excess, to weakness of character, indecision, effeminacy, cowardice, and sloth. A scientifically arranged symmetry between the two would produce the perfect character.

In the literary and æsthetic schools there were two elements of the subjects taught, both with an ethical effect, matter and form. The literature studied in the schools was expected to be full of improving suggestions and life-histories of heroes worthy of imitation, couched in the form most attractive to young minds, in order that they might appreciate and love its teaching and examples. The music which the boys played or heard, the songs which they sang, the dances which they performed or watched, the art which they copied or observed, must be such as would influence their characters for good—mould them, that is, in accordance with the national ideal. For Hellenic morality was

æsthetic ; they followed the course which appealed to
their imagination and sense of beauty. It was therefore the object of education to make the children see
and feel beauty in virtue, and good art in good ethics,
in order that they might find satisfaction for their
æsthetic cravings—the dominant instinct of a Hellene
—in living good and upright lives.

For the unanimous feeling of Hellas based ethics
not upon duty, but upon happiness—upon the satisfaction, that is, of the instincts. But this eudæmonistic
attitude was qualified by an important consideration
which is often forgotten. Owing to the solidarity of
Hellenic life, the happiness which was sought was
primarily not that of the individual but that of the
community. The readiness of the average Hellene,
during the best period of the country, to sacrifice everything on behalf of his city is very remarkable. The
real, if unformulated, basis of his ethics came thus to be
not personal pleasure, but duty to the State. When the
individualism of the Socratic age overthrew this basis,
the Hellenes fell back from the happiness of the State
to the happiness of the self, and both patriotism and
personal morality suffered from the change.

It was the sense of duty to the State, the resolution
to promote the happiness of the whole citizen-body,
which made parents willing to undergo any sacrifice in
order to have their sons educated in the way which
would best minister to this ideal. The bills of the
masters of letters and music and of the paidotribai, and
the lengthy loss of the son's services in the shop or on
the farm in Attica, the break-up of family life at Sparta,
must have been a sore trial to the parents and have
involved many sacrifices. Yet there is no trace of
grumbling. The Hellene felt that it was quite as much

his duty to the State to educate her future citizens properly as it was to be ready to die in her cause, and he did both ungrudgingly. If the laws which made the teaching of letters ·compulsory at Athens fell into desuetude, it was only because the citizens needed no compulsion to make them do their duty. Nor had the State to pay the school bills ; for every citizen, however poor, was ready to make the necessary sacrifices of personal luxuries and amusements in order to do his duty to the community by having his children properly taught. The State only interfered to make schooling as cheap and as easy to obtain as possible.

The solidarity of Hellenic life, which converted eudæmonism into patriotism, was carefully encouraged by the educational system. Sparta, with this object, invented the boarding-school, where boys learnt from early years to sink their individualities in a community of character and interests. The Athenians and most of the other Hellenes, on the other hand, had day-schools. This fact might seem to militate against the principle which I have stated. But Hellenic custom qualified the system of day-schools in a particular way. There were no home-influences in Hellas. The men-folk lived out of doors. The young Athenian or Ephesian from his sixth year onwards spent his whole day away from home (excepting possibly for an interval for the mid-day meal), in the company of his contemporaries, at school or palaistra or in the streets. When he came home, there was no home-life. His father was hardly ever in the house. His mother was a nonentity, living in the women's apartments ; he probably saw little of her. His real home was the palaistra, his chief companions his contemporaries and his paidagogos. He learned to dissociate himself from his family and associate himself with his fellow-citizens.   No doubt he lost much by this system, but the solidarity of the State gained.

The duties of citizenship were also impressed upon the boys in other and more direct ways, especially its supreme duty, at any rate in those days, of military service.   The schools of Sparta and Crete were one long training for war.   The other States set apart two years of the boy's life, those from eighteen to twenty, as a period of conscription, during which he was at the service of his city and under the orders of the military authorities, learning tactics and the use of arms, and being practised in the life of camps and forts.   The young recruit took a solemn oath of allegiance to his country and its constitution : the sacredness of his civic duties was impressed upon him from the first.   The first function of his new officers was to take him on a personally conducted tour, so to speak, of the national temples, that he might realise something of the religious life and history of his country.   His weapons were solemnly presented to him in the theatre of Dionusos, before the assembled people ; they were sacred, and to lose them in battle or disgrace them by cowardice was not only dishonourable, it was impious.   Nor were the boys allowed to grow up in ignorance of the constitution of their city : the ephebos of eighteen had to be acquainted with the laws, some of which he had probably learnt in the music-school, set to a tune. Every means was taken of making the boys realise that they were members of a community, to whose prosperity and happiness their own advantage or pleasure must be subordinated.   In this way grew up the strong Hellenic sense of an obligation of utter self-sacrifice on behalf of the State.

But education had also to consult the happiness of
the children as well as the happiness of the community,
although in a lesser degree. This may seem a startling
statement to make with regard to Spartan education.
Nevertheless, I believe it to be strictly true. It must
be remembered that all our accounts of the rigours and
horrors of Spartan methods come from Athenian writers
who in all probability had never been to Lakedaimon.
Xenophon, who had his sons educated there, gives a
much milder, and wholly eulogistic, account. The
somewhat hedonistic Attic visitor must have watched
Spartan games and exercises with much the feelings of a
French visitor at an English public school ; he found
it difficult to realise that the boys underwent such hardships of their own free will. Then we must remember
what the Spartan boys were. They were a picked breed
of peculiar toughness, strength, and health ; for centuries
every invalid had been exposed at birth or rejected
as incapable of the school-system. Generation after
generation had been trained to be thick-skinned and
stout-hearted ; pluck and endurance were hereditary,
and asceticism was a national characteristic. The whole
system, with its perpetual fighting, its rough games, its
hardships, its fagging and " roughing-it " in the woods, is
just what boys of this sort might be expected to evolve
for themselves because they liked it. I have already
pointed out, in my account of the Spartan schools, how
very similar are many of the customs which grew up at
the older English public schools, mainly on the boys'
own initiative. If English boys, brought up on the
whole much less roughly, evolved such customs of their
own free will, the young Spartans may reasonably be
supposed to have accepted them gladly. One significant
token of this survives. The violent and sometimes

fatal floggings of the epheboi at the altar of Artemis
Orthia were entirely voluntary on the part of the
victims ; yet there was no lack of candidates even in
Plutarch's days.   The Spartan school-system was, in
fact, an exact expression of the national characteristics,
and accordingly was entirely acceptable to the Spartan
boys.

That the Athenian system was designed to suit the
wishes of the Athenian children is less difficult to
establish.   It is only necessary to think what the
primary schools were like.   When once the letters and
rudiments of reading and writing had been mastered,
the process perhaps being aided by metrical alphabets
and dramatised spelling, the boys began to read, learn
by heart, and write down the fascinating stories of
adventure and the romantic tales of Homer.   There
was no grammar to be studied ; that, when invented,
came at a later age as a voluntary subject.   There were
no years wasted over " Primary Readers " consisting of
dull and second-rate stories.   The boys began at once
upon the best and most attractive literature in their
language, and it remained their study for many years,
and was still remembered and loved in after life.   Nor
can it be doubted that the music- and art-schools were
attractive to Athenian boys, sons of a people who filled
their whole city with art, and made their year a round
of musical festivals.   A large part, too, of Athenian
schooling was what now would be called play ; for the
Hellene recognised the importance of physical exercise
in the upbringing of the young, and included it in his
conception of education.

The effect upon Hellenic culture of thus making
education attractive was far-reaching.   Instead of
regarding with aversion or a bored indifference the

subjects which they had studied at school, the Hellenes had an affection for them and continued to practise and improve themselves in them. Throughout their lives they were eager to hear recitations of Homer. At banquets they sang the songs and played the music on the lyre which they had learnt at school. Elderly men would return to a music-master, to improve their style, or rush off to hear a Sophist lecture on geography or astronomy. The exercises of the palaistra were pursued till old age made them impossible. Grown citizens retained throughout an affection for education, and went on educating themselves all their lives. Thus an Hellenic city formed a centre of widely diffused culture, a home where literature and art and music and research could flourish surrounded by appreciation and capable criticism. Children, too, seeing how much their elders were preoccupied with education, found it even more attractive than its designers had made it, since they were not constrained by nursery-logic to see in it one of the plagues of youth from which " grown-ups " were set free. No doubt the Hellenic schoolmaster was much assisted in his endeavour to make education attractive by the intellectual curiosity which was a feature of all those States where the intellect was systematically trained. The young Athenian or young Chian was exceedingly eager to learn. In fact, his eagerness was excessive ; he was too much in a hurry ; he desired to have his information given to him ready-made, not having the patience to think or to undertake researches on his own account. Hence the phenomenal success and educational unsoundness of those prototypes of the modern " crammer," the Sophists, who supplied their pupils with a superficial knowledge of many subjects ready-made, and already dressed in striking phrase-ology. This intellectual appetite for the accumulation of facts made secondary education at Athens attractive without much effort on the part of the teachers, but it was not allowed to influence the primary schools ; a sound and symmetrical development of mind and body, artistic taste and moral character, had to precede the accumulation of facts. This latter stage too was universally treated as optional. In unintellectual districts it found no place, and even in Athens it was only for those who felt a desire for it ; it was not forced upon the unwilling and incapable. For education was regarded as the development of the latent powers of the individual personality, it was no vain attempt to excite or implant non-existent faculties. Every one had a body, which he must make as efficient as possible, for the service of the State ; every one, in an æsthetic people, had a taste which could be developed ; every one had enough intellect to learn his letters ; and every one, above all, had a character to be formed. But not every one could be an international athlete or a first-class artist or musician, and not every one had sufficient mental gifts to combine the accumulation of facts with profit or enjoyment.

In fact, Hellenic sentiment was distinctly adverse to great development in any one direction : the Hellenes had a reasonable horror of undue specialisation at school. The object of education was to make symmetrical, all-round men, sound alike in body, mind, character, and taste, not professional athletes who were mentally vacuous and without any appreciation of art, nor great thinkers of stunted physique, nor celebrated musicians who lacked brains. Opponents of the Spartan system tried to condemn it on this ground, as a specialisation intended only to produce good soldiers ; but the pro-Spartans seemed to have claimed in return that it developed both character and good taste in judging art and music, even if it produced small capacity for painting or playing, while Laconian terseness involved a greater depth of mental exercise than Athenian verbosity.

Thus Hellenic education was not intended to produce professional knowledge of a single subject ; such technical instruction was deemed unworthy of the name of education, and was excluded from the schools. The subjects studied were for the most part a means, not an end. Just as a walk is sometimes taken not for the sake of reaching any particular place, but in order to keep the muscles of the body in good condition, so education in Hellas was meant to develop and exercise the muscles of mind, imagination, and character, not to inculcate so-called " useful " information. The literature read at school was imaginative poetry, like that of Homer or Simonides, not the practical prose treatises upon Agriculture and Economics which utilitarian motives would have demanded. For the poetry was both attractive to the boys and improving for their characters, while the handbooks, however excellent, only enhanced their financial prospects. The immediate future of the individual boy may, it is true, depend somewhat largely upon the utilitarian knowledge which he has learnt at school, although a sound education in the Hellenic sense of the word will prove more advantageous to him in the long run ; but the future of a State depends upon the character of its citizens. Thus a truly national education like that of Sparta or of Athens seeks to train the characters of the future citizens ; having formed their characters, it leaves them with well-justified confidence to gain what technical instruction they need for themselves. At a national crisis it was not skill in trade or profession, not good cobbling, nor good weaving, that Athens required of her citizens ; but pluck, energy, self-sacrifice, obedience, and loyalty.   Money was, it is true, required for building the triremes and for fortifying the city : it was therefore well that Athenian trade and manufactures should prosper.   But Athens recognised, and rightly, that her financial resources would be better served if she trained her boys to be industrious and thrifty and ascetic, if she made it repugnant to their taste to fling their money away upon luxury and self-indulgence, than if she founded the finest system of technical instruction possible.

But whether Sparta and Athens could have ignored technical and utilitarian subjects so wholly in their schools, if they had been educating the whole population of the State, is another question.   It must be remembered that the Spartan and Athenian citizens who attended the schools were only a fraction of the inhabitants of Laconia and Attica.   They corresponded pretty closely to the upper classes, the aristocracy and gentlemen, of a modern State.   The bulk of the middle and lower classes in a Hellenic State were either foreign immigrants, who possessed no civic rights and did not usually attend the schools, or serfs and slaves.   Athens, like mediæval Florence, was only a democracy in the very limited sense that her full citizens—a governing class, that is, and a mere fraction of the population—had equality of civic rights among themselves : the rest had no rights at all.   Sparta was a " mixed constitution " ; but that did not mean that the middle and lower classes, the Perioikoi and Helots, had any share in it whatever.

Consequently education in Hellas is the education of a small upper class, not of the whole population of the State.   The schools of Hellas were not necessarily for the wealthiest inhabitants of the country, for there were plenty of rich Metoikoi and poor citizens at Athens; not necessarily for the boys who had most leisure, for the sausage-seller goes to school as well as a Nikias or Alkibiades; but for a hereditary aristocracy of birth, for that is what Hellenic "citizenship" means. The boys who attended the lessons of Dionusios or Elpias were the sons and grandsons of a cultured class, no matter how humble their circumstances might be; their families had lived in Attica, they believed, from time immemorial, and were probably descended from the local deities. They had the views of an hereditary caste, including a certain preoccupation with physical and military activities, and a contempt for trade.

For the duties of such an aristocracy did not consist in heaping up riches; their position was comparatively independent of their financial successes. Their work was, in brief, to govern and to fight. They composed the electorate of the State, which chose the magistrates; they alone were members of the public Assembly; they alone were eligible for office. They sat as dikastai— jurymen and justices in one—in the law-courts; they made the laws and they administered them. The national honour and morality lay in their hands, for they controlled alike the foreign and the home policy of the State. They formed, too, the cultured circle which governed natural taste; it was their criticism which shaped the art of the vase-painters, the architects, the sculptors, the bronze-makers, and the countless other artistic tradesmen, the style of the orators, the literature of dramatists and dithyrambists, the music of the choric composers. When governors and administrators were needed for the outlying districts of the Athenian or Spartan Empires, or if officers were required to lead local levies to battle, any citizen, rich or poor, might be sent.   The citizens, too, formed the core of the fleets and armies in the best days of Hellas. The object of Hellenic education was to produce this type of citizen—a man capable of governing, of fighting, and of setting the taste and standards of his country.

Thus the schools of Hellas correspond in England not to the national schools, but to the " public schools." I do not mean to assert that the English public-school boy stands, in after life, in the position of the Hellenic citizen to the bulk of the population.   English democracy rests on a wider basis than Athenian or Florentine, and, in theory at any rate, the exclusive power of the " upper classes " is at an end.   None the less it is true that from among the boys educated at the public schools comes a very considerable part of the generals and military officers, of the clergy, of the squires, of the Justices of the Peace and other administrators of the law, of the governors and officials required by the Indian Empire and the various dependencies and Crown Colonies, of the members of Parliament and statesmen at home.   If the influence of the public schools of England upon the governing and fighting of the nation is less than that which the schools of Hellas were able to exercise, their influence upon national taste and standards in art and culture and literature is probably in no way inferior.   It is therefore their duty to train their pupils' characters, that they may be fit and able administrators, governors, and justices ; and their tastes, that their criticism and demands may rightly direct the culture of the nation. In striving after these ends, the public schools of England may, I think, take not a few hints from the like-motived schools of Hellas.

INDEX

THE END

WILLIAM M. CALDER III received his B.A. from Harvard College in 1954, his M.A. from Harvard University in 1956, and his Ph.D. from the University of Chicago in 1958. From 1958 to 1960 he was Instructor, from 1960 to 1964, Assistant Professor, and from 1964 on, Associate Professor of Greek and Latin at Columbia University. Professor Calder was a Guggenheim Fellow and Fulbright Research Scholar in West Germany in 1964–65, and was Guest Professor of Classical Philology at the University of Rostock in the Democratic Republic of Germany in 1968. His published works include *The Inscription from Temple G at Selinus* (1963), *Index Locorum zu Kühner-Gerth* (1965), and numerous articles and reviews in learned journals of the United States and Europe.